Professor W. B. Lockwood, who holds the Chair of Germanic and Indo-European Philology in the University of Reading, has written widely on linguistic topics. His publications include *An Introduction to Modern Faroese* (1955); *An Informal History of the German Language* (1965); *Historical German Syntax* (1968); *Indo-European Philogy: Historical and Comparative* (1969); and *A Panorama of Indo-European Languages* (1972)

LANGUAGES OF THE BRITISH ISLES
PAST AND PRESENT

THE LANGUAGE LIBRARY

EDITED BY ERIC PARTRIDGE AND SIMEON POTTER

W. B. Lockwood

LANGUAGES OF THE BRITISH ISLES PAST AND PRESENT

ANDRE DEUTSCH

First published 1975 by
André Deutsch Limited
105 Great Russell Street London WC1

Printed in Great Britain by
William Clowes & Sons, Limited
London, Beccles and Colchester

ISBN 0 233 96666 8

For Martin,
who said there must be
Gypsies in it.

Contents

🐚🐚🐚🐚🐚🐚

Preface

🔲🔲🔲🔲🔲🔲

THE present volume has been conceived as an introduction to the rich linguistic heritage of Great Britain and Ireland. To this end, accounts are given of the external history of the languages concerned, after which their structure is described in outline and illustrated by a range of reading passages. Bibliographies are selective, and intended as stepping stones to further study.

I am indebted to Professor T. de Bhaldraithe, Mr P. S. Noble, Dr Ceinwen Thomas, Mr R. L. Thompson and Professor D. Thomson, who obligingly dealt with my various queries, and last, but not least, to Professor Simeon Potter for important advice on a number of points.

I express the hope that this compilation, unpretentious though it is, may nevertheless evoke further interest in the languages of these islands, and particularly in those minority languages still surviving. I shall feel rewarded if from such interest there should flow some appreciation of the standpoint of those who use these languages, value them, and are loath to abandon them in their hour of need.

W. B. LOCKWOOD

PART I

ANTECEDENTS

🌀🌀🌀🌀🌀

CHAPTER ONE

Before the written records

🌀🌀🌀🌀🌀

THERE is, as yet, no means of knowing through what aeons of time man has lived in these islands. He has certainly seen Ice Ages come and go – the fragments of the human skull from the Thames gravel at Swanscombe may be a quarter of a million years old. It makes no odds, therefore, if we suppose that man was here at the beginning. His earliest sounds will have been as simian as his features. But the power of oral expression increased, an integral factor in man's gradual emancipation from the animal state, and when his speech was at last perfected, he was then man indeed. These islands have been part of the scene of the general evolution of human speech.

Who can say how many tribes of *homo loquens* have made their homes in this land? Looking back over uncounted millennia, the imagination dimly comprehends peoples without number preceding us in ages unrecorded. And each and every people must have possessed its own mother tongue. Only the details are lost, for though archaeology has brought much understanding of even the remotest past, for our purposes the bones and flints of prehistoric man are mute. Of the transition from brutish call to human utterance we know nothing, nor of those myriad languages which came into being, had their day and passed on, long before the dawn of history.

Yet some of the archaeologist's finds permit at least a general

11

linguistic inference. Some 25,000 years ago, we are told, the last European Ice Age was passing its climax. Most of Britain had been under the ice sheet; only the country south of the Thames appears to have remained free, a tundra zone joined to the Continent by a land bridge fifty miles wide across the Straits of Dover. With the amelioration of the climate, herds of reindeer and bison now found pasture on steppes where ice had once permanently covered the ground. The game-hunters followed with harpoon and spear. We are ignorant of the real names of these people, but still we know them well, for they were of the same stock and culture as those Cro-Magnon men whose exquisite animal drawings have become the fame of Altamira and Labastide. Portrayed are the victims of the chase, and the presence of the pictures in the deepest recesses of the caves indicates their occult significance. Artistry of this calibre bears witness to the advanced ritualistic practices of a very mature society, not without parallels familiar to anthropologists from many parts of the modern world. The bearers of such a culture will undoubtedly have spoken a fully developed language, comparable in principle to any found today. It will have been abundant in expressions pertaining to their way of life. It will certainly have possessed a special vocabulary and dignified phraseology for use in hymns and incantations, differentiated from ordinary speech and aesthetically satisfying. Eloquence would be a hallmark of eminence in a society which, if analogies among primitives today be any guide, must have invested language with an aura of magic.

Meanwhile the climate in our latitudes continued to grow warmer. As the ice melted, the level of the sea rose, so that about 10,000 years ago Ireland was separated from Britain, which itself was being separated from the Continent. Palaeolithic man was still present, but more advanced cultures appear, pointing to new influxes from the Continent. The Old Stone Age was passing, the Middle Stone Age with its quickening evolutionary tempo was at hand. Several waves of mesolithic immigration have been identified and named after some significant source of their cultures, as Tardenoisian, Azilian or Maglemosean, much as Old-Stone-Age cultures have been labelled Aurignacian, Gravettian, Solutrean, Magdalenian.

About 5,000 years ago, the neolithic revolution began. Hitherto man in these parts had been a nomadic hunter and food gatherer. In the New Stone Age he raised crops and animals. Again, these new developments were the work of immigrants who introduced their skills from the Continent. They settled in areas most favourable to their mode of life, chiefly on the uplands of the South and East. It was at this time that Salisbury Plain began to develop into a centre of trade and culture.

The first metal objects found in Britain are dated to about 2000 BC; the Bronze Age had reached these islands. Closely associated with this development were the Beaker people, immigrants ultimately (it is thought) from Central Europe and, judging by grave finds, a martial race. They were most probably responsible for the building of Stonehenge, at the time the largest structure of its kind north of the Alps. About the same period, other settlers were reaching Ireland and the west coast of Britain. They were also builders of megaliths and, as workers in gold, entertained trading relations with the Beaker people. The British Isles in the second millennium BC were apparently prosperous and progressive, adding lustre to barbarian Europe.

As the historical period draws nearer, the archaeological record becomes fuller. Important for our purpose is the evidence of continuing immigration seen in changing burial customs and continental-type artifacts. Then, towards the middle of the first millennium, incursions on a large scale become the order of the day. Now prehistory and history meet: for the first time the newcomers can be ethnically and linguistically identified. They were Celts, bearers of the Iron Age Hallstatt culture, to be followed in the third and second centuries BC by other Celts possessing the La Tène culture which had succeeded that of Hallstatt on the Continent. Finally, in the early part of the first century BC, a third influx affected the south-east. These Celts can actually be named, for their migration was reported to Julius Caesar a generation later, as told in his *Gallic War*: they were the Belgae, who crossed to Britain from the Low Countries.

We have seen that language was fully developed when Britain again became habitable after the last glaciation. We have seen, too, that archaeology has revealed the presence of many different peoples who, at various times, settled in this country. The number of different languages must likewise have been very considerable. It is known from our own day that, where existence is primitive, man lives in small societies, each with its own distinctive speech. Of this the bewildering conglomeration of native Australian languages is a classical example, for here almost every tribe, however diminutive, has developed its own characteristic language. This was almost uni-

13

versally the case in the New World. Only where states had been formed, as those of the Aztecs in Mexico or the Incas in Peru, were languages found to be used over a wide range and by really large numbers. The rule elsewhere was, as it generally still is, a multiplicity of divergent tongues, most of them used by no more than a few thousand or even a few hundred speakers. And the same goes for much of Negro Africa.

The reason for such heterogeneity is not hard to find. The unstable character of primitive society, with its small units and restless wanderings involving the fragmentation of some groups and the fusion of others, was by its nature conducive to rapid linguistic change. Given such conditions, what of the survival rate of the languages in question? The fragmentation of a group speaking a uniform language would give rise to varying dialects which could eventually become so distinct as to constitute separate languages. Likewise the fusion of groups speaking different languages could lead to the emergence of new forms of speech, each again a language unto itself. It will surely have been exceptional if, in these primordial circumstances, any language continued as recognizably the same for more than, say, five hundred years. Such will have been the rate of change in Stone-Age Britain, too. Granted, as we approach the historical era, the amount of diversity would tend to decrease. Impressive monuments like Stonehenge prove that by the second millennium BC very large social entities had come into being. Such progress would make for linguistic stability and encourage the rise of major languages serving a wide area. This would be the general position when the Celtic invasions led to a degree of linguistic uniformity which cannot have been known in these islands previously. In the hazy dawn of history we perceive three main languages, dominating by far the greater part of the country: British Celtic, Irish Celtic and, as the chief representative of the older stock, Pictish.

There can be little doubt that, by and large, the pattern of evolution in the British Isles was a replica of contemporary developments on the continent of Europe. Here, too, the diversity of languages characteristic of early societies was being superseded by the greater homogeneity imposed by more advanced states. The last phase of this trend may be observed in the full light of history in the conquests of the Latin language. Ancient Italy was traditionally a land of many tongues. Beside Latin, native to the province of Latium, were Ligurian, Venetian, Etruscan, Umbrian, Oscan, Messapian, Sicilian, not to mention intrusive Gaulish in the north and colonial Greek in the south. Spain was similarly multilingual before the Roman conquest obliterated all the indigenous languages – with the sole exception of Basque.

CHAPTER TWO

Pre-Celtic languages; Pictish

🐚🐚🐚🐚🐚🐚

As already stated, the Celtic languages had largely obliterated the tongues previously spoken in these islands even before the coming of the Romans. In the present chapter, we consider the evidence for the survival of such languages into Roman and post-Roman times.

In Britain, the pre-Roman period is prehistoric. The Ancient Britons undoubtedly possessed traditions relating to their origins and past history which would include accounts of their arrival in this country. But the most influential guardians of this knowledge, the druids, were slaughtered by the Romans in the early years of the conquest. Four centuries of Roman domination extirpated all memory of former times. Ireland, however, remained outside the Roman Empire. Society here evolved more gradually, there was no violent break with the past, and the druids transmitted their knowledge as of yore. Even when Christianity came in the fifth century, it came gently. Eventually many traditions were set down in writing. A twelfth-century compilation, *The Book of the Conquest of Ireland*, is regarded as the culmination of lost works on the subject going back to the eighth century. It is unfortunately true that, in this work, fact, legend and editorial fiction can but rarely be disentangled with certainty, but the basic theme of the book and the accounts of numerous invasions must be a reflection, however distorted, of genuine folk-memories.

In the latest fundamental study of these problems, that by O'Rahilly (see 'Literature', page 18), it is argued that there is positive evidence for four invasions: those of the Cruthin, the Érainn (also called Fir Bolg), further a group of tribes, of whom the Lagin were the best remembered, and lastly the Goidels. The name Cruthin may be regarded as a gaelicization of *Priteni*, ie, 'Britons', found in Ptolemy's *Geography*, the Irish material of which is dated to 100 AD or perhaps somewhat earlier. The name Érainn presupposes an early **Ēwernī* comparable to Ptolemy's *Iverni*, while Fir Bolg, (lit. 'Men of Bags'), which can hardly be an original sense, has been conjecturally equated with Belgae, the name of a well-known Celtic people. The tribal name Lagin, which survives in the name of Leinster province, has not been explained. The name Goidel is problematic, too; it appears, however, to be a borrowing from Welsh *Gwyddel* 'Irishman', a term attested since the end of the seventh century.

What is known, or what can be deduced, about the languages of these various invaders? The Goidels are, of course, the Gaels whose Celtic language is well known. Whether the Lagin were a branch of the Gaels is not certain, but the other two were apparently not Gaelic. In the case of the Cruthin, there is the testimony of their name which, in its original form *Priteni*, reveals itself as non-Gaelic, since Gaelic at that time did not possess the sound *p*. There is evidence for the Érainn, too. An early tenth-century work, Cormac's *Glossary*, speaks of a style of diction called *iarnbélre*, (lit. 'iron speech': *iarn*, *bélre*), which employed 'hard', ie, unusual, words, as *onn* for 'stone' instead of *cloch*. But as 'hard' is pretty obviously a secondary explanation induced by *iarn* 'iron', it has been suggested that *iarnbélre* stands for an original **Érnbélre* 'speech of the Érainn (*Iverni*)', the corruption possibly encouraged by some association with *Iar*, known to have been an Ivernic personal name. In this way, *onn* is explicable as an Ivernic loan word in Gaelic.

If the Cruthin and Érainn were not Gaelic-speaking, what did they speak? O'Rahilly regarded them as Celts akin to those found in Britain, but given the present state of knowledge such a view is necessarily tentative. One must also seriously reckon with the possibility that they may have been pre-Celtic. It may be emphasized that pre-Celtic in this context does not necessarily imply non-Indo-European. The Celts are the first Indo-Europeans known to have reached the British Isles, but that is not to say that other Indo-Europeans may not have preceded them.

It hardly seems likely, however, that we shall ever be in a position to affirm anything less hypothetical. Yet it is certain that we actually possess linguistic material older than the Celtic invasions, though paradoxically it cannot be positively identified in any given instance. But such material must be present, to a greater or lesser extent, in our oldest river names. Most of these cannot be etymologized – examples are the Thames, Severn, Ouse, Tees – and in view of the known conservative character of such names, it must be assumed that some at least are pre-Celtic.

Antecedents

LITERATURE

T. F. O'Rahilly, *Early Irish History and Mythology* (1946).
E. Ekwall, *English River Names* (1928).

PICTISH

Indubitable evidence for the survival of pre-Celtic speech in the British Isles comes from North Britain. Its last guardians were the Picts.

Not very much is known about this people. *Picti* are first referred to in AD 297, when, together with *Hiberni*, they are characterized as enemies of the *Britanni*. Later sources substitute *Scotti* (*Scoti*) for *Hiberni*, hence the familiar Picts and Scots. The latter were certainly Irish, but who were the Picts? The origin of the name *Picti* is problematic. Latin *pictī* means 'painted, tattooed' and the name would be thus understood by those who read Latin. The insoluble question is this: Is *Picti* really the epithet it seems to be, or is it a corruption of a genuine Pictish name unknown to us? One aspect is, however, clear. In denoting all the inhabitants north of the Clyde and Forth, the term *Picti* embraces two distinct peoples, the one Celtic, the other non-Celtic.

The Celtic component was that population which settled thickly, perhaps in the first century BC, in the Lowlands and along the eastern seaboard beyond the Forth; the British Celtic speech of this population may be further qualified as Pictish Celtic. The non-Celtic component may be equated with those traditional inhabitants of the Highland zone whose territory was known to Agricola in the second half of the first century AD as Caledonia. In a linguistic connotation the term Pictish refers to the language of this component only.

About the middle of the fifth century, the Scots of Ulster began to despoil the Picts of their patrimony in Argyll, where they set up their own kingdom of Dalriada. In the next century, however, the Picts emerge as a powerful force, apparently under a single king. Though perhaps only loosely united under him, they seem to have preserved their unity down to the extinction of the Pictish royal line in or about 843. The territory of this, the historic Pictish kingdom, is known as Pictland. The Forth–Clyde line formed the border with its neighbours to the south, the Angles of Northumbria and the Britons of Strathclyde. In the west, the position seems to have been less stable,

18

the Scottish intruders in Argyll apparently extending their sway northward along the coast and among the islands.

The relations between Celtic and non-Celtic in the territory which became known as Pictland are little understood. British Celtic names are not uncommonly borne by Pictish notables, implying at least strong British Celtic influence, if not indeed outright superiority. This would certainly be expected in the first phase of contact when the iron-using Celts established themselves in what was still a Bronze-Age backwater. But how things subsequently developed is not clear. There is evidence that the language of the kings of Pictland was not Celtic. It is expressly stated in Bede's *Ecclesiastical History* (i.i) that five tongues were in use in Britain: Latin and the languages of the *Bretti, Scotti, Picti* and *Angli*. From his monastery in Jarrow, Bede was in a position to have first-hand information about such matters. Northumbria's neighbours to the north and north-west were Pictland and (British-speaking) Strathclyde respectively. Now, elsewhere (v.xxi) Bede describes a Northumbrian embassy to the Pictish king Naiton, *c.* 710, and reports that a letter brought by the envoys was first translated into Pictish. If the king's language had been Celtic, Bede would surely have called it British, for the Celtic of Pictland was simply a British dialect, to all intents and purposes identical with that of Strathclyde with which it was possibly still in contact. It may be noted, too, that the forms of British Celtic names used by the Picts reveal changes comparable to those taking place elsewhere in British Celtic, notably the loss of inflexional endings. This fact indicates a local continuation of Celtic during the time of the historic Pictish kingdom. All the same, one has the impression that it was Pictish, not Celtic, which was in the ascendancy during this last phase.

Throughout its existence the kingdom of Pictland appears to have been subject to Scottish influence emanating from Argyll. In 565 or thereabouts, Christianity was introduced from this quarter by Columba. The cultural supremacy of Argyll explains why many Pictish names are Gaelic or at least gaelicized. But there is no evidence that the Pictish language itself was seriously threatened until the beginning of the ninth century. It was at this time that the settlements of the Norsemen in Shetland, Orkney, in the Hebrides, and on the mainland in Sutherland and Caithness led to the disappearance of Pictish in these parts. Viking raiders shook the precarious stability of the Pictish state, creating a power vacuum into which the men of Argyll were able to move. In or about 843, under

Kenneth mac Alpin, Argyll and Pictland were united as a Scottish kingdom centered on Scone. The linguistic consequence of the political change was the triumph of Gaelic at the expense of Pictish and Pictish Celtic. The extremely exiguous historical sources for the next two centuries are silent on questions of language. When the record becomes fuller, Pictish appears as a thing of the past, while Gaelic had made advances on all fronts. It must have possessed considerable *élan* and we therefore suppose that Pictish, already weakened in the north and west, rapidly succumbed after the union of the kingdoms. One can only guess that Pictish probably became moribund within two or three generations after that event, which would bring the date of its final demise to somewhere about the year 1000.

THE RECORDS OF PICTISH

The Picts have been characterized as a significant political force. In that day and age, such a people was naturally not without notable cultural achievements. In this respect the Picts are remembered and admired for their remarkable sculpture with its unique symbolic motifs, as yet unexplained. They followed the writing conventions of the Scots, using Ogam letters (p. 80) for inscriptions, but the Latin alphabet for other purposes. No manuscript material of Pictish age has survived, but twenty-two short inscriptions on stone, in the main not earlier than 700 AD, remain as contemporary witnesses to a vanished language. Otherwise Pictish is attested in numerous personal and place names.

Although the inscriptions are frequently damaged, enough remains to give an impression of the language. When the personal names are extracted, the residue is entirely incomprehensible. Thus the Lunnasting stone in Shetland reads *ettocuhetts ahehhttann hccvvevv nehhtons*. The last word is clearly the commonly occurring name *Nechton* (known to Bede as *Naiton*), but the rest, even allowing for the perhaps arbitrary doubling of consonants in Ogam, appears so exotic that philologists conclude that Pictish was a non-Indo-European language of unknown affinities. In this respect, Pictish could be described as the analogue of Basque. The older view that Pictish was essentially Celtic is no longer tenable.

The personal and place names of the Picts, in so far as they are not Celtic of one sort or another, are as intractable as the inscriptions.

20

Pre-Celtic languages; Pictish

The chief source of the former is a list of the Pictish succession of kings, best preserved in a fourteenth-century manuscript. Examples of names are *Bridei, Derelei, Bargoit*, forms corroborated by other historical records. Other examples, as *Bliesblituth* or *Uscombuts*, occur only in the list and cannot be independently confirmed, so that the possibility of their being corrupt is not excluded, especially as the manuscript itself is so late. Among place names (in Irish-style orthography) may be mentioned *Fib* 'Fife', *Athfotla* 'Atholl'. Finally, certain classical authors provide onomastic material, presumed Pictish, first and foremost Ptolemy, who records the names of thirty-eight different peoples and places in his famous *Geography*. Some of the names are definitely Celtic, but the majority cannot be thus explained, including the names of the four chief tribes: *Caledonii, Vacomagi, Taixali, Venicones*.

LITERATURE

F. T. Wainwright (editor), *The Problem of the Picts* (1955).
Isabel Henderson, *The Picts* (1967).

PART II

BRITISH CELTIC

◙◙◙◙◙◙

CHAPTER THREE

Ancient British

◙◙◙◙◙◙

It is not to be doubted that the Roman invaders of Britain found a linguistically homogeneous population throughout the major part of the country. Nor had the newcomers any difficulty in identifying the language, for it was, as Tacitus in his *Agricola* explicitly states (XI), not very different from that spoken in Celtic Gaul. As a modern writer might say: British and Gaulish were regional varieties of a common tongue. They were essentially oral media, and normally unwritten. Neither variety could therefore have been in any sense standardized, but would vary, sometimes considerably, from place to place.

It is probable that this form of Celtic was introduced into Britain by the bearers of the Hallstatt culture towards the middle of the first millennium BC. It was certainly the language of the later La Tène immigrants of the third and second centuries BC and, of course, also of the Belgic invaders of the early first century BC (p. 13) and of those many refugees who crossed over to Britain from Gaul after the subjugation of that country by the Romans in 58–50 BC. British was apparently universal south of a line from the Clyde to the Forth, though Lowland Scotland was perhaps not occupied until the first century BC. About the same time, British would spread further up the east coast, at least as far as the Moray Firth. As far as may be surmised, the pre-Celtic language was thus now confined to the Highland zone (p. 18).

23

The British language was soon affected by the Roman occupation. Latin became the language of prestige and many of its words, especially such as denoted objects or concepts of Roman civilization hitherto unknown to the natives, were borrowed into British (pp. 155–157). Latin was certainly very widely spoken here and will actually have replaced British to a considerable extent, particularly in the towns of the lowland south and east, which were essentially Roman creations and centres of latinization; the wilder uplands of the north and west, on the other hand, remained solidly British-speaking. When the legions were recalled in 410 AD or thereabouts, the native Celtic element again came to the fore. It seems noteworthy that Vortigern, the shadowy leader of the British in the sub-Roman period, bore a transparently Celtic name (*vor-* 'eminent', *tigern* 'king') and it seems very likely that at this time the British language was reviving in the east and south. But whatever the trend, it was to have no tangible effect on subsequent linguistic history. By the middle of the century, the fearsome Germanic tribesmen – Angles, Saxons, Jutes – had begun their invasion in earnest and by the time they had finished, a couple of centuries later, their dialects had obliterated vernacular Latin and British alike over the greater part of the country south of the Cheviots. Of Latin there was now not a trace, while British survived to any mentionable extent only in the extreme south-west (Devon and Cornwall), in Wales with Monmouth and West Hereford, and in the far north-west (North Lancashire, Westmorland, Cumberland), this last area adjoining the equally British-speaking western half of the Scottish Lowlands which eventually formed the historic kingdom of Strathclyde. The eastern half of the Lowlands, however, had fallen to the Angles in the last phase of the invasions and English now reached as far as Edinburgh, but British continued in use in north-eastern Scotland, apparently disputing territory with Pictish.

Subsequent development in Devon and Cornwall and in Wales are considered in Chapters Four and Five. Everywhere else British died out early in the Middle Ages. In the north-west, as far as the Solway, the evidence of place names suggests that some British persisted until the ninth century at least, to be finally supplanted not by Anglo-Saxon, but by the Norse of the Vikings who settled thickly in these districts (p. 202). Further north, in Strathclyde, the language survived somewhat longer, and may not have become entirely extinct until the early twelfth century; it succumbed to Gaelic, first introduced into Argyll from Ireland in the fifth century (p. 117). Whether this late form of British, which may be called Cumbric, was ever used for literary purposes is unknown, but three words of it are preserved as technical terms in an eleventh-century Latin legal document. The fate of British in north-eastern Scotland is particularly obscure. From about the ninth century the area became Gaelic-speaking, but possibly British here yielded, in part at any rate, to resurgent Pictish (p. 19).

We should not close this account of the fate of the Ancient British language without a reference to that remarkable exodus of Britons across the Channel into Gaul which took place during the confused period of the Anglo-Saxon invasions. The destination of the emigrants was Armorica, later renamed Brittany. The new arrivals retained the use of their British speech which imposed itself over much the greater part of the province and came to be known as Breton. Though it had been in slow retreat westwards since the early Middle Ages, the language maintained itself well until recently. In spite of the total lack of recognition on the part of the authorities, it was estimated in 1945 that as many as a million persons were then conversant, more or less, with Breton, though admittedly a large percentage of these belonged to the higher age-groups, the younger generation having often gone over to French exclusively. Since then the number of those speaking Breton has certainly declined; according to some reports the decline has been catastrophic, but exact figures are not available because French census returns are not concerned with such matters. Excepting children under school age, speakers of Breton are normally bilingual. Today the language is confined to the rural districts of Basse-Bretagne west of a line from St Brieuc to Vannes. The philological analysis of Breton shows that it originated in south-western Britain (p. 53).

THE RECORDS OF ANCIENT BRITISH

The British language of antiquity is attested chiefly in the names of places and persons handed down by classical authors, as Caesar or Tacitus; for place names particularly Ptolemy's *Geography*, composed about 150 AD from somewhat older materials (p. 16), and a gazetteer of Britain compiled about 300 AD and known as the *Antonine Itinerary*, are particularly important. A number of British names survive also in contemporary Latin inscriptions found in this country. Lastly, a fair number of British elements are to be found in our modern place names. This rather exiguous material can often be elaborated, thanks to the deductions of comparative Celtic philology. We have already seen that the Celtic of Gaul was similar to that of Britain. The records of Gaulish are, in general, of the same order as those of British, but are much fuller – including, as they do, a considerable number of inscriptions – and often supplement our scanty knowledge of British. The known daughter languages – Welsh, Cornish, Breton – also permit many conclusions as to the nature of the parent language. Comparison with the Irish branch of Celtic likewise plays a significant part in the theoretical restitution of the Ancient British language.

It becomes apparent that British was highly inflected, at a stage of evolution roughly comparable to Classical Latin, and apparently also to the oldest Irish. On the other hand, the language was soon to find itself in a period of transition, reaching by the sixth and seventh centuries a considerably more analytical stage, particularly as regards nominal inflexion, less so in the verbal categories. This development is so reminiscent of the evolution of spoken Latin at this time that one feels entitled to postulate a high degree of typological influence on British from this quarter. Such a view is not based solely on the assumptions of comparative philology. As far as the nominal inflexion is concerned there are clear indications from the ancient sources themselves. We may take examples. British *abonā* f. will have declined rather like Lat. *puella* (p. 160), but by the end of the Roman period it had changed to *avon*, having lost its case ending. This word is still with us today in the name *Avon*, which simply means 'River', cf. Welsh *afon* 'do'. Similarly British *Sabrinā* appears later as *Severn*, though in this case the etymology is unknown; the name may have been taken over by the Britons from a pre-Celtic population (p. 17).

Among semantically transparent names are *Dubrīs* (apparently with latinized locative ending), 'Waters', now *Dover*, cf. Welsh *dwfr* and *Uxellodūnum* (the modern Maryport) 'High Fort' (*uxello-* cf. Welsh *uchel* 'high', *dūnum* with a latinized ending for British *dūnon*, cf. Welsh *din* 'fort'). The term *combe* 'valley, dell' exists in the local English of the West Country and in place names throughout England, as *Babbacombe*. It is a Celtic survivor and though not actually encountered in the sparse records of Ancient British, its form in that language was certainly *cumbā*, for the word is so found in the closely related Celtic of Gaul. The basic sense of personal names may also be recognizable in whole or in part. Thus the name-stem *Maglocun-* is interpreted 'Princely Hound' ie, 'Princely Defender' (*maglo-* 'prince', lit. 'great (person)', *cun-* 'hound'), the latter occurring again in *Cunobelinus* (Shakespeare's *Cymbeline*). Particularly interesting is *Boadicea*, now recognized as a corruption of *Boudīcā* 'Victoria'. All three names survive in later Welsh tradition as *Maelgwn, Cynfelin, Buddug*.

It will be appropriate to consider here a development which led to the remarkable system of initial mutations still strikingly characteristic of the derivative languages (pp. 35–43). We saw above that British *abonā* eventually changed to *avon*. This change of *b* to *v* is found whenever the consonant occurs between vowels or between a vowel and a sonant, as *r*, thus *Sabrinā, Dubrīs*, now *Severn, Dover*. As most initial consonants in Ancient British were in practice followed by a vowel or a sonant, an initial *b* would find itself *de facto* in a comparable position whenever the preceding word ended in a vowel, and the pronunciation was likewise changed to *v* in such cases also. Thus *bodīnā* (fem.) 'army', *oinā bodīnā* 'one army' had by the end of the fifth century evolved to *boðīna, ūna voðīna*, which in the next century further changed to *buðīn, ūn vuðīn*. A masculine noun, on the other hand, was not so affected, since the masculine form of 'one' ended in a consonant, thus *bardos* 'poet', *oinos bardos* 'one poet', becoming by the end of the period *barð, ūn barð*. Since the phonetic environments were now identical for both words, the mutation of initial *b* to *v* came to be felt as a property of the feminine gender. Our examples survive in present-day Welsh as *byddin, un fyddin, bardd, un bardd* – the preliterary stages, as quoted, are of course not actually recorded, but have been reconstructed in accordance with the findings of comparative philology. Seven consonants were prominently involved in this softening or lenition, as it is technically called, namely *p, t, c, b, d, g* and *m*. Other changes worked, to a more limited extent, in an opposite direction, when by a process known as provection consonants were hardened, eg, *b* became *p*. Yet other changes led to nasal and spirant mutations. All these developments appear to have taken place within a short period of time, ie, during the second half of the fifth and the first half of the sixth centuries.

It is remarkable that a related system arose in Irish about the same

British Celtic

time (p. 82). As a phonetic feature, mutations occasionally occur in other languages, as locally in Greek or Italian, but nowhere else apparently have they been developed to such an extent and come to dominate the structure of the language as they do in Insular Celtic. This aspect seems quite unique.

LITERATURE

K. Jackson, *Language and History in Early Britain* (1953, last reprint 1971).

CHAPTER FOUR

Welsh

🉑🉑🉑🉑🉑🉑

WELSH, which is closely related to Cornish and Breton (p. 25), is descended from the British spoken in Wales where it had been isolated since the early seventh century. At that period, however, the border lay further east than at present and included not only Monmouth, but also the country west of the Severn, with most of Shropshire and parts of Cheshire. But the Saxons pressed forward, and in the late eighth century, Offa built his famous Dyke to mark the new political boundary, though Welsh remained in use east of the Dyke for many centuries. The Welsh tribesmen were now well protected by their terrain, but the newcomers infiltrated along the north coast, to be, however, subsequently repulsed or assimilated, as is shown by such place names as *Prestatyn*, a wallicized form of Old English *Prēostatūn* 'Priests' Town' as in *Preston*, Lancashire. There had been some Irish colonization in both North and South Wales in the Dark Ages, and later scattered Norse settlements were made in coastal regions, but the former had long since disappeared, while the latter soon declined and constituted no threat to Welsh independence or the Welsh language.

The scene changed abruptly, however, with the coming of the Normans. In 1070 William himself led an army to Chester and along the Welsh frontier unopposed, and his Lords Marchers sorely harassed the Welsh. In the north, Rhuddlan was seized and fortified, and by 1085 there were Norman castles also at Montgomery and Caerleon. In 1088 a castle arose at Cardiff and within a decade the whole of the more accessible south had fallen. As a consequence, the Welsh language was displaced to a certain extent, particularly in South Pembrokeshire and part of the Gower, by Flemish and English (p. 235). But the Normans could not overcome the Welsh princes in the mountains of the northern part of the country, which remained independent until 1282, when Llewelyn, the last native ruler, was slain in the vain struggle against Edward I.

In the decades that followed, English law was gradually introduced into Wales, but no attempt was made to impose uniformity in customs or administration, and Welsh intellectual life continued undisturbed. The Norman households were by this time being assimilated into Welsh society. Latin was used now much as in England (p. 157), but otherwise Welsh remained the natural literary language and, apart from enclaves in the south, the ordinarily spoken medium everywhere. Literature in Welsh continued to flourish, its leading exponent in the fourteenth century, the poet Dafydd ap Gwilym, having European significance. It was not until Tudor times that the cultural and linguistic traditions of Wales were first seriously jeopardized.

By the Act of Union, which came into force in 1536, Wales was to be administered as a part of England. The Act contained a provision that English alone could be used in the administration of the law and that no one could hold an official position in Wales unless he was able to use the English tongue. Even if, for practical reasons, the whole of this provision could not be implemented immediately, it nevertheless opened the door to anglicization. At one stroke, the national language was robbed of its status, and its prestige inevitably began to decline. The gentry were the first to abandon the native language, but the bulk of the peasantry and the artisan class remained Welsh monoglots down to the beginning of the nineteenth century; the bearers of Welsh culture were now the lower orders. Only on the border with England did Welsh continue to yield ground, though slowly, as it had doubtless done here since Norman times at least.

After 1800, however, the linguistic cohesion of the country was progressively weakened. The industrialization of the south attracted so many workers from outside Wales that Welsh began to be replaced by English, particularly in the main centres, such as Cardiff and Swansea, whose influence penetrated far into the surrounding districts. The smaller towns on the north coast, too, became largely anglicized during the second half of the century. It was also during the nineteenth century that a knowledge of English as a second language spread among those who retained the use of Welsh. This development was accelerated after about 1850 and greatly encouraged by compulsory schooling after 1870, for English was the avowed medium of instruction, in fact the acquisition of English was often seen as the main purpose of the schools.

In the present century, anglicization has proceeded apace, as statistics show. According to a survey made in 1879, Welsh was then spoken by 934,000 persons out of a total of 1,150,000 over three years of age, or 81 per cent. The census of 1891 recorded 880,000 Welsh speakers out of a population of 1,600,000 or 54 per cent. However, the number of speakers increased in spite of the proportional decline: (1901) 930,000, (1911) 977,000, (1921) 985,000 or 50 per cent, 43 per cent, 37 per cent of the total population respectively. But then the fall became absolute: (1931) 909,000, (1951) 715,000, (1961) 659,000 or 36·8 per cent, 29 per cent, 26 per cent. In 1891, as many as 494,000 were returned as Welsh-speaking only, close on a third of the population. Ten years later, monoglot Welsh accounted for no more than 15 per cent, in 1911 for 9 per cent, in 1921 for 6 per cent, in 1931 for 4 per cent, but since the First World War virtually all these have been small children who had not yet learned English. In 1951, a total of 41,000, in 1961 a mere 26,000 were returned as solely Welsh-speaking.

Although the Welsh speakers had generally become bilingual by the early years of this century, and in spite of the rapid advance of monoglot English in the towns, Welsh remained the dominant oral medium over the greatest part of rural Wales for another generation at least. But then the modernization of farming led to redundancy. Agricultural workers left for the towns, or for England, and their going was a loss to Welsh. Their empty cottages, however, provided attractive retirement homes for purely English people. Anglicization has now seized the country districts of Wales, too.

The mass media are probably playing the decisive part. The English-language newspaper or magazine did not materially affect the use of Welsh as a spoken language, but the English radio and, most of all, the English television, have brought the foreign tongue in its most appealing form into every Welshman's home. So great, indeed, is the impact of television that small children who, a generation ago, would have been monoglot Welsh speakers, are now able to use English and often prefer it in imitation of their favourite pop stars. The limited amount of broadcasting time available for Welsh-language programmes is poor compensation in the circumstances. Hitherto Welsh Wales could assimilate at least the small children who moved in from outside, but today even this is questionable. Everybody is expected to know English, no one is expected to know Welsh; that is the prevailing attitude.

The spread of English in Wales during the last century caused much controversy which has lasted until the present day. The problem is basically that of all minor languages in the modern world whose existence is endangered by a major competitor. The advantages of a knowledge of English required little demonstration, and many Welshmen began to feel their Welsh as a hindrance to their advancement and welcomed anglicization. But others looked at their heritage in a more positive way. They saw the language as the natural expression of the national life, with as much right to survive as any other. They deplored the disabilities placed upon the language and eventually achieved some success in the educational field, where Welsh was admitted as a grant-earning subject in 1890. Further progress has been made since then, particularly in the schools, where Welsh is now widely used as a medium of instruction, though mostly only at the primary stage. The language has also obtained a degree of official recognition. The Welsh Language Act (1967) affirmed the equal validity of Welsh with English in the administration of justice and the conduct of government. Welsh has also acquired a certain respectability.

But the Welsh language remains *de facto* in a very inferior position. It is virtually excluded from business and commerce, even in those parts which have a majority of Welsh speakers. Where Welsh survives, it is chiefly as an oral medium. The written or printed medium is overwhelmingly English. Walk down a street in Caernarvon, the only sizable town where the majority of the population still speaks Welsh. On all sides, the language is being spoken, and when the tourists have gone, it is the dominant language. But the signs and notices, the advertisements on the hoardings and in the shop windows are, to all intents and purposes, as English as they are in England. Here the Welsh language is disinherited. It seems as though the genius of the place has become its ghost.

There are signs that the use of the Welsh language has so far declined that a restoration of its fortunes is scarcely to be hoped for, the courageous exertions of its devotees notwithstanding. All the evidence shows that, in this modern world, a language is not likely to survive unless it is made official in an exclusive sense: it must have a monopoly on its own territory. This territory requires its own national administration and its own educational system operating through the national language. As a corollary it will have its own mass media, that is to say, its own radio and television and a daily press using that language. Its speakers may learn as many foreign languages as they wish, but the national life is expressed solely in the national language. Only then can the language maintain itself and assimilate outsiders. Had Wales been able to remain as linguistically cohesive as it was in 1800, there might have been a chance and a desire to form a Welsh-speaking state today. But times and facts have changed. If such a proposition were to materialize today for Wales, or even for part of it, that would surely be miraculous.

Though the outlook must be bleak, we remember that Welsh is, numerically, by far the strongest of the three Celtic languages still used in Britain, and it has therefore possibilities which the others have not. At first sight, for instance, one might expect it to have in any case a longer span of life than we can predict for either Irish or Scottish Gaelic (pp. 78, 119). It is worth noting, however, that survival in the Gaelic fringes has been due in no small measure to the isolation of the communities employing these languages and the continuation of their traditional, simple way of life. But such factors are less relevant for Wales: the whole country is easily accessible nowadays and older styles of life have little or no place in the principality today, so that greater numbers now may be no guarantee that Welsh will, in the end, fare much better than Gaelic. We may emphasize that the transition from bilingual Welsh and English to monolingual English can take place with startling rapidity and is in fact a feature of the contemporary scene. Meanwhile the selfless struggle to save the language goes on – for where there's life, there is also hope.

Spoken Welsh has, in this century, absorbed countless English words and adopted much English idiom, but the literary language continues in substantially its classical form. It looks back on a long and distinguished history. Apart from names occurring in various sources, Old Welsh is attested in glossaries, in short prose passages and in some verses preserved in manuscripts from the late eighth century until about 1100. Then, in the Middle Welsh period, from 1100 to 1400, the language appears profusely as the vehicle of a rich and varied medieval literature, both religious and profane, and developing a remarkably standardized form. Many genres are represented, including law and history. The poetry is especially extensive, and often characterized by elaborate metres. Some of the traditional matter really belongs to the Old Welsh period, but though the language is in part archaic, it has also been modernized. The oldest literary tradition is found in the heroic poetry of Taliesin and Aneirin; going back to the late sixth century, it deals with the struggles of North British princes against the invading Angles.

The language of the fifteenth and sixteenth centuries may be termed Early Modern Welsh. The second half of this period witnessed great changes in intellectual life, and prose now came to dominate. Printing began in 1546 with a book of miscellaneous information, including the Paternoster and Ten Commandments; for lack of a title the work is known from its opening words *Yn y lhyvyr hwnn* – 'In this book'. Other publications quickly followed, including a Welsh–English dictionary in the next year. In 1567 a Welsh grammar appeared. The publication of the whole Bible in 1588 was a landmark. The translation was the work of William Morgan, essentially in the normalized language of the bards: archaic therefore, but dignified. It became a household book and provided an effective standard, even though its forms were often far from those of the spoken dialects. Then, in the eighteenth century, came the Methodist reformers, who appealed to the Welsh in their own language, and the ensuing religious revival brought forth an immense literature on devotional topics. In more recent times, in this century especially, books written in Welsh have become available in a wide range of subjects. A weekly and periodical press, much of it serving denominational interests, has for long been a feature of Welsh publishing, but has declined considerably during the past fifty years. There has never been a daily newspaper in Welsh, or in any other minor language of these islands for that matter.

Only a few words of Welsh provenance have found their way into Standard English, and these chiefly relate to the Welsh scene, as *eisteddfod*, lit. 'session' and *corgi*, lit. 'dwarf dog' (*cor, gi*, r. *ci*). Older loans are *coracle* (W. *corwgl*), *flannel*, dial. *flannen* (W. *wlanen* lenited form of *gwlanen*, from *gwlân* 'wool') and *flummery* (W. *llymru*). Welsh words may survive locally in areas long since anglicized, as *gwas* 'lad', *hiraeth* 'longing'.

Most place names in Wales are Celtic, common formative elements being *aber* 'estuary', *allt* 'slope', *bryn* 'hill', *caer* 'fort', *cwm* 'valley', *glan* 'bank, shore', *maes* 'field', *nant* 'brook', *pen* 'head(land), summit', *pentref* 'village', *tref* 'home, town'. The ubiquitous *llan* is a now obsolete word for 'church', eg, *Llandrindod* 'Church of the Trinity', *Llanfair* 'Church of Mary' (r. *Trindod, Mair*). Some of our best-known surnames are of Welsh origin, as *Lloyd*, variants *Lhuyd*,

Floyd (W. *Llwyd* 'Grey') and those containing older Welsh *ap* for *map* 'son' (now *mab*) as *Powell* or *Price* (W. *Ap Hywel* 'Son of Howell', *Ap Rhŷs* 'Son of Rees').

SKETCH OF WELSH

The following sketch describes the standard literary language. Most spoken Welsh, however, is broadly dialectal, the dialects differing from the written standard and each other, sometimes very considerably, in phonology, including the mutations, in accidence and in syntax.

Phonetics

The spelling of Welsh is very well suited to represent the sounds of the standard language.

Vowels are generally short, but may be long, especially in stressed monosyllables. The vowels *a, e, i, o* are as in English, *u = i* in South Welsh, but in North Welsh represents a central vowel between [i] and [u]; *w* is [u], as *bws* 'bus'; *y* is [ə], except in final syllables when it is [i], as also in the combination *wy* [ui], and when long it may be pronounced [iː]. Vowels coalesce to form numerous diphthongs. Stress normally falls on the last syllable but one; the last syllable, however, carries a pitch accent.

Among consonants we note the following conventions: *c* is [k], *ch* [χ], *th* [θ], *dd* [ð], *f* [v], *ff* [f], *nh* [nh], *ng* [ŋ], *ngh* [ŋh]; *ll* and *rh* are voiceless *l* and *r* respectively; *i* and *w* can be consonantal, eg, *cariad* [karjad] 'love' (noun), *gwely* [gweli] 'bed', also in such words as *gwlad* 'country', *gwnaf* 'I do'. Notice *si* is [ʃ] before back vowels, as *siarad* [ʃarad] 'speaking'.

Initial Mutations

Welsh continued the practice of initial mutation which arose in Late British times (p. 27). The changes observed in the literary language are shown in the table at the top of the following page.

We give a selection of examples to illustrate this all-pervading feature. The soft mutation has the most extensive ramifications; it occurs in nouns, eg, after *dy* 'thy', *ei* 'his': *dy ben* 'thy head' (r. *pen*), *ei dad* 'his father' (r. *tad*), after several prepositions: *drwy gae* 'through a

Radical	Soft	Nasal	Spirant
p	*b*	*mh*	*ph*
t	*d*	*nh*	*th*
c	*g*	*ngh*	*ch*
b	*f*	*m*	
d	*dd*	*n*	
g	*--*	*ng*	
m	*f*		
ll	*l*		
rh	*r*		

field' (r. *cae*), *heb fuwch* 'without a cow' (r. *buwch*), after certain numerals: *dau ddyn* 'two men' (r. *dyn*), when preceded by an adjective: *hen wraig* 'old woman' (r. *gwraig*), when vocative: *dewch yma blant* 'come here children' (r. *plant*), when fem. sg. taking the article: *y ferch* 'the daughter' (r. *merch*), when the object of an inflected verbal form: *etholasant lywydd* 'they elected a president' (r. *llywydd*), after an intervening word which disturbs the usual word order, as *yr oedd yno rosynnau* 'there were there roses', usual order *yr oedd rhosynnau yno*.

The soft mutation likewise affects adjectives, eg, when agreeing with a feminine singular noun: *mam dda* 'a good mother' (r. *da*) – a noun used as an adjective is similarly treated: *cadair freichiau* 'armchair' (r. *breichiau* 'arms') – or when occurring after *yn*, predicatively or adverbially: *y mae yn dlws* 'it is pretty' (r. *tlws*), *canodd hi yn brydferth* 'she sang beautifully' (r. *prydferth*), further in comparisons, as *mor fawr â* 'as big as' (r. *mawr*), and after certain adverbs, eg, *go fach* 'rather small' (r. *bach*). There are changes in verbs, too, particularly after various particles, as redundant: *fe welais* 'I saw' (r. *gwelais*), relative: *y ceffyl a brynasom* 'the horse which we bought' (r. *prynasom*), interrogative: *a glywaist* 'didst thou hear?' (r. *clywaist*), negative: *ni ddarllenasoch* 'you did not read' (r. *darllenasoch*), further after *pan* 'when': *pan fwyf yn hen* 'when I am old' (r. *bwyf*).

Generally speaking, any mutable consonant is affected as above in the conditions described, but *ll* and *rh* are sometimes exceptions. They do not mutate, eg, in adjectives after *yn*, hence *eistedd yn llonydd* 'sit still', or in feminine singular nouns taking the article: *y rhwyf* 'the oar'. The negative particles cause the spirant mutation of *p*, *t*, *c*, see below.

The conditions in which the nasal and spirant mutations take

Welsh

place are more restricted. The former is present only after *fy* 'my':
fy mhlentyn, fy nhad 'my child, my father' (r. *plentyn, tad*), after *yn*
'in' which itself may be modified: *yng Nghymru* 'in Wales', *ym
Mangor* 'in Bangor', *yn Nulyn* 'in Dublin', *yng Ngroeg* 'in Greece'
(r. *Cymru, Bangor, Dulyn, Groeg*), and finally certain numerals
cause change when used with 'days' or 'years', as *saith niwrnod*
'seven days' (r. *diwrnod*), *un mlynedd ar bymtheg* 'sixteen years' lit.
'one years on fifteen' (r. *blynedd*). The spirant mutation occurs,
eg, after the numerals *tri* 'three' and *chwe* 'six': *tri pheth* 'three things'
(r. *peth*), after *ei* 'her': *ei theulu* 'her family', (r. *teulu*), after sundry
other words, as *a* 'and': *cryf a thal* 'strong and tall' (r. *tal*), and after
a few prepositions: *tua Phumlumon* 'towards Plynlimmon' (r. *Pum-
lumon*). After negative particles, *p, t, c* are subject to this mutation:
na cheffyl na chart 'neither horse nor cart' (r. *ceffyl, cart*).

It is evident that mutation may occasionally have a semantic
function; contrast *ei blant* 'his children' with *ei phlant* 'her children',
further homophonous *eu* 'their' followed by the radical form, therefore *eu plant* 'their children'.

Words beginning with a vowel take an *h*-prefix after *ei* 'her', *ein*
'our', *eu* 'their', as *ei heli* 'her ointment', *ein harglwydd* 'our lord',
eu holwyn 'their wheel' (r. *eli, arglwydd, olwyn*), further after *'m*
'me' (p. 40); notice also *un ar hugain* 'twenty one' lit. 'one on
twenty' (r. *ugain*).

Nouns

There are two genders, masculine and feminine. Nouns do not
decline, but the formation of the plural is complicated.

A number of nouns form the plural by internal vowel change, as
oen m. 'lamb', pl. *ŵyn, troed* m. or f. 'foot', *traed, asgwrn* m. 'bone',
esgyrn, carreg f. 'stone', *cerrig, Cymro* m. 'Welshman', *Cymry, dafad*
f. 'sheep', *defaid, march* m. 'stallion', *meirch*. Generally, however, a
plural ending is used with or without further change to the singular.
The usual endings are *-au, -iau, -on, -ion, -i, -ydd, -oedd, -edd, -ed,
-od, -s, -ys*. Examples: *llyfr* m. 'book', *llyfrau, gair* m. 'word',
geiriau, Iddew m. 'Jew', *Iddewon, mab* m. 'son', *meibion, ffenestr* f.
'window', *ffenestri, chwaer* f. 'sister', *chwiorydd, môr* m. 'sea',
moroedd, gwraig f. 'woman', *gwragedd, pryf* m. 'worm; insect',
pryfed, cath f. 'cat', *cathod, lemwn* m. 'lemon', *lemwns, brws* m.
'brush', *brwsys*; notice also the common type *ffermwr* m. 'farmer',

37

ffermwyr. Conversely, the singular is sometimes formed from the plural by means of the suffixes *-en*, *-yn*, as *llygoden* f. 'mouse', *aderyn* m. 'bird', pl. *llygod, adar*. Not infrequently alternative plurals are admitted, eg, *tref* f. 'town', pl. *trefi* or *trefydd*.

Though there are no cases, nouns can be genitive by position, as *gramadeg yr iaith* 'the grammar of the language' lit. 'grammar of-the language'. Notice that *gramadeg* takes no article. Further, on the same lines *brenin nef* 'the king of heaven', *pren gwybodaeth da a drwg* 'the tree of the knowledge of good and evil', also *elfennau amaethyddiaeth* '(the) elements of agriculture', *Prifysgol Rhydychen* 'Oxford University' lit. 'University of-Ford of-Oxen' (*rhyd, ychen*). This distinctive construction is paralleled elsewhere in Insular Celtic, though in Gaelic the genitive may still be morphologically distinct.

Adjectives

Most adjectives are invariable, though a number have a distinct feminine singular formed by internal vowel change, eg (feminine singular normally softened, p. 36), *dwfn* m., *ddofn* f. 'deep', *gwyn, wen* 'white', *melyn, felen* 'yellow'. Some adjectives may, optionally in high style, make plural forms, either by internal vowel change, as *hardd* 'beautiful', plural *heirdd*, or by adding the endings *-ion, -on* with or without further change, as *tlawd* 'poor', *gwyn* 'white', plural *tlodion, gwynion, du* 'black', plural *duon*. Adjectives can be used substantively, as *y tlodion* 'the poor'.

The comparative and superlative of short adjectives are regularly formed by adding *-ach* and *-af* to the positive: *doeth* 'wise', *doethach, doethaf*, often with various internal changes, as *tlawd* 'poor', *tlotach, tlotaf*. There is also an equative degree, commonly formed in the case of short adjectives by *cyn* and the suffix *-ed*, thus *cyn ddoethed â* 'as wise as', *cyn dloted â* 'as poor as'. Most longer adjectives have analytic comparison: *beiddgar* 'bold', *mwy* ('more') *beiddgar, mwyaf* ('most') *beiddgar, mor feiddgar â* 'as bold as'. Several adjectives have irregular comparison: *da* 'good', *gwell* 'better', *gorau* 'best', *cystal â* 'as good as', *drwg* 'bad', *gwaeth* 'worse', *gwaethaf* 'worst', *cynddrwg â* 'as bad as'.

Numbers

1 *un*, 2 *dau*, 3 *tri*, 4 *pedwar*, 5 *pump*, 6 *chwech*, 7 *saith*, 8 *wyth*, 9 *naw*, 10 *deg*, 11 *un ar ddeg*, 12 *deuddeg*, 13 *tri ar ddeg*, 14 *pedwar ar ddeg*,

15 *pymtheg*, 16 *un ar bymtheg*, 17 *dau ar bymtheg*, 18 *deunaw*, 19 *pedwar ar bymtheg*, 20 *ugain*, 21 *un ar hugain*, 30 *deg ar hugain*, 40 *deugain*, 50 *hanner cant*, 60 *trigain*, 70 *deg a thrigain*, 80 *pedwar ugain*, 90 *deg a phedwar ugain*, 100 *cant*, 1000 *mil*.

Nouns immediately following the numeral are used in the singular: *deg llo* 'ten calves' lit. 'ten calf', but also expressed *deg o loi* lit. 'ten of calves'.

Numbers 2, 3 and 4 have feminine forms: *dwy, tair, pedair*; when standing before the noun, 5, 6 and 100 are *pum, chwe* and *can*, eg, *pum llong* beside *pump o longau* 'five ships'; 10 is *deng* before words beginning with *g, d, m, n*, hence *deng munud* 'ten minutes'.

In counting, 18 is *tri* (or *tair*) *ar bymtheg*, and higher numbers are commonly expressed in tens, eg, 50 *pum deg*, 60 *chwe deg*, 66 *chwe deg a chwech*.

Definite Article

The full form of the article is *yr*, used before words beginning with a vowel or *h*, as *yr ysgol* 'the school', *yr haul* 'the sun'. Before other letters, the form *y* is found: *y plant* 'the children', *y gyllell* 'the knife' (r. *cyllel* f.). When the preceding word ends in a vowel, the article is *'r*, as *dyma'r ysgol* 'here is the school', *pwy sydd yn dysgu'r plant?*' 'who is teaching the children?'. On mutations caused by the article, see p. 36.

There is no indefinite article.

Pronouns

The independent pronouns are *mi* 'I, me', *ti* 'thou, thee', *ef* 'he, him', *hi* 'she, her', *ni* 'we, us', *chwi* 'you', *hwy(nt)* 'they, them'. Emphatic forms are common, as *myfi, tydi, efe, hyhi, nyni, chwychwi, hwynt-hwy*. They ordinarily follow the noun of which they are the subject, first and second singular then being *fi* or *i, ti*, eg, *yr wyf fi* (or *i*) 'I am', *yr wyt ti* 'thou art', *y mae ef* 'he is'.

The possessive pronouns are *fy* 'my', *dy* 'thy', *ei* 'his, her', *ein* 'our', *eich* 'your', *eu* 'their', thus *fy mêl* 'my honey', *dy fêl* 'thy honey' (on mutations caused by the possessive, see pp. 36, 40). The noun in this construction may be followed by an affixed pronoun: sg. 1 *i*, 2 *di*, 3 m. *ef*, etc., as for the independent pronoun, hence also *fy mêl i*, etc.

Pronouns may be infixed, as in the case of possessives when they follow a word ending in a vowel, eg, *a* 'and'; sample paradigm: *a'm tad* 'and my father', *a'th dad* 'and thy father', *a'i dad* 'and his father', *a'i thad* 'and her father', *a'n tad* 'and our father', *a'ch tad* 'and your father', *a'u tad* 'and their father'. Infixed pronouns also occur as the object between a particle and the verb, the forms being *'m* 'me', *'th* 'thee', *'s* 'him, her', *'n* 'us', *'ch* 'you', *'s* 'them'; only *'th* causes mutation: *Duw a'th fendithio* 'God bless thee' (r. *bendithio*), but *'m* prefixes *h* to a word beginning with a vowel: *a'm hafal* 'and my apple' (r. *afal*).

Pronouns coalesce with certain prepositions, eg, *gan* 'with': *gennyf* 'with me', *gennyt* 'with thee', *ganddo* 'with him', *ganddi* 'with her', *gennym* 'with us', *gennych* 'with you', *ganddynt* 'with them'. These may be emphasized by the addition of the affixed pronoun: *gennyf fi* or *i*, *gennyt ti*, *ganddo ef*, *ganddi hi*, *gennym ni*, *gennych chwi*, *ganddynt hwy*. Other examples include *ar* 'on': *arnaf* 'on me', *arnat* 'on thee', *arno* 'on him', *arni* 'on her', *arnom* 'on us', *arnoch* 'on you', *arnynt* 'on them', emphatic *arnaf fi*, etc., *rhag* 'before': *rhagof* 'before me', *rhagot* 'before thee', *rhagddo* 'before him', *rhagddi* 'before her', *rhagom* 'before us', *rhagoch* 'before you', *rhagddynt* 'before them', emphatic *rhagof fi*, etc.

Verbs

Verbs have four synthetic tenses in the indicative (present, imperfect, preterite, pluperfect) and may have two in the subjunctive (present, imperfect), though in most cases nowadays only the present is formally distinguished from the indicative. There are no participles and no infinitive, but great use is made of the verbal noun. Impersonal tenses commonly correspond to the English passive. With most verbs, the synthetic present and imperfect generally have future and conditional meaning respectively. Except in the case of certain common verbs, synthetic conjugation is confined to the literary language where it has stylistic relevance, the spoken language preferring periphrastic formations consisting of tenses of the verb 'to be' (*bod*) with the verbal noun. The periphrastic tenses are all freely employed in writing also.

Synthetic inflexion is rather complex. There are several conjuga-

Welsh

tions and a fair number of anomalous forms. We give as our example a regular verb:

Verbal noun: *caru* 'loving'.
Indicative:
Pres. sg. 1 *caraf*, 2 *ceri*, 3 *câr*, pl. 1 *carwn*, 2 *cerwch*, 3 *carant*; impers. *cerir*.
Imperf. sg. 1 *carwn*, 2 *carit*, 3 *carai*, pl. 1 *carem*, 2 *carech*, 3 *carent*; impers. *cerid*.
Pret. sg. 1 *cerais*, 2 *ceraist*, 3 *carodd*, pl. 1 *carasom*, 2 *carasoch*, 3 *carasant*; impers. *carwyd*.
Pluperf. sg. 1 *caraswn*, 2 *carasit*, 3 *carasai*, pl. 1 *carasem*, 2 *carasech*, 3 *carasent*; impers. *carasid*.

Subjunctive:
Pres. sg. 1 *carwyf*, 2 *cerych*, 3 *caro*, pl. 1 *carom*, 2 *caroch*, 3 *caront*; impers. *carer*.
(Middle Welsh only: imperf. sg. 1 *carhwn*, 2 *carhut*, 3 *carhei*, pl. 1 *carhem*, 2 *carhewch*, 3 *carhynt*; impers. *cerhit*).

Imperative:
sg. 2 *câr*, 3 *cared*, pl. 1 *carwn*, 2 *cerwch*, 3 *carent*.

Examples of periphrastic tenses involving the verb 'to be' below: pres. *yr wyf yn caru* lit. 'I am in loving', pres. habitual or fut. *byddaf yn caru* lit. 'I am-wont-to-be in loving' or 'I shall-be in loving', imperf. *yr oeddwn yn caru* lit. 'I was in loving', imperf. habitual *byddwn yn caru* lit. 'I used-to-be in loving', perf. *yr wyf wedi caru* lit. 'I am after loving', pluperf. *yr oeddwn wedi caru* lit. 'I was after loving'.

The affirmative verb is sometimes preceded by a meaningless particle *fe*, as *fe garaf* 'I love'. Another such particle *y, yr*, is used with the present and imperfect of the verb 'to be'. Pronouns may also be found, as *caraf fi* or *i* 'I love' (p. 39).

The verb ordinarily stands at the head of the sentence, except in emphatic order, and a plural noun takes a singular verb: *y mae'r genethod yn cysgu* 'the girls are sleeping' lit. 'is the girls in sleeping'.

The interrogative is indicated by the particle *a*, the negative commonly by *ni*, before vowels *nid*, see below.

The verb 'to be'

Verbal noun: *bod* 'being'.

Indicative:

Pres. sg. 1 *yr wyf* or *yr ydwyf*, 2 *yr wyt* or *yr ydwyt*, 3 *y mae*, pl. 1 *yr ŷm* or *yr ydym*, 2 *yr ych* or *yr ydych*, 3 *y maent*; impers. *yr ys* or *yr ydys*.

The above are the forms employed in the periphrastic tenses of finite verbs; the affirmative particle *yr* is always found, but *y* is sometimes omitted, hence *mae, maent*. In certain circumstances the third singular is spelt *mai* '(that) it is'. The forms *y mae, y maent* are replaced by *yw* or *ydyw, ŷnt* or *ydynt* in given contexts, eg, when the complement is definite: *Meurig yw'r pobydd* 'Maurice is the baker', further by the relative (*y*) *sydd* or *sy*, commonly occurring in sentences like *Meurig sy'n bobydd* 'Maurice is a baker' lit. '(it is) Maurice who-is in baker', emphatic in comparison with synonymous *y mae Meurig yn bobydd*, with predicative use of *'n, yn*.

In the interrogative, the particle *a* precedes, the usual forms being sg. 1 *a ydwyf?* 2 *a wyt?* 3 *a ydyw?* pl. 1 *a ydym?* 2 *a ydych?* 3 *a ydynt?*

In the negative *nid* precedes, eg, sg 1 *nid wyf* or *nid ydwyf*, etc., the third persons being singular *nid yw* or *nid ydyw*, pl. *nid ŷnt* or *nid ydynt*.

When used with an indefinite noun in question and answer and in a negative statement, the form *oes* 'is, are' is needed: *a oes llaeth yn y botel? oes, y mae* 'is there any milk in the bottle? yes, there is', *nid oes llwyau yma* 'there are no spoons here'.

Pres. habitual or fut. sg. 1 *byddaf*, 2 *byddi*, 3 *bydd*, pl. 1 *byddwn*, 2 *byddwch*, 3 *byddant*; impers. *byddir*.

Imperf. sg. 1 *yr oeddwn*, 2 *yr oeddit*, 3 *yr oedd* or *yr ydoedd*, pl. 1 *yr oeddem*, 2 *yr oeddech*, 3 *yr oeddynt*; impers. *yr oeddid*.

Imperf. habitual sg. 1 *byddwn*, 2 *byddit*, 3 *byddai*, pl. 1 *byddem*, 2 *byddech*, 3 *byddent*; impers. *byddid*.

Pret. sg. 1 *bûm*, 2 *buost*, 3 *bu*, pl. 1 *buom*, 2 *buoch*, 3 *buant* or *buont*; impers. *buwyd*.

Pluperf. sg. 1 *buaswn*, 2 *buasit*, 3 *buasai*, pl. 1 *buasem*, 2 *buasech*, 3 *buasent*; impers. *buasid*.

Subjunctive:

Pres. sg. 1 *bwyf*, 2 *bych*, 3 *bo*, pl. 1 *bôm*, 2 *boch*, 3 *bônt*, or sg. 1 *byddwyf*, 2 *byddych*, 3 *byddo*, pl. 1 *byddom*, 2 *byddoch*, 3 *byddont*; impers. *bydder*.

Imperf. sg 1 *bawn*, 2 *bait*, 3 *bai*, pl. 1 *baem*, 2 *baech*, 3 *baent*, or sg. 1 *byddwn*, 2 *byddit*, 3 *byddai*, pl. 1 *byddem*, 2 *byddech*, 3 *byddent*; impers. *byddid*.

Imperative:

Sg. 2 *bydd*, 3 *boed* or *bydded*, pl. 1 *byddwn*, 2 *byddwch*, 3 *byddent*; impers. *bydder*.

The irregular verb *gwneuthur*, more popularly *gwneud*, 'doing', is in limited use as an auxiliary. It was commoner in this function in older style: *dyfod a wnaeth hithau* 'she also came' lit. 'coming which did she-also', as medieval *dyvot a oruc hitheu* (p. 44).

There is no verb 'to have', possession being commonly expressed by the verb 'to be' with the preposition *gan* 'with', eg, *y mae gennym dŷ* 'we have a house' lit. 'is with-us house', alternatively *y mae tŷ gennym*.

READINGS

Medieval Welsh

Though archaic, the language is structurally not far removed from the modern standard (p. 34). Literary Middle Welsh was itself a highly standardized language and written in a fairly regular orthography.

Verses from the twelfth-century *Llyfr Du Caerfyrddin* (Black Book of Carmarthen):

> *Kintevin   keinhaw amsser,*
> Springtime (is) fairest   season,
> *Dyar   adar, glas   callet,*
> Loud (are) birds green (are) groves,
> *Ereidir in rich,   ich iguet,*
> Ploughs in furrow ox yoked,
> *Guirt   mor, brithottor   tiret.*
> Green (is) sea   are-made-variegated lands.
> (the countryside shows many colours.)

> *Pan   ganhont cogev   ar blaen guit   guiw*
> When sing   cuckoos on top   of-trees splendid
> *Handit muy vy llauuridet.*
> Grows more my despair.
> *Tost   muc; amluc   anhunet,*
> Sharp (is) smoke evident (is) sleeplessness
> *Kan   ethint uy kereint in   attwet.*
> Since went my kinsmen into rest.
> (Since my kinsmen have passed away.)

From the story of Culhwch and Olwen, *Mabinogion* (Tales), thirteenth century:

Dyvot   a   oruc hitheu.   A   chamse sidan flamgoch
Coming which did she-also. And robe   of-silk flame-red
ymdanei.   A   gwrddorch rud   eur am   vynwgyl y
about-her. And neck-torque of-red gold about neck   of-the
vorwyn. A   mererit gwerthfawr yndi a   rud emeu. Melynach
maiden. And pearl   precious   in-it and red gems. More-yellow
oed y   phenn no   blodeu y   banadyl. Gwynnach oed y
was her head than flowers of-the broom. Whiter   was her
chnawt no   distrych tonn.   Tegach oed   y   dwylaw ae
flesh   than foam   of-wave. Fairer were her hands and-her
byssed no   channawan gotrwyth o blith man graean fynnawn
fingers than shoots   of-melilot amidst fine gravel of-spring
fynhonws. Na   golwc hebawc mut   na golwc gwalch
welling. Neither eye   of-hawk mewed nor eye   of-falcon
trimut   nyt oed olwc degach nor eidi. Gwynnach oed
thrice-mewed not was eye   fairer than-hers. Whiter   were
y   dwyvron no   bronn alarch gwynn. Cochach oed y
her breasts than breast of-swan white. Redder were her
deurud nor   fuon cochaf. Y sawl ae   gwelei kyflawn
cheeks than-the roses reddest. Whoever who-her saw   full
vydei oe   serch. Pedair meillonen gwynnyon a   vydei yn y
was of-her love. Four clovers   white   which were in her
hol   ford bynnac y delhei. Ac am hynny y gelwit
step (sprang up) way ever   she-came. And for that was-called
hi Olwen
she O. (*ol* 'step', *wen* 'white').

Modern Welsh

A hymn by Ann Griffiths (1776–1805):

Wele'n   sefyll   rhwng y   myrtwydd
Behold (in) standing amid the myrtle-trees
Wrthrych teilwng o'm holl   fryd:
Object   worthy of my whole mind:
Er   mai o   ran wy'n   adnabod
Although (it-is) of (in) part I-am (in) recognizing
Ei fod   uwchlaw gwrthrychau'r   byd:
His being above objects   of-the world:

44

Welsh

Henffych fore
Hail   o morn
Y   *caf*   *ei   weled fel y mae.*
On-which I-shall-be-allowed his seeing as he-is.
(I shall be allowed to see him.)

Rhosyn Saron   yw ei enw,
Rose   of-Sharon is   his name,
   Gwyn a   gwridog,   teg o bryd:
   White and red-cheeked fair of aspect:
Ar ddeng mil   y mae'n rhagori
On ten   thousand he-is (in) excelling
   O wrthrychau penna'r   byd:
   Of objects   chief of-the world:
   (He is better than ten thousand choicest things on
   earth.)
      Ffrind pechadur
      Friend of-sinner
   Dyma'r   llywydd ar y   môr.
   Here-is the captain on the sea.

Beth sydd imi   mwy a   wnelwyf
What is-it to-me more which I-do
(What more have I to do)
   Ag   eilunod gwael y   llawr?
   With idols   base of-the world?
Tystio'r   wyf nad   yw eu   cwmni
Testifying I-am that-not is   their company
   I'w   gystadlu   â'm   Iesu mawr:
   To its comparing with my Jesus great:
      O! am aros
      O! for staying (to abide)
   Yn ei gariad   ddyddiau f'oes.
   In his love (all) days   of-my life.

(Mutations: *wrthrych* r. *gwrthrych, fryd* r. *bryd, ran* r. *rhan, fod* r. *bod,
fore* r. *bore, weled* r. *gweled, bryd* r. *pryd, ddeng* r. *deng, wrthrychau* r.
gwrthrychau, wnelwyf r. *gwnelwyf, gystadlu* r. *cystadlu, gariad* r.
cariad, ddyddiau r. *dyddiau.*)

From the national anthem *Hen Wlad fy Nhadau – Land of my Fathers,*

45

composed in 1856 by Evan James (bardic name, Ieuan ap Iago) of Pontypridd:

Mae hen wlad fy   nhadau   yn annwyl imi,
Is   old land of-my ancestors dear   to-me,
Gwlad beirdd   a   chantorion, enwogion o fri;
Land of-bards and-singers,   renowned of fame;
Ei   gwrol ryfelwyr, gwlatgarwyr tra   mad,
Her manly warriors, patriots   most true,
Tros ryddid   collasant eu   gwaed.
For freedom they-shed their blood (it was for freedom).

 Cytgan 'refrain':
 Gwlad! Gwlad! Pleidiol wyf i'm   gwlad.
 Land! Land! Partial I-am to my land.
 Tra   môr   yn fur i'r   bur hoff bau,
 While sea (which is) wall   to the fine dear country,
 (While there is a sea as a rampart for)
 O bydded i'r   heniaith   barhau!
 O let-be to the old-tongue continuing!

(Mutations: *wlad* r. *gwlad, nhadau* r. *tadau, chantorion* r. *cantorion, fri* r. *bri, ryfelwyr* r. *rhyfelwyr, ryddid* r. *rhyddid, fur* r. *mur, bur* r. *pur, bau* r. *pau, barhau* r. *parhau.*)

Y Rhaeadr – The Cataract – by Dewi Wyn o Eifion (Dafydd Owen); an example of an *englyn*, a traditional form, usually of four lines, as here:

 Uchel-gadr   raeadr dŵr   ewyn   hydrwyllt,
 Lofty mighty cataract of-water of-spray strong-wild,
  Edrych arno'n   disgyn!
  Look on-it (in) descending!
 Crochwaedd y   rhedlif crychwyn,
 Loud-call   of-the torrent rippling-white
  Synnu,   pensyfrdanu dyn.
  Wonderment bewilderment of-man.

(Mutation: *raeadr* r. *rhaeadr.*)

A glimpse of the Welsh in the Middle Ages, based on accounts by Giraldus Cambrensis (*Gerallt Gymro* = Gerald the Welshman), late twelfth century:

Y mae'r gwragedd yn ogystal â'r gwŷr yn torri   eu   gwallt yn
Are the women   as-well-as the men (in) cutting their hair in
gylch gyda'u   clustiau a'u   llygaid.
circle with their (round their) ears   and their eyes.
Gwisga'r   gwragedd benwisg   o liain gwyn wedi'i   godi'n
Wear   the women   head-dress of cloth white after its placing in
dorchau yn debyg i dwrban y   Persiaid. Cymer pawb   ofal
coils   like   to turban of-the Persians. Takes everyone care
mawr o'u   danedd gan eu   rhwbio'n gyson   â   chollen
great of their teeth by their rubbing regularly with hazel
werdd a'u   sychu â   darn o frethyn   nes eu
green and their wiping with piece of woollen-cloth until their
bod yn wyn fel ifori; ac yn eu   gofal amdanynt ni fwytânt
being white like ivory and in their care for-them not they eat
seigiau poeth. Eillia'r   gwŷr eu   barfau ac eithrio'r
meals hot.   Shave the men their beards and excepting the
trawswch   yn unig.
moustache only.
Y mae'r bobl   yn dangos medr arbennig ar eu
Are the people (in) showing of-skill special   on their
hofferynnau cerdd – y delyn, y pibau, a'r   crwth.
instruments of-music the harp, the pipes, and the crowd.
Lluosog   iawn yw'r   beirdd yn eu   plith
Numerous very are the bards in their midst (among them)
a'r   rheini'n   cyfansoddi barddoniaeth ardderchog.
and (the) those (in) composing poetry   excellent.
Hoffant   gyflythreniad yn fawr iawn. Yn eu   cerddoriaeth
They-like alliteration much very. In their music
byddant   yn canu   yn unsain, ond
they-are-wont (in) singing (are wont to sing) in unison, but
mewn llawer llais, modd a   chywair.   Mewn
in   many-a voice, mode and key (many voices, etc.). In
cwmni   o gantorion clywir   cynifer o gyweirnodau ac o
company of singers   is-heard as-many of keynotes   and of
leisiau amrywiol ag a   welir o
voices different as which is-seen of
bennau   ond i gyd   yn y   diwedd
heads (as there are heads to be seen) but together in the end
 yn gorffen   gyda B fflat.
(in) finishing with B flat.

Rhydd pawb   bris uchel ar ach   pur a   llinach
Gives everyone price high on pedigree pure and lineage
fonheddig. Gofala'r gwerinwr   mwyaf di-nod
noble.   Cares the common-man most   without-note (lowly)
am ei daflen achau.   *Oherwydd y*
for his table of-pedigrees (genealogical tree). Because-of the
pwyslais hwn ar achau   a   pherthynas teuluol y maent
emphasis this on pedigrees and relationship family they-are
yn barod i ddial   unrhyw gam a   wnaethpwyd   i'w
ready   to avenging of-any wrong which has-been-done to their
tylwyth, boed y   cam   yn hen neu'n ddiweddar.
kindred, let-be the wrong old   or later (whether old or recent).

(Mutations: *Gymro* r. *Cymro, gylch* r. *cylch, benwisg* r. *penwisg, liain*
r. *lliain, debyg* r. *tebyg, dwrban* r. *twrban, ofal* r. *gofal, gyson* r. *cyson,*
chollen r. *collen, werdd* r. *gwerdd, frethyn* r. *brethyn, wyn* r. *gwyn,*
fwytânt r. *bwytânt, bobl* r. *pobl, hofferynnau* r. *offerynnau, gyflythreniad*
r. *cyflythreniad, fawr* r. *mawr, delyn* r. *telyn, chywair* r. *cywair,*
gantorion r. *cantorion, gyweirnodau* r. *cyweirnodau, leisiau* r. *lleisiau,*
welir r. *gwelir, bennau* r. *pennau, bris* r. *pris, fonheddig* r. *bonheddig,*
daflen r. *taflen, pherthynas* r. *perthynas, barod* r. *parod, ddial* r. *dial,*
gam r. *cam, wnaethpwyd* r. *gwnaethpwyd, ddiweddar* r. *diweddar.*)

Edward Lhuyd, pioneer of Celtic studies:

Prif ffigur y   mudiad   hynafiaethol yng Nghymru ar
Chief figure of-the movement antiquarian in   Wales   on
ddiwedd yr   ail   ganrif ar bymtheg   ac yn
end   of-the second century on fifteen (seventeenth) and in
y ddeunawfed ganrif oedd Edward Lhuyd. Fe'i ganed   yn
the eighteenth century was Edward Lhuyd. He-was-born in
y   flwyddyn 1660 (mil chwe chant chwe deg) ym mhlwyf
the year   1660   in parish
Lappiton. Gŵr bonheddig o   blas   Llanforda   oedd ei
Lappiton. Gentleman   from mansion of-Llanforda was his
dad, a'i   fam   yn un o Brysiaid Gogerddan,   gogledd
father and his mother one of Prices of-Gogerddan, north
Ceredigion.
Cardigan(shire).
Deuchreuodd ei addysg   yn Ysgol Ramadeg Croesoswallt
Began   his education in School Grammar Oswestry

48

a   dichon iddo   fod   yn athro yno   cyn   mynd i
and perhaps to-him being master   there before going to

Goleg   yr   Iesu,   Rhydychen. Yn ddiweddarach dewiswyd
College of-the Jesus, Oxford.   Later   was-chosen

ef yn geidwad i   Amgueddfa Ashmole.   Gyda chymorth
he keeper   to Museum   Ashmolean. With help

tanysgrifiadau aeth Lhuyd ar daith   fawr wyddonol
of-subscriptions went Lhuyd on journey great scientific

trwy'r   gwledydd Celtaidd i gyd. Astudiodd   yn ddiflino yr
through the countries Celtic   all.   He-studied untiringly the

ieithoedd Celtaidd, casglodd lawysgrifau, agorodd lygaid
languages Celtic   collected manuscripts, opened eyes

rhai   anwybodus a   rhagfarnllyd i werth gwareiddiad
of-those ignorant and prejudiced to value of-civilization

yr   Ucheldirwyr a'r   Gwyddelod, mewn cyfnod pan
of-the Highlanders and the Irish   in   period when

ystyrid   hwy'n farbariaid, a   rhoddodd glod   i'r
were-considered they barbarians and gave   praise to the

gwledydd Celtaidd am gadw   eu   traddodiad a'u
countries Celtic   for keeping their tradition and their

harferion.
customs.

Ffrwyth y   daith   hon oedd cyhoeddi   yn
Fruit   of-the journey this was the-publishing in

1707 (*mil saith gant saith*) *waith   mawr Lhuyd,*   Archaeologia
1707   of-work great of-Lhuyd, *Archaeologia*

Britannica, *ystordy   o wybodaeth werthfawr am*
Britannica, store-house of knowledge valuable about

eirfa   a   gramadeg yr   ieithoedd Celtaidd. Dyma'r
vocabulary and grammar of-the languages Celtic.   This-is the

ymdriniaeth gyntaf â tharddiad yr   ieithoedd hyn.
treatment   first of origin   of-the languages these.

Bu   farw   yn 1709 (mil saith gant naw) a
Was dead (he died) in 1709   and

chladdwyd ef yn eglwys Mihangel Sant, Rhydychen.
was-buried he in church of-St Michael, Oxford.

(Mutations: *Nghymru* r. *Cymru, ddiwedd* r. *diwedd, ganrif* r. *canrif,*
bymtheg r. *pymtheg, ddeunawfed* r. *deunawfed, flwyddyn* r. *blwyddyn,*
chant r. *cant, mhlwyf* r. *plwyf, blas* r. *plas, dad* r. *tad, fam* r. *mam,*

Brysiaid r. *Prysiaid, Ramadeg* r. *Gramadeg, fod* r. *bod, Goleg* r. *Coleg,*
ddiweddarach r. *diweddarach, geidwad* r. *ceidwad, chymorth* r. *cymorth,*
daith r. *taith, fawr* r. *mawr, wyddonol* r. *gwyddonol, ddiflino* r. *diflino,*
lawysgrifau r. *llawysgrifau, lygaid* r. *llygaid, werth* r. *gwerth, farbariaid*
r. *barbariaid, glod* r. *clod, gadw* r. *cadw, harferion* r. *arferion, gant* r.
cant, waith r. *gwaith, wybodaeth* r. *gwybodaeth, werthfawr* r.
gwerthfawr, eirfa r. *geirfa, gyntaf* r. *cyntaf, tharddiad* r. *tarddiad,*
farw r. *marw, chladdwyd* r. *claddwyd.*)

From a Ministry of Education circular, *Dysgu Iaith yn Ysgolion*
Cynradd (*Language Teaching in Primary Schools*):

   Ers   talm   bellach   datganodd y   Bwrdd
   Since period now (a long time ago now) expressed the Board
   Addysg   y   farn   mai   iaith   yr   aelwyd a
   Education the opinion that-it-is language of-the hearth which
   ddylai fod   yn gyfrwng   addysg   yn
   ought being medium (ought to be the medium) of-education in
   ysgolion babanod. Gwedir   yr egwyddor hon amlaf
   schools of-infants. Is-offended the principle this most-often
   lle   ceir   lleiafrif   o blant   o   gartrefi
   where there-is minority of children from homes
   Cymraeg   am na threfnir   yn fynych i'w   cadw
   Welsh(-speaking), for not is-arranged frequently to their keeping
   gyda'i gilydd,   a'u   haddysgu trwy   gyfrwng eu
   with each other and their educating through medium of-their
   mamiaith.   Fe'u llyncir   yn y   mwyafrif
   mother-tongue. They-are-absorbed in the majority
   di-Gymraeg,   a'u   gosod felly   o dan
   without-Welsh and their placing so (they are so placed) under
   anfantais.   Gall iaith   ysgol   yn gyflym iawn ddisodli
   disadvantage. Can language of-school swiftly   very oust
   iaith   y   cartref o'i   safle   fel iaith   gyntaf.
   language of-the home from its position as language first.
   Ni ellir   amddiffyn arferiad   sy'n   gadael i
   Not can-be defending of-practice which-is (in) allowing to
   blant   mewn ynrhyw ran o Gymru golli'r   Gymraeg
   children in   any   part of Wales the-losing of-the Welsh
   fel eu   hiaith   gyntaf. Dyletswydd ysgolion   yw eu
   as their language first.   Duty   of-schools is   their

cynorthwyo,   *nid yn unig i* *gadw'r*
assisting (to assist them) not only   to the-keeping of-the
iaith   *gyntaf, ond hefyd i'w* *meithrin fel cyfrwng*
language first,   but also to its fostering as medium
mynegiant   *a*   *diwylliant.*
of-communication and culture.

(Mutations: *farn* r. *barn, ddylai* r. *dylai, fod* r. *bod, gyfrwng* r. *cyfrwng, blant* r. *plant, gartrefi* r. *cartrefi, threfnir* r. *trefnir, fynych* r. *mynych, haddysgu* r. *addysgu, dan* r. *tan, gyflym* r. *cyflym, ddisodli* r. *disodli, gyntaf* r. *cyntaf, ellir* r. *gellir, ran* r. *rhan, Gymru* r. *Cymru, golli* r. *colli, Gymraeg* r. *Cymraeg, hiaith* r. *iaith, gadw* r. *cadw.*)

Coryglau-Coracles:
  A wyddoch chwi beth yw corwgl? Cwch bach yw ef. Dim
  Do-know you what is coracle? Boat little is it. Nothing
ond lle *i* *un dyn sydd*   *ynddo. Gellwch weld*
but room for one man which-is in-it.   You-can seeing
coryglau *ar afon Tywi rhwng* *Caerfyrddin a'r*   *môr, ac*
of-coracles on river Tywi between Carmarthen and the sea and
ar afon Teifi rhwng   *pentref Cenarth*   *ac Aberteifi. Pysgota*
on river Teifi between village of-Cenarth and Cardigan. Fishing
eogiaid *y*   *maent yn y*   *coryglau. Bydd dau gorwgl,*
of-salmon at-which they-are in the coracles. Are two coracles
un bob ochr i'r   *afon, yn mynd ar hyd*   *yr*
one each side to the river (in) going on length of-the (along the)
afon am ddwy neu dair milltir. Bydd rhwyd fawr o   *un cwch*
river for two or three miles. Is   net   big from one boat
i'r   *llall, a* *bydd yn cael* *ei*   *llusgo*   *trwy'r*
to the other and is   (in) getting of-its dragging through the
dŵr. Y *rhwyd honno*   *fydd yn dal*   *y*   *pysgod.*
water. The net   that (that net) is   (in) catching of-the fish.

(Mutations: *wyddoch* r. *gwyddoch, weld* r. *gweld, gorwgl* r. *corwgl, ddwy* r. *dwy, dair* r. *tair, fawr* r. *mawr, fydd* r. *bydd.*)

LITERATURE

A number of books cater for the beginner in Welsh, among which A. S. D. Smith, *Welsh Made Easy* (three booklets) has been many times reprinted. Works of reference are the two publications by J. M. Jones, namely *An Elementary Welsh Grammar* (1922), for morphology, and *Welsh Syntax. An Unfinished Draft* (1931). H. M. Evans and W. O. Thomas, *Y Geiriadur Mawr* (*The Large Dictionary*) (1958) gives up-to-date coverage. A number of bilingual volumes on subjects of Welsh interest are published by *Gwasg Prifysgol Cymru* (*The University of Wales Press*).

The nature of dialect in Welsh is fully illustrated in O. H. Fynes-Clinton, *The Welsh Vocabulary of the Bangor District* (1913).

On the older language consult J. Strachan, *An Introduction to Early Welsh* (1909), a work containing grammar, texts and glossary; further D. S. Evans, *A Grammar of Middle Welsh* (1964). J. M. Jones, *A Welsh Grammar, Historical and Comparative* (1913, last reprinted 1955) treats the phonology and accidence of the language from the earliest times.

Welsh speakers may be referred to S. J. Williams, *Elfennau Gramadeg Cymraeg* (1959), G. M. Richards, *Cystrawen y Frawddeg Gymraeg* (1938), H. Lewis, *Datblygiad yr Iaith Gymraeg*, argraff. diwygiedig (1946), D. S. Evans, *Gramadeg Cymraeg Canol* (1951), ail argraff. (1960), and T. A. Watkins, *Ieithyddiaeth* (1961).

CHAPTER FIVE

Cornish

𝕊𝕊𝕊𝕊𝕊𝕊

CORNISH is descended from the British of the extreme south-west, and is closely related to Welsh, but more so to Breton (p. 25). British had been isolated in the Devonian Peninsula since the early seventh century; Ogam inscriptions (p. 80) show that Irish communities had emigrated to Cornwall in the Dark Ages, but these settlers were probably soon assimilated. The area of the modern Devon was reached by the advancing Saxons at the middle of the seventh century and generally occupied about the early eighth century. But the Britons appear to have retained, in part at least, some measure of autonomy, for Athelstan is reported to have driven them from Exeter *circa* 936, about which time the Tamar became the boundary between Saxon and Celt. Cornwall now lost its independence, though the local inhabitants were not dispersed. But their new masters were everywhere in control; at any rate, the Domesday survey (1086) shows that the men who then held manors in Cornwall bore English names. However, the province offered no natural obstacles to influence from beyond and, not surprisingly, the linguistic frontier moved slowly westward as the Cornish speakers of east Cornwall exchanged their dialects for English. Details of this movement are obscure, but it probably began by the end of the tenth century and, by the sixteenth, Cornish was predominantly spoken only in west Cornwall. Andrew Boorde in his *Fyrst Boke of the Introduction of Knowledge* (1542) reports: 'In Cornwall is two speches, the one is naughty ('bad') Englysshe, and the other is Cornysshe speche. And there be many men and women the which cannot speake one worde of Englysshe, but all Cornyshe'.

After this, however, the language declined rapidly. In the Elizabethan Age, Cornish sea-faring men brought back a knowledge of English, which now became widely known in those parts where the native language was still in use. That area, however, was now very small, for as a diarist noted in 1644, Cornish was then confined to

53

the districts west of Truro. We hear of religious services being conducted in Cornish until 1678. It is likely that, by this date, the last
Cornish monoglots were no more, and the remaining speakers, now
bilingual, were soon to go over to English exclusively. After 1700,
Cornish was no longer being passed on to children. In 1776, four or
five old persons in Mousehole, near Penzance, could speak Cornish,
but these will have been among the last, so that the language would
be extinct before the end of the century. Its last strongholds were the
country parishes from St Ives to Land's End and along the shores of
Mount's Bay.

Cornish was never used as an official written language. In the
Middle Ages, Latin and French were the languages of administration,
later superseded by English, as in England itself. Nor was there any
printing in Cornish until the development of scholarly interest,
beginning with Lhuyd in 1707. Nevertheless, the remains of Cornish
are not inconsiderable. Apart from names found in various sources,
Old Cornish is attested chiefly in a tenth-century manuscript recording
the manumissions of Cornish slaves from whose names, and those of
witnesses, some 200 words can be gleaned; and in a twelfth-century
manuscript which preserves a Cornish–Latin vocabulary of 961 items
datable to about 1100. The language is best known, however, from
the Middle Cornish period, in particular from five religious dramas
of the fifteenth century. In somewhat later language is a mid-sixteenth-
century collection of homilies translated from English and another
religious drama, dated 1611. The language of these latter texts may
be called Modern Cornish, to the records of which we add scraps of
prose and verse, besides many single sentences and numerous
glossaries committed to writing before the language became extinct,
and, most valuable of all, Edward Lhuyd's 'Cornish Grammar' contained in his *Archaeologia Britannica* (1707).

As may be expected, the Cornish language lived longest on the lips
of farmers and fishermen. In its last stages, at any rate, Cornish
inevitably came to be looked down upon as something inferior, old-
fashioned, useless, the hallmark of ignorance or simplicity. Nicholas
Boson, born at Newlyn in 1624, relates in a little essay entitled
Nebbaz Gerriau dro tho Carnoack (A Few Words about Cornish)
that his mother attempted to prevent him from picking up Cornish
by forbidding servants and neighbours to talk to him in that language.
This particular mother, however, failed, and Boson became one of
the few men to write anything in Modern Cornish.

In this century, enthusiasts have banded themselves into Cornish Societies, taught themselves the Cornish language and produced a number of compositions in it. Their revived Cornish is, however, a normalization of Middle Cornish in unified spelling. The prime mover in this revival was R. M. Nance (1873–1959).

A small residue of Celtic words remains in local use in Cornwall, as *crowst* 'meal taken to work, picnic lunch', *wheal* 'tin-mine' (Co. *crowst, whŷl*) or *pajerpaw* 'newt' lit. 'four foot' (Co. *pajer, paw*), clearly a noa name. Occasionally a Cornish term has passed into Standard English, as *(sea)gull* (Co. *gullan*) or the fish name *wrasse* (a seventeenth-century misspelling of dial. *wraffe*, ultimately Co. *wrâgh* lenited form of *gwrâgh* lit. 'old woman').

Cornwall's Celtic past is everywhere evident in its place names, as *Hayle* (Co. *hayl* 'estuary') or *Mullion* (Co. *mullyon* 'clover'). The modern forms of many names are, however, corrupt, as *Marazion*, a misunderstanding of a badly written *Marajiou* (or similar spelling, compare (lenited) *Varha Jou* in the reading passage on p. 68), from earlier (sixteenth century) *Marghas Dêth-Yow* lit. 'Market of-Thursday'. A further distortion of the same is seen in *Market Jew Street*, the name of the street leading from the centre of Penzance towards Marazion. Local surnames, too, are often Celtic; they are chiefly toponymical in origin, as in the jingle:

> By *Tre, Pol,* and *Pen,*
> You shall know the Cornishmen.

The meanings are: *tre* 'farmstead', *pol* 'pool', *pen* 'head(land), summit', and examples include *Trelawny, Polwhele, Pentreath.*

SKETCH OF MIDDLE CORNISH

The orthography of the Cornish manuscripts is irregular and inconsistent, and as a consequence phonetic values are often in doubt. We here follow the unified spelling adopted by the Cornish Societies (above).

Phonetics

Vowels are short for the most part, but may be long, length being generally indicated by the circumflex: *clêth* 'ditch'. There are the usual five vowels *a, e, y* (used for *i* as commonly in the manuscripts), *o, u*, further *ü* (generally written *u, ue* or *uy*) approximately [y(ː)], as *ügans* [ygans] 'twenty', *tüs* [tyːs] 'people', cf. Welsh *ugain, tud*. The unified spelling uses the same symbol for what was perhaps [əː], as in *lün* 'full', *üs* 'is', perhaps [ləːn, əːs], cf. Welsh *llawn, oes*. The common spellings *eu, ou*, are often retained in unified spelling, especially in verbal endings; they may be pronounced [u(ː)], thus *kerough* [keruχ] 'love!', *gour* [guːr] 'husband'. Short vowels may often have been obscure in unstressed syllables, but no certain rules emerge and the matter may be disregarded here. There are six diphthongs: *aw, ew, ow, yw, ey, oy*. Stress normally falls on the last syllable but one.

Orthographic conventions for consonants are as in English, except that *gh* is [χ] and *th* always voiceless, *dh* being used for its voiced counterpart, this last being a modern refinement due to Lhuyd, the traditional texts having only *th*. Notice *w* in such words as *gwlâs* 'country', *gwraf* 'I do', cf. Welsh.

Initial Mutations

Cornish continued the practice of initial mutation developed in Late British times (p. 27), though the changes are not consistently marked in the manuscripts. The mutations often correspond to those occurring in Welsh, but in this as in other spheres, the two sister languages have often gone their separate ways, so that considerable variations are also found. We tabulate the commonest mutations:

Radical	Soft	Hard	Spirant
p	*b*		*f*
t	*d*		*th*
c, k	*g*		*h*
b	*v*	*p*	
d	*dh*	*t*	
g	– or *w*	*c, k*	
m	*v*		

In certain cases, the soft mutations *v, dh, –* or *w* are replaced by *f, t, h*.

We give a selection of examples, beginning with the extensive soft mutation, or lenition. It occurs in nouns, eg, after *dha* 'thy', *y* 'his': *dha ben* 'your head' (r. *pen*), *y dâs* 'his father' (r. *tâs*), after several prepositions: *drê gew* 'through a field' (r. *kew*), *dhe vugh* 'to a cow' (r. *bugh*), after the numerals *deu* 'two' and *mýl* 'thousand': *deu dhên*

56

'two men' (r. *dên*), commonly when masculine plural or feminine singular after the article: *an wesyon* 'the fellows' (r. *gwesyon*), *an vyrgh* 'the daughter' (r. *myrgh*).

The soft mutation likewise affects adjectives, eg, when agreeing with a masculine plural or feminine singular noun: *flêghes vŷghan* 'little children' (r. *bŷghan*), *mam vâs* 'good mother' (r. *mâs*), or in comparison: *mar vrâs del* 'as big as' (r. *brâs*). Changes in verbs are found after various particles, as relative: *nŷ a wêl* 'we see' lit. 'we who sees' (r. *gwêl*), interrogative: *a glewsys?* 'did you hear?' (r. *clewsys*), negative: *nŷ derrys* 'I did not break' (r. *terrys*), perfective: *re dhypsyn* 'we have eaten' (r. *dypsyn*), further after *pan* 'when': *pan dhethons* 'when they came' (r. *dethons*).

The conditions in which the hard and spirant mutations occur are more restricted. The former is chiefly found after *ow* commonly used with verbal nouns (p. 61): *ow tôs* '(at) coming' (r. *dôs*), and in a few other instances, as after *mar* 'if': *mar pŷth* 'if it shall be' (r. *bŷth*). The spirant mutation occurs after *trŷ* 'three': *trŷ fyth* 'three things' (r. *pyth*), and after *ow* 'my', *hy* 'her', *aga* 'their': *ow fysk* 'my fish' (r. *pysk*), *hy thŷlu* 'her family' (r. *tŷlu*), *aga hês* 'their cheese' (r. *kês*).

Less usual mutations include the changing of *b* to *f* and *g* to *h*, as after adverbial *yn*, thus *yn frâs* 'greatly' (r. *brâs*), *yn harow* 'roughly' (r. *garow*); in analogous circumstances *d* changes to *t*, as *yn ta* 'well' (r. *da*). Other miscellaneous changes include *d* to *j*, as *an jêth* 'the day' (r. *dêth*) and *d* to *n*, as *an nor* 'the world' (r. *dor*), this latter an instance of the nasal mutation, exceptional in Cornish, but a regular feature of Welsh.

Nouns

There are two genders, masculine and feminine. Nouns do not decline, but the formation of the plural is complicated.

A number of nouns form the plural by internal vowel change, as *dans* m. 'tooth', pl. *dyns*, *margh* m. 'horse', *mergh*, *trôs* m. 'foot', *treys*, *ascorn* m. 'bone', *eskern*, *davas* f. 'sheep', *deves*, *edhen* f. 'bird', *ydhyn*. Generally, however, a plural ending is used with or without further change in the form of the singular. The usual endings are *-ow*, *-yow*, *-on*, *-yon*, *-yn*, *-y*, *-yth*, *-eth*, *-es*, *-as*, *-s*, also *-ens*, *-yar*. Examples: *lyver* m. 'book', *lyvrow*, *ger* m. 'word', *gerryow*, *Yethow* m. 'Jew', *Yethewon*, *map* m. 'son', *mebyon*, *hanow* m. 'name',

British Celtic

hynwyn, fenester f. 'window', *fenestry, whôr* f. 'sister', *wheryth, gwrêk* f. 'woman', *gwrageth, prŷf* m. 'worm; insect', *pryves, cath* f. 'cat', *cathas, doctour* m. 'doctor', *doctours, car* m. 'friend', *kerens, pren* m. 'tree', *prennyer.* Conversely, the singular is sometimes formed from the plural by means of the suffix -*en*, as *logosen* f. 'mouse', pl. *logas.*

Though there are no cases, nouns can be genitive by position, as *grammer an yêth* 'the grammar of the language' lit. 'grammar of-the language'. Notice that *grammer* takes no article. Further, on the same lines *myghtern nêf* 'the king of heaven', *gwedhen gothvos da ha drôk* 'the tree of the knowledge of good and evil'. The construction is paralleled in other Celtic (p. 38).

Adjectives

Adjectives as such are invariable for gender and number, but when used substantively they take the plural ending -*yon*, thus *boghosek* 'poor', pl. *an voghosogyon* 'the poor'.

The comparative and superlative usually have the same termination -*a* added to the positive: *têk* 'fair', *tecca* 'fairer, fairest', the single final consonant of the positive being regularly doubled. Analytic comparison also occurs: *skyansek* 'wise', *moy* ('more') *skyansek, moyha* ('most') *skyansek.* There is some irregular comparison, eg, *mâs* or *da* 'good', *gwell* 'better', *gwella* 'best', *drôk* 'bad', *gwêth* 'worse', *gwêtha* 'worst'.

Numbers

1 *onen*, 2 *deu*, 3 *trŷ*, 4 *peswar*, 5 *pymp*, 6 *whêgh*, 7 *seyth*, 8 *êth*, 9 *naw*, 10 *dêk*, 11 *ünnek*, 12 *deudhek*, 13 *tredhek*, 14 *peswardhek*, 15 *pymthek*, 16 *whetek*, 17 *seytek*, 18 *êtek*, 19 *nawnjek*, 20 *ügans*, 21 *onnen warn ügans*, 30 *dêk warn ügans*, 40 *deu ügans*, 50 *hanter cans*, 60 *trŷ ügans*, 70 *dêk ha trŷ ügans*, 80 *peswar ügans*, 90 *dêk ha peswar ügans*, 100 *cans*, 1000 *mŷl.*

Nouns immediately following the numeral are used in the singular: *dêk lugh* 'ten calves' lit. 'ten calf', but also expressed *dêk a lughy* lit. 'ten of calves'.

Numbers 2, 3 and 4 have feminine forms: *dyw, tŷr, peder*, and 5 and 6 have the reduced forms *pym, whê*, cf. Welsh.

Cornish

Before a noun 1 is *ün*, governing the soft mutation of a feminine singular: *ün venen* 'one woman' (r. *benen*).

Definite Article

This is *an*, eliding to *'n* after words ending in a vowel: *an tâs ha'n map* 'the father and the son', *dhe'n venen* 'to the woman'. On mutations caused by the article, see p. 57.

There is no indefinite article.

Pronouns

The independent pronouns are *mŷ* 'I, me', *tŷ* 'thou, thee', *ef* 'he, him', *hŷ* 'she, her', *nŷ* 'we, us', *whŷ* 'you', *ŷ* 'they, them'. They often follow the verb of which they are the subject, first and second sg. then being *vŷ*, *sŷ*, eg, *ôf vŷ* 'I am', *ôs sŷ* 'thou art', *yû ef* 'he is' (see also p. 62).

The possessive pronouns are *ow* 'my', *dha* 'thy', *y* 'his', *hy* 'her', *agan* 'our', *agas* 'your', *aga* 'their', thus *ow mêl* 'my honey', *dha vêl* 'thy honey' – on mutations caused by the possessive, see pp. 56–57. The noun in this construction may be followed by an affixed pronoun: sg. 1 *vŷ*, 2 *sŷ*, 3 m. *ef*, etc., as for the independent pronoun, hence also *ow mêl vŷ*, etc. Affixed pronouns frequently appear in an emphatic form, as *avŷ*, *dhesŷ*, *eef*, *hyhŷ*, *nynŷ*, *whywhŷ*, *ynsŷ*.

Pronouns may be infixed, as in the case of possessives when they follow a word ending in a vowel, eg, *ha* 'and'; sample paradigm: *ha'm tâs* 'and my father', *ha'th dâs* 'and thy father', *ha'y dâs* 'and his father', *ha'y thâs* 'and her father', *ha'gan tâs* 'and our father', *ha'gas tâs* 'and your father', *ha'ga thâs* 'and their father'. Infixed pronouns also occur as the object between a particle and the verb, as *'m* 'me', *'th* 'thee', *'n* 'him', *'s* 'her', *'n* 'us', *'s* 'you, them'; only *'th* may cause mutation: *Dew rê'th fenyggo* 'God bless thee' (r. *benyggo*).

Pronouns coalesce with certain prepositions, eg, *gans* 'with': *genef* 'with me', *genes* 'with thee', *ganso* 'with him', *gensy* 'with her', *genen* 'with us', *genough* 'with you', *gansa* 'with them'. These may be emphasized by the addition of the affixed pronoun: *genef vŷ*, *genes sŷ*, *ganso ef*, *gensy hŷ*, *genen nŷ*, *genough whŷ*, *gansa ŷ*. Other examples include *war* 'on': *warnaf* 'on me', *warnas* 'on thee', *warnodho* 'on him', *warnedhy* 'on her', *warnan* 'on us', *warnough* 'on you', *warnedha* 'on them', emphatic *warnaf vŷ*, etc., *rak* 'before': *ragof* 'before me', *ragos* 'before thee', *ragtho* 'before him', *rygthy* 'before her', *ragon* 'before us', *ragough* 'before you', *ragtha* 'before them', emphatic *ragof vŷ*, etc.

Verbs

Verbs have four synthetic tenses in the indicative (present, imperfect, preterite, pluperfect) and two in the subjunctive (present, imperfect). There is a past participle passive. There is no infinitive, but great use is made of the verbal noun. Impersonal tenses commonly correspond to the English passive. With most verbs, the synthetic present and imperfect generally have future and conditional meaning respectively. The particle *rê* is used before a preterite to give perfective meaning: *rê gerys* 'I have loved' (see below). It is likely that, as in Welsh, synthetic conjugation was typical of higher style, the ordinarily spoken language preferring periphrastic constructions consisting of the tenses of the verb 'to be' (*bôs*) or especially the verb 'to do' (*gwrüthyl*) with the verbal noun.

Synthetic inflexion is rather complex. There are several conjugations and a fair number of anomalous forms. We give as our example a regular verb:

Verbal noun: *cara* 'loving'.
Indicative:
Pres. sg. 1 *caraf*, 2 *keryth*, 3 *car*, pl. 1 *keryn*, 2 *kerough*, 3 *carons*; impers. *keryr*.
Imperf. sg. 1 *caren*, 2 *cares*, 3 *cara*, pl. 1 *caren*, 2 *careugh*, 3 *carens*; impers. *kerys*.
Pret. sg. 1 *kerys*, 2 *kersys*, 3 *caras*, pl. 1 *kersyn*, 2 *kersough*, 3 *carsons*; impers. *caras*.
Pluperf. sg. 1 *carsen*, 2 *carses*, 3 *carsa*, pl. 1 *carsen*, 2 *carseugh*, 3 *carsens*; impers. *carsys*.

Subjunctive:
Pres. sg. 1 *kyrryf*, 2 *kyrry*, 3 *carro*, pl. 1 *kyrryn*, 2 *kyrreugh*, 3 *carrons*; impers. *kerrer*.
Imperf. sg. 1 *carren*, 2 *carres*, 3 *carra*, pl. 1 *carren*, 2 *carreugh*, 3 *carrens*; impers. *carres*.

Imperative:
sg. 2 *car*, 3 *cares*, pl. 1 *keryn*, 2 *kereugh*, 3 *carens*.

Past participle:
kerys.

Examples of periphrastic tenses involving the verb 'to be' below: present *esof ow cara* lit. 'I am at loving', present habitual or future *bydhaf ow cara* lit. 'I am-wont-to-be at loving' or 'I shall-be at loving', imperfect *esen ow cara* lit. 'I was at loving', imperfect habitual *bedhen ow cara* 'I used-to-be at loving', etc. Similarly in the passive: *ôf kerys* 'I am loved', etc.

The personal forms of the verb are generally preceded in affirmative sentences by a meaningless particle *y*, before *h* or vowels *yth*, as *y caraf* 'I love', *yth ôf kerys* 'I am loved'. Pronouns may also be found, as *y caraf vŷ* 'I love' (p. 59).

An impersonal construction, where the verb remains in the third singular, is commonly used: *mŷ a gar* 'I love' lit. 'I who loves', *an benenes a gar* 'the women love' lit. 'the women who loves'.

In the personal construction, the verb ordinarily stands at the head of the sentence, except in emphatic order, and a plural noun takes a singular verb: *yma an mowysy ow cusca* 'the girls are sleeping' lit. 'is the girls at sleeping'.

The interrogative is commonly indicated by the particle *a*, the negative by *ny*, before vowels *nyns* (see the verb 'to be' below).

The verb 'to be'

Verbal noun: *bôs* 'being'

Indicative:
Pres. (short form) sg. 1 *ôf*, 2 *ôs*, 3 *yû*, pl. 1 *ôn*, 2 *ough*, 3 *yns*; impers. *ôr* – these are found when the complement is a noun or adjective, (long form) sg. 1 *esof*, 2 *esos*, 3 *üsy*, pl. 1 *eson*, 2 *esough*, 3 *üsons*; impers. *eder* – these are found with an expression indicating position. In affirmative sentences the particle *yth* or *y* usually precedes: *yth ôf soudor* 'I am a soldier', *yth eson y'n tre* 'we were at home'. The third singular *yma*, pl. *ymons*, in a few contexts *ma*, *mons*, are variously employed in affirmative sentences either instead of, or as alternatives to, the forms above.

In the formation of periphrastic tenses the short form appropriately occurs with the past participle, the long form with the construction involving the verbal noun: *yth ôf gwelys* 'I am seen', *yth esof ow tysky Kernewek* 'I am learning Cornish' lit. 'I am at learning of-Cornish'.

British Celtic

The form *üsy* may have a relative function: *rê'n enef üsy y'm corf* 'by the soul which-is in my body'.

Interrogative sg. 1 *ôf*? *esof*? etc.; on the interrogative particle, see below. In the negative, *nyns* precedes the verb, eg, *nyns ôf*, *nyns esof*.

When used with an indefinite noun in question and answer and in a negative statement, the form *üs* 'is, are' is needed: *üs lêth y'n bottel*? *üs, yma* 'is there any milk in the bottle? yes, there is', *nyns üs loyow omma* 'there are no spoons here'.

Pres. habitual or fut. sg. 1 *bydhaf*, 2 *bydhyth*, 3 *bŷth*, pl. 1 *bydhyn*, 2 *bydhough*, 3 *bydhons*; impers. *bydher*.

Imperf. (short form) sg. 1 *ên*, 2 *ês*, 3 *ô*, pl. 1 *ên*, 2 *eugh*, 3 *ens*; impers. *ôs* (long form) sg. 1 *esen*, 2 *eses*, 3 *esa*, pl. 1 *esen*, 2 *eseugh*, 3 *esens*; impers. *edes*. On the use of short and long forms, see under Pres. above.

Imperf. habitual sg. 1 *bedhen*, 2 *bedhes*, 3 *bedha*, pl. 1 *bedhen*, 2 *bedheugh*, 3 *bedhens*; impers. *bedhes*.

Pret. sg. 1 *büf*, 2 *bês*, 3 *bê*, pl. 1 *bên*, 2 *beugh*, 3 *bons*; impers. *bês*.

Pluperf. sg. 1 *bŷen*, 2 *bŷes*, 3 *bŷa*, pl. 1 *bŷen*, 2 *bŷeugh*, 3 *bŷens*; impers. *bŷes*.

Subjunctive:
Pres. sg. 1 *bŷf*, 2 *bŷ*, 3 *bo*, pl. 1 *bên*, 2 *beugh*, 3 *bons*; impers. *bôer*.
Imperf. sg. 1 *bên*, 2 *bês*, 3 *bê*, pl. 1 *bên*, 2 *beugh*, 3 *bens*; impers. *bês*.

Imperative:
Sg. 2 *byth*, 3 *bedhens*, pl. 1 *bedhen*, 2 *bedheugh*, 3 *bedhens*.

Verbal forms are often followed by the appropriate pronoun: *vŷ* 'I', *sŷ* 'thou', *ef* 'he', etc., thus *ôf vŷ* 'I am', etc. There are, however, certain alternative forms notably sg. 1 *-ma*, *-a*, 2 *-ta*, 3 *-va*, *-a*, hence *ôma* 'I am', *êna* 'I was', *osta* or *ôta* 'thou art', *esta* 'thou wast', *ôva*, *bêva* 'he was', *yûa* 'he is'.

The affirmative particle survives before a consonant, as *a vydhaf*? 'shall I be?', contrast *üs lêth . . .*? above.

The perfect is formed without mutation: *rê büf* 'I have seen', but mutation regularly takes place after the affirmative particle, as *y fydhaf* 'I shall be'.

The verb 'to do'

Verbal noun: *gwrüthyl*, also *güthyl*, *gül*.

62

Cornish

Indicative:
Pres. sg. 1 *gwraf*, 2 *gwrêth*, 3 *gwra*, pl. 1 *gwren*, 2 *gwreugh*, 3 *gwrons*;
impers. *gwrer* – the only impersonal form of this verb.
Imperf. sg. 1 *gwren*, 2 *gwrês*, 3 *gwrê*, pl. 1 *gwren*, 2 *gwreugh*, 3 *gwrens*.
Pret. sg. 1 *gwrük*, 2 *gwrüssys*, 3 *gwrük*, pl. 1 *gwrüssyn*, 2 *gwrüssough*,
3 *gwrüssons*.
Pluperf. sg. 1 *gwrüssen*, 2 *gwrüsses*, 3 *gwrüssa*, pl. 1 *gwrüssen*, 2
gwrüsseugh, 3 *gwrüssens*.

Subjunctive:
Pres. sg. 1 *gwryllyf*, 2 *gwrylly*, 3 *gwrello*, pl. 1 *gwryllyn*, 2 *gwrellough*,
3 *gwrellons*.
Imperf. sg. 1 *gwrellen*, 2 *gwrelles*, 3 *gwrella*, pl. 1 *gwrellen*, 2 *gwre-
lleugh*, 3 *gwrellens*.

Imperative:
Sg. 2 *gwra*, 3 *gwrens*, pl. 1 *gwren*, 2 *gwreugh*, 3 *gwrens*.

Past participle:
Gwrês or *gwrŷs*.

Examples of auxiliary use: *mŷ a wra cara* 'I love' lit. 'I who does
loving', *a wneugh cara* 'do you love?' lit. 'do you loving?'.

There is no verb 'to have' and possession may be expressed by the
verb 'to be' with the prepositions *gans* 'with' or *dhe* 'to', eg, *yma
genen chŷ* 'we have a house' lit. 'is with-us house' or *yma dhyn chŷ*
lit. 'is to-us house', alternative order *yma chŷ genen*, *yma chŷ dhyn*.
More often, however, a construction is used which consists of
(partly unique) forms of the verb 'to be' with an infixed (dative)
pronoun preceded by a particle, thus *(nŷ) a'gan büs chŷ* lit. '(we) who
to-us is house'.

READINGS

From the *Origo Mundi*, Third Act. Fifteenth century:

REX DAVID
    Damsel, er dha jentylys, dysqua dhym a'th   kerensa
    Damsel, of thy courtesy, show to-me of thy love,

Rag bythqueth mŷ ny welys benen   dhym a   well-blêkya
For (n)ever I   not saw woman to-me who better pleased
                    Whath yn nep lê.
                    Yet   in any place.
Rôf   dhys   ow thour, hêl ha chambour, bydhaf dha
I will-give to-thee my tower, hall and chamber, will-be thy
wour,
husband,
                    Warbarth nŷ a dryk   nefra.
                    Together we shall-live for-ever.

BATHSHEBA:

Ow arluth kêr caradow, myghtern ôs   war oll an bŷs.
My lord   dear beloved, king   thou art on all the world.
Assa vŷa   plegadow genef gwrüthyl bôth   dha   vrŷs,
How would-be willing   by-me doing   consent of-thy desire,
A callen hep   keladow ha dowt ow   bôs hellerghys.
If I could without secrecy and fear of-my being found-out.
Mar cothfa an casadow   dystough   y fŷen   ledhys.
If   learnt the hateful (fellow) straightway I-would-be killed.

(*Bersaba transeat domum cum Rege David* – Let Bathsheba go home
with King David)

REX DAVID:

Bersaba, flowr oll   a'n   bŷs, certus rag dha
Bathsheba, flower of-all of the world verily for thy
  gerensa
  love (love of thee)
Syr Urry a vŷth ledhys. Mŷ a'n tê   rê'm   lêouta!
Sir Uriah shall-be killed. I   it-swear by my troth!
Rag oll ow yeunes pupprŷs tŷ   a vŷth pür wŷr nefra.
For all my longing always thou shalt-be right truly for-ever.
Groweth y'n   gwely a-hês, may hyllyf genes   cusca.
Lie   on the bed   down, that I may with-thee sleep.

BATHSHEBA:

Mŷ ny allaf dha nagha, lemen pup tra-oll   grontya,
I   not can thy refusing, but   every thing-all granting,

64

(I cannot refuse thee, but grant everything)
Dhyworthyf a   wovynny.   Ow arluth whêk-oll,
Of-me   which thou mayest-ask. My lord   sweet-all,
  ladh e,
  kill him,
Ken   ef a wra ow shyndya, mar clewvyth   a'gan gwary.
Before he does my injuring, if   he shall-hear of-our sport.

(Mutations: *welys* radical *gwelys, well-* r. *gwell-, -blêkya* r. *-plêkya,
thour* r. *tour, wour* r. *gour, dryk* r. *tryk, vŷa* r. *bŷa, vrŷs* r. *brŷs, callen* r.
gallen, fŷen r. *bŷen, gerensa* r. *kerensa, vŷth* r. *bŷth, wŷr* r. *gwŷr,
hyllyf* r. *gyllyf, allaf* r. *gallaf, dhyworthyf* r. *dyworthyf, wovynny* r.
govynny, wra r. *gwra.*)

From the *Life of Silvester*, a minor play inserted into the *Life of
Meriasek*, ms. dated 1504:

(*Hic Episcopus Poli pompabit* – Here the Bishop of Poly shall
  parade)

Mŷ yû epscop a dhevŷs   ha perlet mür ow   râsow,
I   am bishop of perfection and prelate great of-my blessings,
Y tedhewys nans yû mŷs   mones yn hans
I-promised now is month (a month ago) going yonder
dhe'n   prâsow
to the meadows
Erbyn   Duk Magus   a brŷs,   dên für yn y
Against (to meet) Duke Magician of eminence, man wise in his
  worthebow.
  answers.
Ow crosser,   ôta   parys lemmyn dhe'm gormynadow?
My crozier-bearer, art thou ready now   at my bidding?

CROZIER-BEARER:
Mŷ yû parys, arluth da,   saw gwan rewl   yma omma
I   am ready, lord good, but bad management is   here
  Na   yllyn lŷfya ken   môs.
  That-not we can dine before going.
Gwâk yû dhym an pengasen.
Empty is to-me the stomach.
    A, mollath Dew   y'n   gegyn,
    Oh, curse   of-God in the kitchen,

65

Scant yû an dewas ha'n   bôs!
Scant is the drink and the food!

(*Descendunt* – They go down)

BISHOP:

Hayl dheugh, Duk   nobyl, Magus!   Mŷ ha'm   crosser
Hail to-you, Duke noble, Magician I   and my crozier-bearer
Presagus
Presagus (Prophet)
rê dhüth   dheugh whŷ dhe sportya.   Na wythyn
I have-come to-you   to   have-sport. Let-us-not-keep
rê   dhe'n   tŷrnans,
too-much to the valley-land,
rag yma dragon dyblans   hag onen vrâs sür   omma.
for is   dragon evidently   and one big surely here.

PRIMUS DUX MAGNUS:

Now wolcum, Fadyr Byschyp! *Ny   dhê   dragon, mŷ a dyp,*
                           Not will-come dragon, I   think,
ogas dhyn nŷ.
near to-us.

Mar tê   yn sŷght, mŷ a'n gôr, yma omma pobel   lowr
If   comes in sight, I   it-know is   here   people enough
rag hy ladha   yredy.
for its killing readily.
(Here the dragon ready in the place – Here the dragon ready on
the plain).

SECUNDUS DUX MAGNUS:

Na drestyen nŷ dhe henna. Arlydhy, dün   alemma.
Let-us-not-trust to that.   Lords   let-us-come away.
Otta hŷ   sür   devedhys! Owt, dredhy bydhyn   marow
Here-it-is surely come!   Out, by-it we shall-be dead
gans flam tân   mês a'y   ganow: ny's   gorta   mŷl
by   flame of-fire out of its mouth: not-it will-stop thousand
dhên ervys!
man armed!

(Mutations: *dhevŷs* г. *devŷs, tedhewys* г. *dedhewys, brŷs* г. *prŷs,
worthebow* г. *gorthebow, yllyn* г. *gyllyn, gegyn* г. *kegyn, dhüth* г. *düth,*

wythyn r. *gwythyn, vrâs* r. *brâs, dhê* r. *dê, dyp* r. *typ, tê* r. *dê, drestyen*
r. *trestyen, dhên* r. *dên.*)

MODERN CORNISH

Modern Cornish is a somewhat more advanced language than
Middle Cornish, but the difference between the two is not great and
of an order comparable to, say, the difference between colloquial
Welsh and strictly literary Welsh today. The spelling is generally
anglicized, except in the work of Lhuyd, who employed his own
'Celtic' alphabet. We adopt the principles already laid down for
Middle Cornish; *yy* is [ji].

The following differences between the two stages of the language
may be noted. Initial mutations include some not marked in the
older language, as *j, v, z*, softened forms of *ch, f, s*; *f* may occasionally change to *h*. A striking feature was the development of *m, n* to
bm, dn in a short stressed syllable, as *tabm* 'piece', *pedn* 'head', Mid.
Co. *tam, pen*. Mid. Co. *s* often became *j*, as *boghosek > boghojak*
'poor', when final it changes to *z*, as *gweles > gwelaz* 'seeing'. In these
last two examples we notice also the regular change of unstressed *e*
to *a* in final syllables. Among other vowel changes may be mentioned
the diphthongization of *ŷ* to *ey*, as *chŷ > chey* 'house'. The sound, or
sounds, represented by *ü* (p. 56) appear as *ê* or *ŷ*, thus *düth > dêth*
'came', *gwrük > grŷg* 'did'. Sometimes *y* is found where *e* would be
expected, as *gwyly*, otherwise *gwely* 'bed'.

Notice the following forms in the text below: *an jey* 'they, them' <
Mid. Co. *ynsŷ* (properly an emphatic form, p. 59), *era, thera* 'was' <
Mid. Co. *esa, yth esa*, and *dhô* 'was' < Mid. Co. *yth ô*.

From the only surviving Cornish folk-tale *John of Chyannor* (*Jûan
Chey an Hor*=John of Ram's House), written down by Nicholas
Boson between 1660 and 1670.

John had worked for three years away from home. In lieu of wages
at £3 a year, his master had taught him three points of wisdom:
never leave the old road for the new, never lodge in an inn where an
old man is married to a young woman, and think twice ere you strike
once. As John was leaving, his master gave him a cake which was not
to be cut until he was happily reunited with his wife. Unbeknown to
John, his unpaid wages were hidden in the cake. On the way home,

John overtook three merchants from his own parish. Then the merchants turned off into a new road, but John would not leave the old one:

Nag ô   an vartshants gyllys pel dhort Jûan, bez ledran
Not were the merchants gone far from John, but thieves
a glenaz ort   an jey. Ha an jey a dhalladhaz dho wŷl   crey
fastened onto them. And they   began   to doing of-cry
ha Jûan a greyaz awêth 'Ledran!' Ha genz an crey a   rŷg
and John cried   also 'Thieves!' And with the cry which did
Jûan gwŷl, an ledran a forsakyaz an vartshants. Ha pa
John doing, the thieves forsook   the merchants. And when
rŷg an jey dhôz   dho Varha Jou,
did they coming to Market of-Thursday (*Marazion*, p. 55),
ena an jey a vettyaz arta. Ha pa   rŷg an jey dhôz   dho'n
there they met   again. And when did they   coming to the
chey lebma gothfŷa   an jey ostya, a medh Jûan 'Mŷ dal
house where were-wont they lodging, said   John 'I   must
gwelaz an   ost'. 'Pendra venta   gwŷl gen an ost?'
seeing of-the host'. 'What will-you doing with the host?'
a medh an jey, 'ybma ma agen ostez ney ha yynk yû hey.
said   they, 'here is our hostess of-us and young is she.
Mar menta gwelaz an   ost, kŷ dho'n gegen.' Ha pa
If you-will seeing of-the host, go to the kitchen.' And when
rŷg ê dhôz   dho'n gegen, ena êv a welaz an ost, ha
did he coming to the kitchen, there he saw   the host, and
dên côth ô ê ha   gwadn a traylya an   bêr. Ha a medh
man old was he and weak at turning of-the spit. And said
Jûan, 'Ybma na vadna vŷ ostya, bez en nessa chey.'
John, 'Here not will I lodging, but in next house.'
Lebmen an ostez an   chey, hey a kynsylyaz   gen
Now   the hostess of-the house, she counselled (plotted) with
nebyn manah a era en tre, dho dhestrŷa
a-certain monk who was in town, to destroying (murdering)
an dên côth en gwyly en termen an nôz, ha gorra
of-the man old in bed in time of-the night and putting
an   fowt war on vartshants. Ha pa   thera Jûan en gwyly,
of-the blame on the merchants. And when was John in bed,
thera toll en tâl an   chey. Ha êv a welaz golow, ha êv
was hole in gable of-the house. And he saw   light and he

a savaz aman amêz e wyly, ha êv a glywaz an manah
stood up out-of his bed, and he heard the monk
laveral, ha traylyaz e geyn dho'n toll, 'Martezen', a medh
speaking and turned his back to the hole, 'Perhaps', said
êv, 'ma nebonen en nessa chey a rŷg welaz
he, 'is someone in next house who did seeing (would see)
agen hager oberow'. Ha genz hedna an gwadn-
of-our evil deeds'. And with this (thereupon) the wicked-
gyrty genz e follat a dhestrŷaz an dên côth. Ha
housewife with her gallant murdered the man old. And
genz hedna Jûan genz e golhan trohaz der an toll mêz a
thereupon John with his knife cut through the hole out of
geyn gûn an manah pŷs pŷr-round.
back of-gown of-the monk (a) piece (quite)-round.

Ha nessa metten an gwadn-gyrty hey a dhalladhaz
And next morning the wicked-housewife, she began
dho wŷl crey ter dhô e thermâz hey destrŷaz. Ha
to doing of-cry that was her husband of-her murdered. And
rak na era dên na flôh en chey bez an vartshants, an jey
since not was man nor child in house but the merchants, they
dhal krêg ragta. Ena an jey a vê kemeryz ha dho'n
must hang for-it. Then they were taken and to the
clogh-prednyer an jey a vê ledyyz. Ha war an diwedh
bell-beams (gallows) they were led. And on the end (at last)
Jûan a dhêth war aga fydn. 'Anjustyz yû', a medh
John came on their head (met them) 'Injustice is', said
Jûan.
John.

Then John told of what he had seen and heard through the gable-
wall and showed the piece he had cut out of the monk's gown:

Ha genz hedna an vartshants a vê frŷez ha an venyn
And thereupon the merchants were freed and the woman
ha'n manah a vê kemeryz ha kregyz.
and the monk were taken and hanged.
Nenna an jey a dhêth warbarh mêz dho Varha Jou ha nenna
Then they came together out of Marazion and then
thera vor dhiberh ha an vartshants
was road of-separation (fork in the road) and the merchants

a venja arta   dho Jûan môz   barh an jey. Bez êv a venja môz
wished again of   John going with them.   But he wished going
dre   dho e   wrêg.
home to   his wife.

   Ha pa   rŷg ê dôz   dho'n   darraz, êv a venja
   And when did he coming to   the door, he would
clywaz   dên aral en gwyly. Êv a waske e
hearing (thought he heard) man other in bed.   He clapped his
dorn war e   dhagyer dho dhestrŷa   an   dhêaw. Bez êv
hand on his dagger to   murdering of-the two.   But he
a brederaz ter   gotha dhodho bôz   avyzyyz
pondered   that it-fell to-him being considered (he ought to
        dhiweth ken   gwesgal enweth. Nenna êv a gnakyaz:
consider) twice   before striking once.   Then he knocked:
'Pyû ez ena?'   a medh hey. 'Thera vŷ ybma', a medh Jûan. Ha
'Who is there?' said   she. 'Was I here', said   John. And
pa   rŷg Jûan dôz   chey, a medh êv,
when did John coming (into the) house said   he,
'Mŷ a venja clywaz dên aral en gwyly'. 'Jûan', a medh hey,
'I thought I heard man other in bed'.   'John,' said   she,
'pa   rŷgough whey môz ker,   thera vŷ gyllyz trey mŷz
'when did   you going away was I gone three month
gen hlôh, ha   lebmen ma dho ney meppig whêg en gwyly.'
with child and now   is to us sonny sweet in bed.'
   Nenna an jey a dorhaz an dezan ha thera naw punz   en
   Then they cut   the cake and were nine pounds in-the
dezan. Ha an mona an jey a gavaz ha'n   dezan an jey
cake. And the money they found and the cake they
a dhabraz ha andella ma diwedh me   daralla dhodhans.
ate,   and so   is end   of-my story about-them.

(Mutations: *vartshants* r. *martshants, dhalladhaz* r. *dalladhaz, wŷl* r.
gwŷl, greyaz r. *creyaz, rŷg* r. *grŷg, dhôz* r. *dôz, Varha* r. *Marha,*
vettyaz r. *mettyaz, gothfŷa* r. *cothfŷa, dal* r. *tal, venta* r. *menta, gegen*
r. *kegen, welaz* r. *gwelaz, vadna* r. *madna, dhestrŷa* r. *destrŷa, wyly* r.
gwyly, glywaz r. *clywaz, geyn* r. *keyn, follat* r. *pollat, golhan* r. *colhan,*
thermâz r. *termâz, dhal* r. *dal, vê* r. *bê, dhêth* r. *dêth, fydn* r. *pydn,*
venyn r. *benyn, dhiberh* r. *diberh, venja* r. *menja, wrêg* r. *gwrêg, waske*
r. *gwaske, dhagyer* r. *dagyer, dhêaw* r. *dêaw, brederaz* r. *prederaz,*
gotha r. *cotha, dhiweth* r. *diweth, gnakyaz* r. *knakyaz, vŷ* r. *mŷ,*

rŷgough r. *grŷgough, hlôh* r. *flôh, dorhaz* r. *torhaz, dezan* r. *tezan, gavaz* r. *cavaz, dhabraz* r. *dabraz*.)

LITERATURE

There is no comprehensive work for the study of Cornish as it is actually attested in the sources. The only up-to-date survey of the medieval language is written in Welsh; this is H. Lewis, *Llawlyfr Cernyweg Canol* (*Handbook of Middle Cornish*), 2nd edition (1946). On the modern language, see H. Jenner, *A Handbook of the Cornish Language* (1904) ('chiefly in its latest stages with some account of its history and literature').

The following publications are concerned with normalized ('revived') Middle Cornish:

R. M. Nance, *Cornish for All* (revised edition 1949, reprinted 1960), contains a Middle Cornish restoration of John of Chyannor.

P. A. S. Pool, *Cornish for Beginners*, 3rd edition 1970, reprinted 1973.

R. M. Nance, *An English–Cornish Dictionary* (1952), *A Cornish–English Dictionary* (1955).

Enquiries about works in or about Cornish may be made to Miss M. E. Mills, Amalwhidden Cottage, Towednack, St Ives, Cornwall.

PART III

IRISH CELTIC

🔯🔯🔯🔯🔯

CHAPTER SIX

Irish

🔯🔯🔯🔯🔯🔯

IN a previous chapter we have seen that archaeological evidence points to large-scale immigration into Britain from the Continent towards the middle of the first millennium BC, the newcomers being identifiable as Celts. For Ireland, however, there is as yet no comparable archaeological record. It is certain that Celts were dominant there in Roman times, but at what date they first established themselves, and by what route they arrived, are quite unknown. It is at any rate clear that the Irish Celts are not simply a recent offshoot of the British Celts we know from history, for even in Roman times their languages must have differed very considerably. Indeed, Irish seems to represent a more archaic type of Celtic than British.

Irish Celtic is traditionally called Goidelic, whence the modern term Gaelic, applied both to the language of the mother country and to its colonial varieties in Scotland and Man.

At an unknown date, perhaps in Roman times, but at the latest during the Dark Ages, Irish absorbed an earlier language or languages spoken in Ireland and thus became the speech of the whole population of the country. Irish was also expansive outside Ireland. From the end of the third century AD, Irish colonies were founded in North and South Wales, and these doubtless survived into the Dark Ages. The north Welsh province of Gwynedd, centred on the modern Caernarvonshire, takes its name from the immigrant Irish *Féni*, while in Demetia, the modern Dyfed (Pembrokeshire and west Carmarthen-

73

shire), an Irish dynasty ruled until the eighth century. The Devonian peninsula also received Irish settlers about this time.

More lasting conquests were made further north. The Isle of Man was occupied not later than the fourth century AD and the indigenous British entirely replaced by Goedelic. In the fifth century, colonists from Ulster set up a kingdom in Argyll. From this large bridgehead they brought the country subsequently called Scotland under their sway, at the same time spreading their language at the expense of Pictish and British. These developments are further considered in Chapters Seven and Eight.

Apart from a few names transmitted by classical authors, Irish is first recorded in a pre-Christian native script in the so-called Ogam inscriptions, the oldest of which belong to the fourth century (p. 80). The Latin alphabet, introduced by the Christian mission in the fifth century, was soon being used to write Irish, first in the glossing of Latin texts, later for original work, the earliest surviving material being datable to the sixth century (p. 81). During the Age of Saints, from the sixth to the eighth centuries, monastic culture flourished in Ireland as nowhere else in Western Christendom, and Irish missionaries were responsible for many religious foundations on the continent of Europe. The oldest manuscripts with Irish materials are preserved in continental libraries.

This remarkable period in Irish history was terminated by the invading Norsemen. Their assaults on Ireland, beginning in 795, led to permanent settlement, particularly at centres on the coast. This influential alien minority for long preserved its identity. But after the decisive defeat of the Norsemen at Clontarf in 1014, assimilation became simply a matter of time. It was doubtless well advanced when even more powerful foreigners descended upon the country. These were the Norman knights with their retinues of French, Flemish and English mercenaries who landed in the south in 1169 and captured Dublin the following year. In 1171, Henry II received the homage of most of the Irish chieftains, thus inaugurating the formal connection with England. The Normans quickly spread out over Ireland and by 1250 had brought two-thirds of the country under their control. Dublin became the seat of the central government, such as it was, and maintained close links with London. Gradually the English language became dominant in the town and its immediate environs. The English-controlled districts were known as the Pale and here English law was in force.

After 1250, however, the Normans lost some of their earlier gains to native Irish rulers, while the Normans outside the Pale were themselves becoming gaelicized. As the Normans in England abandoned French in favour of English, in Ireland they went over to Gaelic. This perfectly natural development was nevertheless, in Ireland, potential treason, as was made explicit in the legislation of the time. The Statutes of Kilkenny (1367) define three classes of persons residing in Ireland: first, the 'loyal subjects' of the Pale, English in law and language; secondly, the 'degenerate subjects' who had adopted the law and language of the Irish; and lastly the 'Irish enemies' themselves. The Statutes forbade subjects of the Crown to follow the law or use the language of the King's enemies. In the historical circumstances of the day, these declarations – clearly an expression of anxiety in the face of resurgent Gaeldom – remained a dead letter, but the spirit which conceived them did not die. It was thus decreed that there were to be two parties in the land, hostile and exclusive: the English minority within the Pale, elsewhere the Irish majority now strengthened by the gaelicized Normans, *Hibernis ipsis Hiberniores* 'more Irish than the Irish themselves' as the bitter reproach had it. The Gaelic advance continued to the end of the fifteenth century. In 1494, the Pale had shrunk to its smallest ever, a thirty-mile strip of coast from Dublin to Dundalk, extending barely twenty miles inland.

But just then, under the Tudors, the balance of power radically altered. The first moves were directed against the great Norman houses and by 1535 these were largely reduced to submission. Then came the turn of the native Gaelic families. In 1556, the Irish of Leix and Offaly were expelled from their clan lands to make room for English settlers – the beginning of the plantation policy – and Ireland was fast becoming Britain's first colony. What yet remained of independent Ireland was, within a few decades, to encounter the military might of Elizabethan England and struggle in vain. The end of Gaelic Ireland was now at hand. The vanquished laid down their arms after the defeat at Kinsale in 1601. Six years later their remaining leaders fled the country, a symbolic episode known as the Flight of the Earls.

As long as Ireland remained essentially Gaelic, the Irish continued to employ their native language widely for literary purposes. Not unnaturally, production suffered as a consequence of the Viking invasions and again under the first impact of the Anglo-Norman conquest, but each time it recovered. Medieval Irish is the vehicle of a literature more ancient than that of any vernacular in Europe, and scarcely less voluminous. Heroic song and saga, legend, historical and legal writings may describe conditions more than a thousand years older than the twelfth-century manuscripts which preserve so much of this unique heritage.

After the Flight of the Earls, the hereditary lands of the fugitives – they lay principally in Ulster – were declared forfeit and planted with English-speaking settlers. This was but a foretaste of the depredations under Cromwell which aimed at the total destruction of native Irish life. By 1655, the English-speaking element was numerically so strong that it could begin to assimilate the Gaelic speakers, chiefly those in the urban areas. But the countryside, and especially the backward western districts, remained predominantly Irish-speaking and still able to assimilate many foreign settlers. But all the time the English element grew in strength and influence. In 1600, English had been the language of a very small minority; by 1800 it had become the normal medium of quite half the total population, estimated to have been about four millions. Irish was now in a very inferior position. Its speakers were recognizably the less fortunate section of the population; Irish was now synonymous with poverty and illiteracy. The language was, of course, totally ignored by officialdom. It was despised not only by the English-speaking section whatever their origin, but ominously also by the leaders of the Gaelic peasantry themselves, foremost among whom was the idolized Daniel O'Connell. Such men believed that Irish was an obstacle to progress and avoided using it wherever possible. The sympathies of the Catholic Church, that most influential institution in Ireland, were likewise on the side of English. Small wonder that English continued to gain ground at the expense of Irish and that a knowledge of English was eagerly sought by those who still used Irish as the primary medium. On the other hand, the rapid rise in numbers to a total population of eight millions in 1841 probably meant that Gaelic was then being used by as many as three millions, more adherents in fact than ever before.

But there was no safety in unprecedented numbers in this case. The famine years of the late forties carried off upwards of a million Gaels, while the survivors saw their main hope of salvation in America. The country was depopulated on a scale and at a speed unparalleled in Europe. Thus the Famine struck the Gaelic language in Ireland a blow from which it could never recover. By the end of the century it was found only in rapidly shrinking enclaves, chiefly in the far west. Only then did a reaction in its favour set in. The nineteenth century had seen the rise of movements for national independence all over Europe – Icelanders and Norwegians, the Baltic peoples, Czechs and Slovaks, and many others proclaimed their sovereign right to decide their own destinies and strove to liberate themselves from the larger powers which controlled them. They perceived in the national language the hallmark of their identity and aimed not merely to free it from any sort of discrimination, but to confer upon it supreme status. In keeping with these trends, a number of intellectuals came to see in the Gaelic language a symbol of Irish nationhood. In 1893, the Gaelic League was formed with the task of restoring the Irish language. But if the patriotic endeavours of the restorers could overcome to some extent the prejudices of the administration, they could make little practical progress in the face of the overwhelming difficulties. The first census of Irish speakers in 1851 had returned 1,524,000, of whom 320,000 had no English. But when the Gaelic League began its work, there were not half as many, most of whom belonged to the oldest generation, and the number of monoglot speakers had dropped to 30,000 in the 1891 census. At best the example of the Gaelic Leaguers could here and there slow down the decline in Irish speaking, but their idealism was gratified when, in 1922, Gaelic was declared to be the national language of the new *Saorstát Éireann*, 'Free State of Ireland', fully recognized for all purposes and formally taking precedence over English, the second official language of the State. This position remains unchanged today. In practice, however, the national language can play little more than a nominal role outside the *Gaeltacht* (as the areas where Gaelic is still naturally spoken are called). It exists as an ideological extra, cultivated by government, chiefly in the educational field, including radio and television. Signs and notices emanating from official sources are frequently bilingual. But for most people, ordinary life goes on without Irish.

After Independence, the national language was introduced into school curricula wherever teachers were available. Irish is now taught in all state schools and has become the usual medium of instruction not only in schools actually situated in the *Gaeltacht*, but also in several outside it. Higher education is available in Irish at some institutions, Galway University College having taken the lead here. As a consequence of this policy, perhaps half a million can now be said to possess some knowledge of Irish Gaelic. But for

most of these, School Irish is on a par with School French. Meantime the number of those who employ Irish as the mother tongue
declines year by year as the *Gaeltacht* dwindles through emigration
and the encroachment of English. The monoglot speakers of Irish
are no more; with insignificant exceptions all have fluent English today, which is strong enough to modify their Gaelic idiom. The 1961
census returned 83,000 Irish speakers living in areas defined as
Gaeltacht, and there may be quite as many emigrant native speakers
who still retain a fluent command of Gaelic. But knowing the language
and actually using it is not the same thing, even in the *Gaeltacht*.
We estimate that not more than 40,000, if indeed as many, habitually
employ the language today. In Munster, Irish has now entered the
stage of final dissolution, Dunquin at the tip of Dingle peninsula
being the only village which yet remains largely Irish-speaking. The
two principal retreats of the language today are Connemara, the
district west of Galway City, and the west-central part of Donegal.
With such small areas, survival in the long term is no longer possible.
One generation yet to come may, in fast decreasing numbers, continue to use the language as the spontaneous domestic medium, but
these will be the last. Native Irish can be expected to become moribund early in the next century and therefore extinct by the end of it.

Since the end of Gaelic Ireland, literature in the native language has
shared the sorry fate of the language itself. There have been some
exceptional men like Geoffrey Keating, who, in the first half of the
seventeenth century, could still employ a standard form of the
language acceptable throughout Gaeldom. But by the second half
of that century, Gaelic society had been weakened to such an extent
that national literature could no longer be produced. Irish gained
next to nothing from the invention of printing. It had first appeared
in print in 1567 in a translation of a Protestant Prayer Book (p. 120).
In 1603 came a New Testament from the same quarter, but what use
were such things to the Catholic Gaels? But then the Catholic side
followed suit, beginning with a Catechism in 1611, perforce printed
abroad. Other devotional works followed, but output remained
minimal. Meanwhile the works of Keating and others circulated in
manuscript. Traditional culture survived best in the south-west and
was expressed in the works of the Munster bards until the Famine
blasted the land. But their diction was no longer the standard used by
Keating. The audience was now a local, rustic one, for whom dialect
was necessary. The literary language had been lost.

This is still the position today: the living language exists solely in its varying dialect forms. Three main types occur, those of Munster, Connaught and Ulster, and mutual comprehension is not easy, particularly as between the extremes of Kerry and Donegal. Such a situation naturally posed serious problems for the restorers. School books were issued in three styles, rough standardizations of the dialects mentioned above. Meanwhile a standard spelling and morphology have been worked out and generally adopted (p. 100). Thanks mainly to official patronage, a modest literature in contemporary Gaelic has come into being, some of it deriving from the rich oral tradition of the Irish-speaking peasantry, and learned societies in particular have found means to print at last the significant writings of an earlier age.

Gaelic has exercised a considerable influence on the English as spoken in Ireland, particularly in rural Ireland. There are not only lexical elements like *boreen* 'lane' or *canavan* 'bog-cotton' (Ir. *bóithrín*, diminutive of *bóthar* 'road', *ceannbhán* lit. 'white head'), but syntactical features as well, of which the creation of habitual tenses as 'I do be, I did be' in imitation of Ir. *bím, bhínn* (p. 109) is a striking enough example: 'I do be at my piano lesson every day.' A fair number of Gaelic words have passed into standard English, as *bog, glen, smithereens* (Ir. *bog* 'soft', *gleann, smidríní* dim. of *smiodar* 'piece'), but even so such words usually retain an Irish connotation, eg, *keen* 'lament', *leprechaun, poteen, shamrock* (Ir. *caoineadh, leiprachán, poitín* dim. of *pota* 'pot', *seamróg* dim. of *seamar* 'clover').

The place and personal names of Ireland remain in large measure Gaelic. Many are semantically transparent, thus *Dublin*, Ir. *Duibhlinn* 'Blackpool' (*dubh* 'black', *linn* 'pool'), also known as *Baile Átha Cliath* 'Town of-Ford of-Hurdles', this its usual name in Gaelic. Surnames mostly contain *ó*, lit. 'grandson' or *mac* 'son' followed by the genitive of the name, as *Flaherty*, properly *O'Flaherty*, Ir. *Ó Flaithbheartaigh* (*flaithbheartach* 'hospitable (man)'), *Macnamara*, Ir. *Mac Conmara* (*cú mara* 'seal' lit. 'dog of-sea').

LITERATURE

B. Ó Cuív (editor), *A View of the Irish Language* (1969). A collection of twelve essays by authoritative writers which provide a satisfying account of the language, literature and culture of the Irish Gael, today and yesterday.

OGAM IRISH

Apart from names transmitted by classical authors, the oldest Irish is recorded in monumental inscriptions, the majority found in the southern half of Ireland, the rest elsewhere in that country, in Scotland and Man, and also in Wales and Cornwall. Some three hundred in number, these inscriptions date from the fourth to the eighth centuries AD. In a few cases the Latin alphabet is used, but generally the script is Ogam, a sort of cipher inspired by the Latin alphabet. It consists of three sets of one to five strokes cut (*a*) to the right of, (*b*) to the left of, (*c*) across a middle line, for consonants, and one to five cross-strokes or notches on the middle line for vowels:

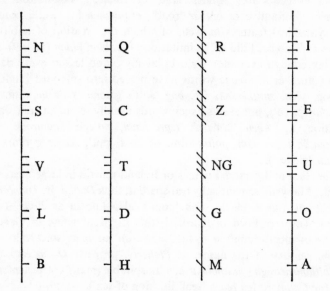

The language disclosed in the earliest of these brief monuments suggests that Irish was then at about the same stage of development as is assumed for British, but with a significant archaism: the retention of original Celtic *kw*, written Q, but which had changed to *p* in British, thus Ogam Ir. MAQ- 'son', Brit. *map*-, implied by Medieval Welsh *map*.

Irish

Ogam writing was adopted by the Picts (p. 20).

Specimen inscriptions with renderings in the later (Classical) Old Irish, comparison showing the exceptionally archaic character of the Ogam records:

DALAGNI   MAQI   DALI
(stone) of-Dallagnas of-son of-Dallas
  Dalláin   maicc Daill

MODDAGNI   MAQI   GATTAGNI   MUCOI   LUGUNI
(stone) of-Modagnas of-son of-Gatagnas of-people of-Luguniyas
  Múadáin   maicc Gaítháin   moccu   Luigni

TRIA   MAQA   MAILAGNI   CURCITTI
(stone) of-three of-sons of-Mailagnas (of-son) of-Curcitiyas
  tri   macc   Mailáin   Cuircthi

LITERATURE

R. A. S. Macalister, *Corpus Inscriptionum Insularum Celticarum* (1945).

SKETCH OF OLD IRISH

We are here concerned with Classical Old Irish, a largely standard-ized literary idiom present in texts of the eighth and ninth centuries. A smaller amount of material in somewhat older language goes as far back as the sixth century. Writing is in Latin letters of a distinctive half-uncial type developed in Ireland itself; it has remained in use to this day (p. 99). The highly complex nature of Old Irish, both phonologically and morphologically, makes the study of its records exceptionally exacting.

Phonetics

The stress falls on the first syllable, except in certain compound forms, as *ro·gab* 'has given', the dot preceding the stressed syllable.

The orthography provides a very inadequate key to the involved phonetic system. Thus *p, t, c* [k] are voiceless occlusives when initial (unless nasalized, see Mutations below) or after *s*, but following vowels they are [b, d, g], following consonants they represent either

81

voiceless or voiced pronunciations; *b, d, g* are voiced occlusives when initial (unless lenited, see Mutations), but following vowels they are the spirants [β, δ, γ], following consonants they represent either occlusive or spirant pronunciations. Geminates (*cc, gg*, etc.) have occlusive pronunciation only. Double consonants are long. In certain positions *m* had a spirant pronunciation [μ], not distinguished in the script.

Consonants (except *h*) have three qualities, not marked in the script, but most often recognizable by changes induced in associated vowels. Thus *r* is neutral in nominative singular *fer* 'man', but palatal in genitive singular *fir* and has a *u*-quality in dative singular *fiur*.

Apart from its use in the digraphs *ph, th, ch* (see Mutations), *h* has no phonetic value, but is often redundantly prefixed to words beginning with a vowel, especially very short ones, as *hi* 'in', properly *i*.

The Old Irish scribes frequently employed the acute accent and their usage is here normalized. The accent has two functions. Firstly, placed over a single vowel, it denotes length. Secondly, it distinguishes a diphthong as opposed to a single vowel accompanied by a vowel glide, though quantities here are uncertain. It is written over the first component in *áe, óe, áo, áu, éo, éu, íu, óu*, but over the second in *aí, oí, uí* to avoid confusion with *ái, ói, úi*, which represent a single vowel accompanied by an *i*-glide, hence *druí* [drui] 'druid', but *rúin* [ruːjń], accusative dative singular of *rún* 'secret'. Similarly the combinations *ai, au*, etc., denote a short vowel accompanied by an *i*- or *u*-glide. The forms *áe, óe* are scribal variants of *aí, oí*; the two originally distinct diphthongs early fell together but the spellings were retained and confused, so that all four are commonly interchangeable.

The letter *i* is commonly written to denote the glide arising between back vowels and a following palatal consonant, as *aig* 'ice', *coin* 'dogs', *súil* 'eye'; an analogous glide arising between a palatal consonant and a following back vowel is written *e*, as *cairtea*, accusative of *carait* 'friends'. By the same token, the letter *a* came to be written after a neutral consonant followed by a front vowel, as *echaib* dat. pl. of *ech* 'horse'.

Initial Mutations

Initial consonants follow a system of mutations not unlike that evolved in British about the same time, ie, between 450 and 550 AD (p. 27).

Two main types occur, known scientifically – with historical justification – as lenition and nasalization, but also commonly referred to as aspiration and eclipsis respectively. A third type – gemination – also occurs, but as a declining category.

In lenition (aspiration) the occlusives *p, t, c* are mutated to the corresponding spirants [φ, θ, χ] written *ph, th, ch*. Similarly the occlusives *b, d, g* are mutated to [β, δ, γ], but this change is not shown in the script. Another unmarked change is that of *m* to [μ] (a sound close to [β]). Further, *s* becomes [h], while *f* disappears; this mutation may be unmarked, or else represented by a *punctum delens* placed above the letter: *ṡ, ḟ*. The pronunciation of *l, n, r* is also variously affected, but not shown in writing.

In nasalization (eclipsis) *n* is prefixed to words beginning with a vowel or *d*, also *g* (but then pronounced [ŋ]); before *b* the nasal is *m*, before *m, n*, also *l, r, s*, the initial is doubled and is thus indistinguishable from gemination (below). The occlusives *p, t, c* are voiced, but this change is not shown in the script, except occasionally in the case of *t* to *d*. By this mutation *f* becomes [β] which may be written *b* or not shown at all. The pronunciation of other consonants is variously modified, but again not shown in the script.

In gemination, the consonant was doubled. This change is not often marked, and eventually the phenomenon disappeared leaving the single radical consonant.

The presence of mutations not explicit in the writing can be demonstrated philologically. The practices of the derivative modern Gaelic languages often throw light on earlier forms, as does the evidence of Middle Irish. Finally, there is the corroborative testimony of British, for initial mutations are an ancient feature of Insular Celtic.

The circumstances in which mutations take place are many and varied, as the selection of examples may illustrate:

Lenition (aspiration) occurs in a dative noun: *do'n choin* 'to the dog' (radical *coin*), in a noun following a nominative feminine singular: *súil chairach* 'eye of a sheep' (r. *cairach*), in the second element of a compound: *findfolt* 'white hair' (r. *folt*), after certain possessive pronouns: *mo thol* 'my will' (r. *tol*), after several prepositions: *do choscrad* 'to destruction' (r. *coscrad*), *fo pheccad* 'under sin' (r. *peccad*), after various particles, as *a* with a vocative: *a choimdiu* 'O Lord' (r. *coimdiu*) or conjunctions, as *ó* 'since': *ó chretsit* 'since they have believed' (r. *cretsit*), frequently after verbal forms: *ni˙fil chumtubairt* 'there is no doubt' lit. 'not-is doubt' (r. *cumtubairt*), in certain relative clauses: *is mó ro˙chés Críst* 'indeed Christ suffered more' lit. 'it-is more which-suffered Christ' (r. *ro˙cés*), *not˙beir* (pronounce *not˙veir*) 'which bears thee' lit. 'which-thee-bears', after *ocus* 'and': *ocus chlaideb* 'and (a) sword' (r. *claideb*).

Nasalization (eclipsis) occurs after the accusative singular: *rath ndé* 'the grace (acc.) of God' (r. *dé*), *lá mbrátha* 'the day (accusative) of judgment' (r. *brátha*), after accusative singular masculine feminine of article: *sechtar in degdais* 'outside the house' (r. *tegdais* f.), after certain possessive pronouns: *for n-étach* 'your garment' (r. *étach*), after certain numerals: *da n-orbe* 'two inheritances' (r. *orbe*), after certain prepositions: *i mbélre naill* 'into another language' (r. *bélre* 'language'), in certain relative clauses: *do˙mmeil* 'which (it) consumes' (r. *do˙meil* '(it) consumes'), *inna túari no˙cari* (pron. *no˙gari*) 'the foods which thou lovest'.

When gemination takes place, the words involved are always written as one; we here separate them by a hyphen. Gemination occurs after certain cases of the article, as accusative plural: *inna-mmaccu* 'the sons' (r. *maccu*), after *a* 'her': *a-mmuntar* 'her household' (r. *muntar*), after various prepositions: *a-ppeccad* 'out of sin' (r. *peccad*).

Nouns

There are three numbers: singular, plural and dual, the latter occurring only in association with the numeral *da* 'two'. There are five cases: nominative, vocative, accusative, genitive, dative, though these are not always morphologically distinct. The vocative is preceded by a leniting (aspirating) particle *a*. There are various declensions described as *o*-stems, *ā*-stems, etc., terms which refer to the structure of ancestral forms. Thus *fer* 'man' is described as an *o*-stem since it descends from Proto-Celtic **wiros*, where *-s* is the (nominative singular) case ending and *wiro-* the stem, further reducible to the root *wir-* and the stem vowel *-o-*. Similarly *delb* 'image' is characterized as an *ā*-stem as it derives from a postulated **delw-ā* (this type without a nominative singular case ending). From the point of view of comparative philology, these two declensions correspond to the *a*- and *ō*-stems of Old English, etc., and to the second and first declensions of Latin, respectively. There are three genders: masculine, feminine, neuter. Sample paradigms:

o-stems, masc. and neut.
Sg. nom. *fer* m. 'man', voc. *fir*, acc. *fer*, gen. *fir*, dat. *fiur*, pl. nom. *fir*, voc. acc. *firu*, gen. *fer*, dat. *feraib*, du. *fer* except dat. *feraib*
Sg. nom. voc. acc. *scél* n. 'tale', gen. *scéuil*, dat. *scéul*, pl. *scél* except dat. *scélaib*, du. as pl.

ā-stems, fem.
Sg. nom. voc. *delb* 'image', acc. *deilb*, gen. *delbae*, dat. *deilb*, pl. nom. voc. acc. *delba*, gen. *delb*, dat. *delbaib*, du. nom. voc. acc. *deilb*, gen. and dat. as pl.

i-stems, all genders
Sg. nom. voc. acc. *cnáim* m. 'bone', gen. *cnámo*, dat. *cnáim*, pl. nom. voc. acc. *cnámai*, gen. *cnámae*, dat. *cnámaib*, du. nom. voc. acc. *cnáim*, gen. *cnámo*, dat. *cnámaib*.
Sg. nom. voc. acc. *súil* f. 'eye', gen. *súlo*, dat. *súil*, pl. nom. voc. acc. *súili*, gen. *súile*, dat. *súilib*, du. nom. voc. acc. *súil*, gen. *súlo*, dat. *súili*.
Sg. nom. voc. acc. *muir* n. 'sea', gen. *moro*, dat. *muir*, pl. *muire* except dat. *muirib*, du. nom. voc. acc. *muir*, gen. *moro*, dat. *muirib*.
(Sg. gen. also commonly in -*a*, hence *cnáma*, etc.).

u-stems, masc. and neut. (originally all genders, as in adjectival declension below).
Sg. nom. voc. acc. *cath* m. 'battle', gen. *catho*, dat. *cath*, pl. nom. *cathae*, voc. acc. *cathu*, gen. *cathae*, dat. *cathaib*, du. nom. voc. acc. *cath*, gen. *catho*, dat. *cathaib*.
Sg. nom. voc. acc. *dorus* n. 'door', gen. *doirseo*, dat. *dorus*, pl. nom. voc. acc. *dorus*, gen. *doirse*, dat. *doirsib*, du. nom. voc. acc. *dorus*, gen. *doirseo*, dat. *doirsib*.
(Sg. gen. also commonly in -*a*, hence *catha*, etc.).

Further, consonant stems notably with gutturals (*ch*, *g*), dentals (*t*, *d*) and a nasal (*n*), of various genders, as:
Sg. nom. voc. *caíra* f. 'sheep', acc. *caírig*, gen. *caírach*, dat. *caírig*, pl. nom. *caírig*, voc. acc. *caírcha*, gen. *caírach*, dat. *caírchaib*, du. nom. voc. acc. *caírig*, gen. and dat. as pl.
Sg. nom. voc. *rí* m. 'king', acc. gen. dat. *ríg*, pl. nom. *rí*, voc. acc. *ríga*, gen. *ríg*, dat. *rígaib*, du. nom. voc. acc. *ríg*, gen. and dat. as pl.

Sg. nom. voc. *tengae* m. 'tongue', acc. *tengaid*, gen. *tengad*, dat. *tengaid*, pl. nom. *tengaid*, voc. acc. *tengtha*, gen. *tengad*, dat. *tengthaib*, du. nom. voc. acc. *tengaid*, gen. and dat. as pl.

Sg. nom. voc. *carae* m. 'friend', acc. *carait*, gen. *carat*, dat. *carait*, pl. nom. *carait*, voc. acc. *cairtea*, gen. *carat*, dat. *cairtib*, du. nom. voc. acc. *carait*, gen. and dat. as pl.

Sg. nom. voc. *cú* m. 'dog', acc. *coin*, gen. *con*, dat. *coin*, pl. nom. *coin*, voc. acc. *cona*, gen. *con*, dat. *conaib*, du. nom. voc. acc. *coin*, gen. and dat. as pl.

Sg. nom. voc. *Ériu* f. 'Ireland', acc. *Érinn*, gen. *Érenn*, dat. *Érinn*.

Adjectives

Adjectives take (singular and plural) declensions which correspond to those of noun stems ending in a vowel, eg, (1) *o*-stems provide the masculine and neuter, *ā*-stems the feminine, (2) *i*-stem endings for all genders, (3) *u*-stem endings for all genders, this last being a very small group.

We illustrate (1), the commonest type:

	masc.	fem.	neut.
Sg. nom.	*becc*	*becc*	*becc* 'little'
voc.	*bicc*	*becc*	*becc*
acc.	*becc*	*bicc*	*becc*
gen.	*bicc*	*bicce*	*bicc*
dat.	*biucc*	*bicc*	*biucc*
Pl. nom.	*bicc*		*becca*
voc.	*biccu*		*becca*
acc.	*biccu*		*becca*
gen.	*becc*		*becc*
dat.	*beccaib*		*beccaib*

The comparative and superlative are generally formed by adding -(*i*)*u* and -*em* or -*am* to the positive: *sen* 'old', *siniu* 'older', *sinem* 'oldest', *ard* 'high', *ardu* 'higher', *ardam* 'highest'. There is also an equative degree, for which the suffix is commonly -*ithir*, hence *sinithir* 'as old', *ardaithir* 'as high'. A few adjectives have irregular comparison, eg, *maith* 'good', *ferr* 'better', *dech* 'best', *olc* 'bad', *messa* 'worse', *messam* 'worst'.

Numbers

1 *oín*, 2 *da*, 3 *tri*, 4 *cethir*, 5 *cóic*, 6 *sé*, 7 *secht*, 8 *ocht*, 9 *noí*, 10 *deich*, 11 *oín deac*, 12 *da deac*, 13 *tri deac*, 14 *cethir deac*, 15 *cóic deac*, 16 *sé deac*, 17 *secht deac*, 18 *ocht deac*, 19 *noí deac*, 20 *fiche*, 21 *oín fichet*, 30 *tricho*, 40 *cethorcho*, 50 *coíco*, 60 *sesco*, 70 *sechtmogo*, 80 *ochtmogo*, 90 *nócho*, 100 *cét*, 1000 *míle*.

Numbers 2 to 4 inflect: nom. acc. masc. neut. *da*, fem. *di*, gen. *da*, dat. *dib*, nom. acc. gen. masc. neut. *tri*, nom. fem. *téoir*, acc. gen. *téora*, dat. masc. neut. *trib*, fem. *téoraib*, nom. masc. neut. *cethir*, fem. *cethéoir*, acc. gen. masc. neut. *cethri*, fem. *cethéora*, dat. masc. neut. *cethrib*, fem. *cethéoraib*. The decads and words for 100 and 1000 are nouns followed by the genitive of the things enumerated. Sample declension: sg. nom. *fiche* m. '20', acc. dat. *fichit*, gen. *fichet*, pl. nom. *fichit*, acc. *fichtea*, gen. *fichet*, dat. *fichtib*.

Definite Article

Sg. nom. masc.	*in*	fem. *ind*	neut. *a*
acc.	*in, -sin*	*in, -sin*	*a, -sa*
gen.	*ind*	*inna*	*ind*
dat.	*ind, -sind*	*ind, -sind*	*ind, -sind*
Pl. nom.	*ind*	*inna*	*inna*
acc.		*inna, -sna*	
gen.		*inna*	
dat.		*-naib, -snaib*	

Du. *in, -sin* (invariable)

Sg. nom. masc. *int* before vowels; *ind, -sind* become *int, -sint* before *ś*. The forms *-sa, -sin, -sind* are found after certain prepositions, as *isna* (accusative plural) 'into the' (*i* 'into'). After other prepositions elided forms occur, hence *dund* (dative singular), *dunaib* (dative plural) 'to the' (*du* 'to'). The forms *ind, -sind* and *inna* are often reduced to *in, -sin, na*.

There is no indefinite article.

Pronouns

The system is exceptionally intricate, as pronouns are regularly incorporated ('infixed') into the verb, when they may cause mutations and other changes. Great use is made, optionally, of emphasizing particles suffixed to the verb; typical forms are sg. 1 -*sa*, -*se*, 2 -*so*, -*siu*, 3 masc. neut. -*som*, fem. -*si*, pl. 1 -(*s*)*ni*, 2 -*si*, 3 -*som*. Infixed pronouns generally appear between the various verbal prefixes and the verb proper (p. 90); they are commonly no more than a single letter: sg. 1 -*m*-, 2, -*t*-, 3 masc. neut. -*a*-, fem. -*s*-, pl. 1 -*n*-, 2 -*b*-, 3 -*s*-. In other cases, eg, after a preposition ending in a consonant or after a relative, the forms are of the following type: sg. 1 -*dom*-, 2 -*tot*-, 3 masc. neut. -*t*-, fem. -*da*-, pl. 1 -*don*-, 2 -*dob*-, 3 -*da*-. Mutations are notably lenition after the first and second person sg. and third neut. sg., nasalization after the third masc. sg., and gemination after -*da*- (fem sg., pl.).

Examples (prefixes occurring in front of the pronouns illustrated below are the particles *no*, *ro* (see p. 89), further *ni* 'not' and the preposition *fo* 'under', *for* 'on', *at* < *ad* 'to', also *in* 'in which'): (first type) *nimcharatsa* (*ni-m·charat-sa*) 'they don't love me', *notcharatso* (*no-t·charat-so*) 'they love thee', *raléicc* (*ra·léicc: ra* < *ro-a*) 'has left him', *nosbeirmis* (*no-s·beirmis*) 'we were carrying her', *nonsoírni* (*no-n·soír-ni*) 'deliver us', *robcarsi* (*ro-b·car-si*) 'has loved you', *fosdidmat* (*fo-s·didmat*) 'they will suffer them', (second type) *fortchomi* (*for-t·chomi*) 'preserve it', *atdobelliub* (*at-dob·elliub*) 'I will visit you', *indammoidet* (*in-da·mmoidet*) 'on which they pride them(selves)'.

Much less frequently the pronoun is suffixed, the forms being sg. 1 -*m*, 2 -*t*, 3 masc. neut. -*i*, fem. -*us*, pl. 1 -*nn*, 2 -*b*, 3 -*us*. In general, only the third person of a verb takes a suffix pronoun, which itself is usually also in the third person: *orti* 'it killed him', *morsus* 'it magnified her', with other pronouns: *noíthium* 'extols me', *noíthiut* 'extols thee', etc.

The pronoun is not used as the subject of an active verb, the inflexional ending of the latter sufficing to identify the person: *baitsim* 'I baptise', *guidmi* 'we pray'. Such verbs may, however, take an emphasizing particle: *baitsimse*, *guidmini*. In view of the restriction of distinctive endings in the passive (p. 90), a subject pronoun is necessary for the first and second persons: *ninincébthar* (*ni-n·incébthar*) 'we will not be reproached', *robhícad* (*ro-b·hícad*) 'you have been saved'.

Independent forms of the pronoun occur in the nominative: *mé* 'I', *tú* 'thou', *é* 'he', *sí* 'she', *ed* 'it', *sní* 'we', *sí* 'you', *é* 'they'; except for *ed*, they may combine with emphasizing particles giving *messe*, *tussa*, *ésom*, *sissi*, *snisni*, *sissi*, *ésom*. The above forms are most often found with the copula (p. 93), eg, *is mé, is messe* 'it is I'. Independent forms also occur in the genitive, when they function as possessives: *mo, m* 'my', *do, d* 'thy', *a* 'his, her', *ár* 'our', *far* 'your', *a* 'their'. The emphasizing particle follows the noun: *mo leborsa* 'my book' (*lebor*).

Pronouns coalesce with certain prepositions forming a kind of conjugation, eg, with *oc* 'at': *ocum* 'at me', *ocut* 'at thee', *oco* 'at him', *oci* 'at her', *ocunn* 'at us', *ocaib* 'at you', *ocu* 'at them', with corresponding emphatic forms *ocumsa, ocutsa, ocosom, ocisi, ocunni, ocaibsi, ocusom*.

Verbs

The verbal system is of almost incredible complexity. There are inflexions which bear comparison with those of Latin and tense formations in which irregularity is almost the rule. Then, by a unique development, the basic verbal forms often find themselves at the centre of complexes where they are prone to undergo modification depending on the position of the stress and the nature of the attached elements (pronouns, particles, p. 88).

Conjugation is synthetic for active and passive. There are five tenses of the indicative (present, future, conditional, imperfect, preterite) and two of the subjunctive (present, past), an imperative for second and third singular and for all three persons plural, further an all-important verbal noun, in some uses coming close to an infinitive, and a past participle passive.

The terminations themselves fall into two categories, absolute and conjunct, the latter occurring in the verbal complex. In some cases absolute and conjunct forms are identical, in others the conjunct forms may be further modified if unstressed. The conditional, imperfect and the past subjunctive are used with the particle *no* and therefore have only conjunct inflexion. The preterite pure and simple, a narrative tense, is not prominent in the records; in practice it is generally used with the particle *ro* and accordingly appears for the most part in the conjunct form, in fact the absolute inflexion is poorly attested for this tense. The particles *no* and especially *ro* play a significant part in the verbal system. The former is chiefly used to support the infixed pronoun, the latter variously qualifies the sense of the verb, in particular giving perfective force to the preterite. Both particles may geminate, *ro* most frequently lenites.

Irish Celtic

Passive inflexion is much reduced. The third singular is used for the first and second persons of both numbers with the addition of the relevant pronouns; only the third plural has a distinct form. Thus present indicative of *léciud* 'leaving': sg. 1 *no-m˙léicther*, 2 *no-t˙léicther*, 3 *léicthir*, ˙*léicther*, pl. 1 *no-n˙léicther*, 2 *no-b˙léicther*, 3 *léictir*, ˙*léicter*. On the other hand, the related deponent inflexion preserves distinct personal endings; for the meaning of the term 'deponent', borrowed from Latin grammar, see p. 167.

A normal verb is formed from five different stems (pres., subj., fut., pret. act., pret. pass.). According to the mode of formation, two main classes are distinguished, strong and weak – the terms have been taken from Germanic grammar. We conjugate an example of each (active and passive) and also give a specimen of deponent inflexion.

Weak Verb

Verbal noun: *léciud* 'leaving', gen. *léictheo*.

Active

Indicative:
Pres. sg. 1 *lécim*, 2 *léci*, 3 *lécid*, pl. 1 *léicmi*, 2 *léicthe*, 3 *lécit*; sg. 1 ˙*lécim*, 2, 3 ˙*léci*, pl. 1 ˙*lécem*, 2 ˙*lécid*, 3 ˙*lécet*.
Fut. sg. 1 *léicfea*, 2 *léicfe*, 3 *léicfid*, pl. 1 *léicfimmi*, 2 *léicfide*, 3 *léicfit*; sg. 1 ˙*léiciub*, 2 ˙*léicfe*, 3 ˙*léicfea*, pl. 1 ˙*léicfem*, 2 ˙*léicfid*, 3 ˙*léicfet*.
Cond. sg. 1 ˙*léicfinn*, 2 ˙*léicfeda*, 3 ˙*léicfed*, pl. 1 ˙*léicfimmis*, 2 ˙*léicfide*, 3 ˙*léicfitis*.
Imperf. sg. 1 ˙*lécinn*, 2 ˙*léicthea*, 3 ˙*léced*, pl. 1 ˙*léicmis*, 2 ˙*léicthe*, 3 ˙*léictis*.
Pret. sg. 1, 2 (?), 3 *lécis*, pl. 1, 2 (?), 3 *léicset*; sg. 1 ˙*léicius*, 2 ˙*lécis*, 3 ˙*léic*, pl. 1 ˙*léicsem*, 2 ˙*léicsid*, 3 ˙*léicset*.

Subjunctive:
Pres. sg. 1 *lécea*, 2 *léce*, 3, etc., as indic.; sg. 1 ˙*léic*, 2 ˙*léce*, 3 ˙*lécea*, pl. as indic.
Past as imperf.

Imperative (abs. and conj.):
sg. 2 *léic*, 3 *léced*, pl. 1 *lécem*, 2 *lécid*, 3 *lécet*.

Passive

Indicative:
Pres. *léicthir*, pl. 3 *léictir*; `*léicther*, pl. 3 `*léicter*.
Fut. *léicfidir*, pl. 3 *léicfitir*; `*léicfider*, pl. 3 `*léicfiter*.
Cond. `*léicfide*, pl. 3 `*léicfitis*.
Imperf. `*léicthe*, pl. 3 `*léictis*.
Pret. *léicthe*, pl. 3 *léicthi*; `*léced*, pl. 3 `*léicthea*.

Subjunctive:
pres. as indic., past as imperf.

Imperative (abs. and conj.): *léicther*, pl. 3 *léicter*.

Past participle: *léicthe*.

Strong Verb
Verbal noun: *brith* 'bearing', gen. *brithe*.

Active

Indicative:
Pres. sg. 1 *biru*, 2 *biri*, 3 *berid*, pl. 1 *bermi*, 2 *berthe*, 3 *berit*; sg. 1
`*biur*, 2 `*bir*, 3 `*beir*, pl. 1 `*beram*, 2 `*berid*, 3 `*berat*. In unstressed
position the conjunct forms are sg. 1 *-bur*, 2, 3 *-bir*, pl. 1 *-brem*,
2 *-brid*, 3 *-bret*.
Fut. sg. 1 *béra*, 2 *bére*, 3 *bérid*, pl. 1 *bérmi*, 2 *bérthe*, 3 *bérit*; sg. 1
`*bér*, 2 `*bére*, 3 `*béra*, pl. 1 `*béram*, 2 `*bérid*, 3 `*bérad*.
Cond. sg. 1 `*bérinn*, 2 `*bértha*, 3 `*bérad*, pl. 1 `*bérmis*, 2 `*bérthe*, 3
`*bértis*.
Imperf. sg. 1 `*berinn*, 2 `*bertha*, 3 `*bered*, pl. 1 `*bermis*, 2 `*berthe*, 3
`*bertis*.
Pret. sg. 1, 2 (?), 3 *birt*, pl. (?); sg. 1 `*biurt*, 2 `*birt*, 3 `*bert*, pl. 1
`*bertammar*, 2 `*bertid*, 3 `*bertatar*.

Subjunctive:
Pres. sg. 1 *bera*, 2 *bere*, 3, etc. as indic.; sg. 1 `*ber*, 2 `*bere*, 3 `*bera*,
pl. as indic.
Past as imperf., except sg. 3 `*berad*.

Imperative (abs. and conj.):
sg. 2 *beir*, 3 *berad*, pl. 1 *beram*, 2 *berid*, 3 *berat*.

Passive

Indicative:
Pres. *berir*, pl. 3 *bertir*; *'berar*, pl. 3 *'bertar*.
Fut. *bérthir*, pl. 3 *bértir*; *'bérthar*, pl. 3 *'bértar*.
Cond. *'bérthe*, pl. 3 *'bértis*.
Imperf. *'berthe*, pl. 3 *'bertis*.
Pret. *brethe*, pl. 3 *brithi*; *'breth*, pl 3 *'bretha*.

Subjunctive:
Pres. *berthir*, pl. 3 *bertir*; *'berthar*, pl. 3 *'bertar*.

Imperative (abs. and conj.): *berar*, pl. 3 *bertar*.

Past participle: *brithe*.

Deponent
The deponent conjugation was falling into disuse even in the earliest period and in many cases the endings are already the same as those of the active conjugation.

Verbal noun: *labrad* 'speaking', gen. *labrado, labrada*.

Indicative:
Pres. sg. 1 *labrur*, 2 *labrither*, 3 *labrithir*, pl. 1 *labrimmir*, 2 *labrithe*, 3 *labritir*; sg. 1 *'labrur*, 2 *'labrither*, 3 *'labrathar*, pl. 1 *'labrammar*, 2 *'labrid*, 3 *'labratar*.
Fut. sg. 1 *labrafar*, 2 *labrafider*, 3 *labrafidir*, pl. 1 *labrafimmir*, 2 *labrafide*, 3 *labrafitir*; sg. 1 *'labrafar*, 2 *'labrafider*, 3 *'labrafadar*, pl. 1 *'labrafammar*, 2 *'labrafid*, 3 *'labrafatar*.
Cond. sg. 1 *'labrafinn*, 2 *'labrafada*, 3 *'labrafad*, pl. 1 *'labrafimmis*, 2 *'labrafide*, 3 *'labrafitis*.
Imperf. sg. 1 *'labrinn*, 2 *'labratha*, 3 *'labrad*, pl. 1 *'labrimmis*, 2 *'labrithe*, 3 *'labritis*.
Pret. abs. hardly recorded for any verb, but sg. 3 will have been *labristir*; sg. 1 *'labrasur*, 2 *'labriser*, 3 *'labrastar*, pl. 1 *'labrasammar*, 2 *'labrisid*, 3 *'labrasatar*.

Subjunctive:
Pres. sg. 1 *labrar*, 2, etc. as for indic.; sg. 1 *'labrar*, 2, etc. as for indic. Past as imperf.

Imperative (abs. and conj.):
sg. 2 *labrithe*, 3 *labrad*, pl. 1 *labrammar*, 2 *labrid*, 3 *labratar*.

Past participle: *labarthe*.

The verb 'to be'
There are two sets of forms distinguished as 'substantive verb' and 'copula'. Whereas the latter, always unstressed, simply links the subject to its predicate, the former usually emphasizes the state of being, thus expressing existence or presence.

(Substantive verb)

Verbal noun: *buith* 'being', gen. *buithe*.

Active

Indicative:
Pres. sg. 3 only: *attá*; sg. 1 ˙*táu*, 2 ˙*taí*, 3 ˙*tá*, pl. 1 ˙*taam*, 2 ˙*taid*, 3 ˙*taat*. In certain environments the conjunct forms are replaced by invariable ˙*fil*, as commonly after the negative: *ninfil* (*ni-n'fil*) 'we are not'. There is also a habitual present tense: sg. 1 *bíuu* 'I am wont to be', 2 (?), 3 *bíid*, pl. 1 *bímmi*, 2 (?), 3 *bíit*; sg. 1 ˙*bíu*, 2, 3 ˙*bí*, pl. 1 ˙*bíam*, 2 (?), 3 ˙*bíat*.
Fut. sg. 1 *bia*, 2 *bie*, 3 *bied*, pl. 1 *bemmi*, 2 *bethe*, 3 *biet*; 1, 2 (?), 3 ˙*bia*, pl. 1 ˙*bíam*, 2 ˙*bied*, 3 ˙*bíat*.
Cond. sg. 1 ˙*beinn*, 2 (?), 3 ˙*biad*, pl. 1 ˙*bemmis*, 2 (?), 3 ˙*betis*.
Imperf. sg. 1 ˙*bíinn*, 2 (?), 3 ˙*bíth*, pl. 1 ˙*bímmis*, 2 (?), 3 ˙*bítis*.
Pret. sg. 1 *bá*, 2 (?), 3 *baí*, pl. 1 *bámmar*, 2 (?), 3 *bátar*; sg. 1, 2 ˙*bá*, 3 ˙*baí*, pl. 1 ˙*bámmar*, 2 ˙*baid*, 3 ˙*bátar*, further unstressed with the particle *ro*: sg. 1 ˙*roba*, 2 (?), 3 ˙*robe*, pl. 1 ˙*robammar*, 2 ˙*robaid*, 3 ˙*robatar*.

Subjunctive:
Pres. sg. 1 *beu*, 2 (?), 3 *beid*, pl. 1 *bemmi*, 2 *bethe*, 3 *beit*; sg. 1 ˙*béo*, 2 ˙*bee*, 3 ˙*bé*, pl. 1 ˙*bem*, 2 ˙*beid*, 3 ˙*bet*.
Past sg. 1 ˙*beinn*, 2 ˙*betha*, 3 ˙*bed*, pl. 1 ˙*bemmis*, 2 ˙*bethe*, 3 ˙*betis*.
Imperative (abs. and conj.):
sg. 2 *bí*, 3 *bíd*, pl. 1 (?), 2 *biid*, 3 *biat*.

Passive (used impersonally)

Indicative:
Pres. *'táthar*; habitual *bíthir*; *'bíther*.
Fut. (?), Cond. (?), Imperf. *'bíthe*, Pret. *bothe*; *'both*.

Subjunctive:
Pres. *bethir*; *'bether*, Past (?).

(Copula)

Pres. sg. 1 *am*, 2 *at*, 3 *is*, pl. 1 *ammi*, 2 *adib*, 3 *it*; sg. 1, 2 *'da*, 3 *'t*, pl. 1 *'dan*, 2 *'dad*, 3 *'dat*.

The other tenses of the copula are expressed by the substantive verb, generally in a reduced form, as imperfect and preterite singular 1, 2 *basa*, 3 *ba*, plural 1, 2 (?), 3 *batir*.

Expressing possession

There is no verb corresponding to 'have', possession being expressed by the verb 'to be' with the dative, as *ronbíth* (*ro-n'bíth*) 'let us have' lit. 'let be to-us', or else with a preposition, as *attá leis* 'he has' lit. 'is with-him' (*la* 'with') or *is doib* 'they have' lit. 'is to-them' (*do* 'to').

Syntax

It is a basic rule of Irish, as of British, that the verb or verbal complex stands at the beginning of the sentence, and a plural noun takes a singular verb. As may be seen from the interlinear translations of the texts below, the syntax of Irish contains a number of exotic features; it is likely that some of these are due to the influence of earlier languages once spoken in Ireland.

READINGS

Eighth-century glosses
    Léic   úait   inna biada mílsi ocus thomil inna-hí-siu
    Let-go from-thee the foods sweet and eat   the-those
do'mmeil do chenél,   arnáp
which-eats thy people (those which thy people eat) that-it-not-be
hé-som con'éit   det-so. Is mó ro'chés   Críst
he   who-yields to-you. It-is more that-suffered Christ (that
              airi   .i. (=ed-ón) bás. Ol   is   amein,
Christ suffered) for-him to-wit   death. Since it-is so,

94

léic úait   inna túari no'cari.   Ni   hed
let-go from-thee the foods which-thou-lovest. It-is-not it (this)
not'beir   i   nem   cía   ba   loingthech.
which-thee-bears into heaven that thou-shouldst-be gluttonous.
Comitecht dund oís nad'chaithi   cach   túari.
Indulgence to-the folk that-not-consumes every (sort of) food.

Lines from an elegy on Labraid Loingsech, apparently comparing
him to the god Lug, famous for his armour ('Lug of the shield' in
our extract). Perhaps eighth century:
Lug scéith,   scál   find,
Lug of-shield, phantom fair,
fo   nimib ni   robe beth   macc n-Áine aidblithir.
under skies not was would-be son of-Aine as-mighty.
(there was no one under heaven as mighty as Aine's son.)
Arddu deeib   doín, dron daurgráinne,
Higher than-gods (a) man strong oak-fruit,
glan gablach án,   aue   Loircc Loíguiri.
pure branched splendid grandson of-Lorcc Loiguire.

A ninth-century couplet:
Is acher in   gaíth in-nocht,
Is keen the wind tonight,
fu'fúasna fairgge finolfolt;
it-tosses sea's   white-hair;
ni'ágor   réimm   Mora Mind
not-I-fear coursing of-Sea Clear (the Irish Sea)
dond láechraid   lainn úa   Lothlind.
by-the warrior-band fierce from Norway (*ie*, 'Vikings').

From Líadan's Lament, ninth century:
Cen   áinius
Without joy
in gním hí do'rigénus;
the deed that I-have-done;
nech   ro'charus   ro'cráidius.
someone whom-I-have-loved I-have-angered.

Ba   mire
It-was madness

nad   n'dernad   a airer-som,
that-not has-been-done his pleasure,
mainbed   omun ríg   nime.
if-not-were fear   of-king of-heaven.
(were it not for fear of . . . it would have been madness not to do
as he wished)

Mé   Líadan,
I (am) Liadan,
ro'carus-sa Cuirither;
I-loved   Cuirither;
is   fírithir ad'fíadar.
it-is as-true is-said (as true as they say).

Céol   caille
Music of-forest
fo-m'chanad   la   Cuirither
sang-to-me (when I was) with Cuirither
la   fogur fairrce flainne.
with sound of-sea deep-blue.

Gair   bá-sa
Brief-time I-was
hi coímthecht Chuirithir;
in company   of-Cuirither;
frissom   ba   maith mo gnás-sa
towards-him was good my company (I was happy in his com-

pany)

Do'ménainn
I-would-have-thought
ni-cráidfed   frim   Cuirither
not-it-would-have-angered towards-me Cuirither
di dálaib   cacha'dénainn.
of matters whatsoever-I-may-have-done.
(what I have done would not have made Cuirither angry with me).

LITERATURE

J. Pokorny, *A Historical Reader of Old Irish* (1923).
R. Thurneysen, *A Grammar of Old Irish* (1947) and supplement, *Old Irish Reader* (1949).

A general text-book for those able to read Welsh is G. M. Richards, *Llawlyfr Hen Wyddeleg* (1936).

MIDDLE IRISH

The Irish written in the tenth century differs considerably from that found in the two preceding centuries. There has been a perceptible break with the classical canon of Old Irish and the language is now termed Middle Irish. The Middle Irish period is regarded as lasting until 1600. The abundant records of this period frequently reflect the naturally evolving language, but towards 1200 a largely standardized literary style arose and was generally followed, especially in poetry, rather less so in prose, until the end of the period. Nowadays this style is often called Classical or Early Modern Irish.

In general, Middle Irish can be said to have more in common with the modern tongue than with Old Irish. The intricate verbal system with its baffling arrangement of infixed pronouns and the like declined, and was superseded by morphologically simpler and more regular forms, the forerunners of those used in Modern Irish. The neuter gender disappears. Though making an archaic impression, Middle Irish as written, say in the twelfth century, does not strike the modern reader as being a foreign language in the way Old Irish does. The specimen below is intended to give some idea of Middle Irish and may be compared with the materials on Modern Irish following in the next section. As in Old Irish, mutations are imperfectly shown and the spelling is variable.

From *Lebor Gabála Érenn – The Book of the Conquest (Taking) of Ireland*, twelfth century:

  Túatha Dé Danann (Peoples of the Goddess Danu) seize power in Ireland:

  Do dechatar docum n-Érenn Día Luain hi kallann Mai   hi
  They-came to   Ireland Monday   on kalends of-May in
  longaib ocus barcaib. Ocus ro dolbsat   temel   trí   láithe
  ships   and barks.   And they-formed darkness three days
  ocus trí   n-aidche dar gréin ocus ésca,   ocus conaitchetar
  and three nights   over sun and moon, and they-demanded
  cath   no rígi   co   Feraib Bolg.   Ocus
  battle or kingship to (of) (the) Fir   Bolg (Men of Bags). And

97

ro figedh   cath   Mag   Tuired   eterro   ocus
was-fought battle of-the-Plain of-the-Hero between-them and
ro machtait   cét   míle   do Feraib Bolg and
were-slaughtered (one) hundred thousand of Fir   Bolg there
íarum. Ro gabsad Túatha Dé Danann íar   sin   ríghe
then took   Túatha Dé Danann after that kingship
n-Éirenn.
of-Ireland.

In their own country *Túatha Dé Danann* had possessed four cities,
Goirias, Finnias, Muirias and Failias, from which they brought to
Ireland four magic things:

A   Goirias tucad   sleagh Logha ocus ní   gebthi
From Goirias was-brought spear of-Lug and not was-taken
fria.   A   Finnias tucad
against-it (there was no resisting it). From Finnias was-brought
claidem Núadat   Airgetlám ocus ní térnadh nech   úadh
sword of-Núada Silver-Arm and not escaped anyone from-it
ó   do berthai   assa   thindtigh bodba. A   Muirias
when it-was-drawn from-its scabbard of-battle. From Muirias
tucadh   coire   in   Dagda: ní teighedh dám
was-brought cauldron of-the Dagda: not went   company
dimdach   úadh. A   Failias tucad   in Lia   Fáil
unsatisfied from-it. From Failias was-brought the Stone of-Fál
co Temraigh   ocus no gesidh fo   cach rí   no gabad
to Temair (Tara) and it-cried-out under each king that-should-
Érinn   ocus úaithi ráiter   Inis Fáil   ut Cinaed cecinit:
take Ireland and from-it is-called Isle of-Fál as Cinaed sang
(composed):
In cloch for stait   mo   dí šáil
The stone on (the) halt of-my two heels (where stand my . . .)
húaidhi ráiter   Inis Fáil;
from-it is-called Isle of-Fál;
etir   dá tráigh thuile   teinn
between two shores of-flood mighty
Mag Fáil   uile for Érinn.
Plain of-Fál all on Ireland (is a name for Ireland).

LITERATURE

G. Dottin, *Manuel d'irlandais moyen* (1913).

Irish

SKETCH OF MODERN IRISH

Phonetics

Irish is traditionally written in a form deriving from Old Irish times (p. 81). This Irish, or Gaelic, alphabet, as it came to be called, is still commonly used in Ireland, though during the last fifty years Roman type has become widespread and is now the more usual. The two types may be compared in the specimens on p. 259.

By the early modern period, many of the ambiguities of the medieval orthography had been overcome. The letters *p*, *t*, *c*, and *b*, *d*, *g*, now represented occlusives only; the corresponding spirants being distinguished either by placing a dot over the letter or by adding *h* after it, thus *b* always [b], but *ḃ* or *bh* [v, w], and similarly *m* [m], but *ṁ* or *mh* [v, w], *s* [s], but *ṡ* or *sh* [h]. In Irish script the dot is generalized, in Roman the *h*. The digraph *fh* (now both scripts), representing the deletion of radical *f*, is silent. Aspiration is thus largely explicit in the modern script. Eclipsis is also regularly shown when the new value of the initial is expressed by prefixing the appropriate consonant (p. 102). The acute accent now denotes a long vowel only.

The most remarkable feature of the orthography is the rule *caol le caol agus leathan le leathan* 'slender with slender and broad with broad.' The basis for this rule is the fact that the modern language retains the fundamental difference between palatal and velar consonants, the difference being expressed by the vowels, a feature already evolving in Old Irish orthography (p. 82). A velar consonant is indicated by a 'broad' vowel *a*, *o*, or *u*, a palatal by a 'slender' *e* or *i*, thus velar *éan* [eːn] 'bird', palatal *éin* [eːń] 'birds'. Vowels flanking a medial consonant or consonants must both be either broad or slender: the loan word 'crystal' appears as *criostal*, 'radio' as *raidió*, where mute *o* and *i* respectively have been added in accordance with the rule. 'Cashmere' is gaelicized *caismíor* (palatal *s* being pronounced [ʃ]). Compare further *Nóra* 'Nora' with velar, but *Nóirín* 'Noreen' with palatal *r*. In *loingeas* 'fleet' (anglicized in *Aer Lingus*) *e* is inserted after the palatal consonant cluster, while *o* indicates the velar *l*. Sometimes *e* is neutral, as in *Gaeltacht* 'Gaeldom', where *lt* are velar. Parts of the system are, however, ambiguous. Contrast *loingeas* (above) with *coitean* [kotʹən] 'common, general', where *o* is the spoken vowel of the first syllable, but *i* (like *e* of the second

99

syllable) merely a silent pointer to the palatal nature of the intervening consonant. Dialect variations may also play a part, eg, *toil* 'will, intention', in Munster and Connaught [til'], in Ulster [tol'].

The orthography is conservative and a poor guide to the current pronunciation, indeed necessarily so, for Irish never acquired a standard pronunciation and all living speech is broadly dialectal. The official reform of 1947, however, removed a large number of inconvenient traditional spellings; typical innovations in the paternoster (p. 259) include: *go naofar* 'be hallowed', *ríocht* 'kingdom', *laethúil* 'daily', *inniu* 'today', *lig* 'lead', *cathú* 'temptation', *ach* 'but', *go síoraí* 'for ever', instead of pre-1947 *go naomhthar, ríoghacht, laethamhail, indiu, leig, cathughadh, acht, go síorraidhe*. The unreformed spelling reflects, in essence, the sounds of the language as it was in the twelfth century.

Stress falls regularly on the first syllable in Ulster and Connaught, but often on the final in Munster.

An account of Gaelic pronunciation involves exceptional difficulties. A standard morphology for written Irish was prescribed in 1958 and generally accepted. It would be equally possible to prescribe a unified pronunciation, but this has not yet been done. Faced with the stark realities – a medley of divergent dialects, each with a phoneme inventory of the order of sixty items, as compared with the forty-four phonemes of English, featured in an orthography which at best can only do rough justice to the complicated phonological facts – our only practicable course here is to devise such approximations as enable us to extend to the Gaelic words at least a modicum of phonetic courtesy. This is indeed the most that can be achieved in the ordinary teaching of Irish as a second language. We therefore set up our own simplified norm on the basis of the new spelling, as follows.

Stress on the first syllable is the general rule.

Vowel Sounds
Reference is to stressed vowels, unless otherwise stated. It will be recognized that many of the spellings are variants necessary to give effect to the rule *caol le caol, etc.* (p. 99).

[a] is represented by *a, ai, ea, eai*, as *agus* [agəs] 'and', *bainne* [bañə] 'milk', *sean* [ʃan] 'old', *seaicéad* [ʃak'e:d] 'jacket'.

[ɑː] is represented by *á, ái, eá, eái*, as *lán* [lɑːn] 'full', *cáis* [kɑːʃ]

100

'cheese', *Seán* [ʃɑːn] 'John', *a Sheáin* [ə hɑːn̩] 'John!', also by *a* before
r plus consonant, as *ard* [ɑːrd] 'high'.

[e] is represented by *e, ei*, occasionally by *ai, oi* as *le* [lʲe] 'with', *leis*
[lʲeʃ] 'with (the)', *saibhir* [sevʲir] 'rich', *oifig* [efʲiǵ] 'office', also *ar* [er]
'on'.

[eː] is represented by *é, éa, éi, ae, aei*, as *gé* [ǵeː] 'goose', *béal* [bʲeːl]
'mouth', *éisteacht* [eːʃtʲəxt] 'listening', *Gael* [geːl] 'Gael', *Gaeilge*
[geːlǵə] 'Gaelic (language)'.

[i] is represented by *i, io, oi, ui*, as *mil* [mʲilʲ] 'honey', *fios* [fʲis] 'knowledge', *oileán* [ilʲɑːn] 'island', *uisce* [iʃkʲə] 'water', in unstressed
syllables also by *ai*, as *Eaglais* [agliʃ] 'Church'.

[iː] is represented by *í, ío, aí, aío, oí, uí, uío*, as *tír* [tʲiːr] 'land', *síoda*
[ʃiːdə] 'silk', *deoraí* [dʲoːriː] 'exile (person)', *deoraíocht* [dʲoːriːxt]
'exile (state)', *oíche* [iːçə] 'night', *suím* [siːm̩] 'I sit', *suíochán* [siːxɑːn]
'seat', also by *ao, aoi*, as *gaoth* [giː] 'wind', *faoileán* [fiːlʲɑːn] 'seagull'.

[o] is represented by *o, oi*, as *bog* [bog] 'soft', *scoil* [skolʲ] 'school',
also *deoch* [dʲox] 'drink' (noun).

[oː] is represented by *ó, ói, eo, eoi*, as *mór* [moːr] 'big', *cóir* [koːr]
'just, true', *ceo* [kʲoː] 'fog', *feoil* [fʲoːlʲ] 'meat', also by medial *omh,
omha, omhai*, as *comhrádh* [koːrɑː] 'conversation', *comharsa* [koːrsə]
'neighbour', *comhairle* [koːrlʲə] 'advice'.

[u] is represented by *u, ui, iu*, as *muc* [muk] 'pig', *muirnín* [murnʲiːn̩]
'darling', *fliuch* [flʲux] 'wet'.

[uː] is represented by *ú, úi, iú, iúi*, as *glún* [gluːn] 'knee', *cúig* [kuːǵ]
'five', *siúcra* [ʃuːkrə] 'sugar', *stiúir* [ʃtʲuːr] 'rudder', also by medial
umh, etc., as *umhal* [uːl] 'humble'.

[ə] is represented by unstressed *a, ea, e, o, u*, see above *passim*.

[ai] is represented by medial *adh, adha, adhai, aidh*, etc., *eadh*, etc.,
agh, etc, as *adhmad* [aiməd] 'timber', *adharc* [airk] 'horn', *raidhse*
[raiʃə] 'abundance', *praghas* [prais] 'price', *aghaidh* [ai] 'face',
saighdiúir [said'uːr] 'soldier', also *eidh, eigh*, as *feidhm* [faim̩] 'function', *leigheas* [lʲais] 'medicine'.

[au] is represented by medial *abh, abha, abhai, eabh*, etc, also *omh*,
etc., as *fabhra* [faurə] 'eyelash', *seabhac* [ʃauk] 'hawk', *meabhair*
[mʲaur] 'intellect', *samhradh* [saurə] 'summer', *domhan* [daun]
'world', further *odh, ogh*, etc., as *bodhar* [baur] 'deaf', *Ogham* [aum]
'Ogam'.

101

[iə] is represented by *ia*, as *fia* [f'iə] 'deer' (sg.).

[uə] is represented by *ua, uai*, as *uan* [uən] 'lamb', *fuaim* [fuəṁ] 'sound'.

An epenthetic vowel may develop between certain consonants, as *ainm* [aṅiṁ] 'name', *balbh* [baləw] 'dumb', *airgead* [ariġəd] 'money'.

Consonants

As already noticed (p. 99), consonants, except *h*, have two contrasting qualities, velar and palatal. With the former the tongue is raised at the back towards the *u*-position and the lips pouted; with the latter the tongue is raised at the front towards the *i*-position and the lips drawn back; or, loosely speaking, the velars are consonants followed by a *w*-glide, the palatals by a *y*-glide.

In our approximation, we give Irish *p, t, c, b, d, g, f, m, n, s*, when velar, values as in English, when palatal the same values with a following *y*, in phonetic transcription [p'], etc, except palatal *s* which is [ʃ]. We notice, however, that *p, t, c* are strongly aspirated. We pronounce velar (dark) *l* as in English *all*, palatal (light) *l* as in English *lee*. We disregard further varieties of *l*, also of *m, n*; the different *r*-sounds we pronounce uniformly as slightly rolled *r*. The consonants *l, n, r* also occur double, but this does not affect the pronunciation. The digraph *ph* has the values of *f*, the digraphs *th, sh* are [h], *ch* velar is [χ], palatal [ç]. Medial *dh, gh*, like *bh, mh*, commonly merge with vowels to form diphthongs (see Vowel Sounds) and final *dh, gh* are silent; otherwise *dh, gh* velar are [ɣ], palatal [j], while *bh, mh* velar are [w], palatal [v]. The digraph *fh* is silent, as are all eclipsed letters (p. 99). Initial [j] is represented by *i*, as *Iúil* [juːl'] 'July'. Consonant clusters are also either velar or palatal; palatal *sm, sp*, however, are pronounced [sṁ, sṗ], as *speal* [sp'al] 'scythe', but *stioróip* [ʃt'iːroːp'] 'stirrup'.

Initial Mutations

These mutations – lenition or aspiration and nasalization or eclipsis – survive vigorously in the contemporary language. The former affects *p, t, c, b, d, g, m, f, s*, as *a phíopa* 'his pipe' (radical *píopa*); *l, n, r*, are also involved, but changes here are not shown in the script (and are ignored by us). The latter affects *p, t, c, b, d, g, f*, which become *bp, dt, gc, mb, nd, ng, bhf*, ie, [b], etc., the eclipsed letters becoming silent, as *ár bpictiúir* 'our picture' (r. *pictiúir*); *n* is prefixed to vowels, as *bhur n-im* 'your butter' (r. *im*). The circumstances in which muta-tions occur are closely comparable to those producing analogous changes in Old Irish (p. 83).

By a change unrelated to the foregoing, *s* may be eclipsed by *t* after the definite article *an* (p. 105).

Words beginning with a vowel take an *h*-prefix under certain conditions, as after the article *na*, after the possessive *a* 'her', etc.

Nouns

Compared with Old Irish, the language of today has a much simpler morphology and new declensional patterns have arisen. There are still three numbers, but the dual, now invariable, is always the same as the dative singular. The nominative and accusative have fallen together, but vocative, genitive and dative may have their own forms, though in the plural the dative is always the same as the nominative-accusative. In many words declension proper has been lost, only singular and plural being morphologically distinct, but otherwise identical forms may be distinguished by mutation, as *an bád* 'the boat', *sa bhád* 'in the boat', *na mbád* 'of the boats', or *an bháid* 'of the boat', *na báid* 'the boats'. The vocative is preceded by an aspirat-ing particle: *a fhir* 'O man!', *a fheara* 'O men!'.

The nouns quoted in the Old Irish section all survive in Gaelic today, and we here quote them in their standard forms, in this way giving a fair impression of the changes which have taken place in the language and of the nature of the present inflexional system:

nom. acc. dat. *fear* m. 'man', voc. gen. *fir*, pl. nom. acc. dat. *fir*, voc. *feara*, gen. *fear*.

nom. acc. dat. *scéal* m. 'story, matter', voc. gen. *scéil*, pl. *scéalta*.

nom. voc. acc. *dealbh* f. 'image, statue', gen. *deilbhe*, dat. *deilbh*, pl. *dealbha* except gen. *dealbh*.

nom. voc. acc. *cnámh* f. 'bone', gen. *cnáimhe*, dat. *cnáimh*, pl. *cnámha*, gen. *cnámh*.

súil f. 'eye', gen. *súile*, pl. *súile*, gen. *súl*.

muir f. 'sea', gen. *mara*, pl. *mara*.

cath m. 'battle', gen. *catha*, pl. *cathanna*.

doras m. 'door', gen. *dorais*, pl. *doirse*.

rí m. 'king', pl. *ríthe*.

teanga f. 'tongue, language', pl. *teangacha*.

cara m. 'friend', gen. *carad*, pl. *cairde*.

Irish Celtic

cú m. 'hound', pl. *cúnna.*
nom. voc. acc. *Éire* f. 'Ireland', gen. *Éireann*, dat. *Éirinn.*

Adjectives

Adjectival inflexion corresponds, in general, to that of the nouns and is similarly much reduced compared with Old Irish. Mutations remain a prominent feature, eg, an adjective is commonly aspirated in the singular vocative *a thiarna mhóir* 'o great lord', in the singular nominative accusative feminine *cloch chruaidh* '(a) hard stone', in singular genitive masculine *ceann an bhóthair fhada* '(the) end (lit. 'head') of the long road', often in the plural nominative accusative dative *fir bhochta* 'poor men'.

Old Irish *becc* 'small' survives today as *beag*, inflecting as follows: singular masculine nominative accusative dative *beag*, vocative genitive *big*, feminine all cases *beag* except genitive *bige*; plural both genders and all cases *beaga* except genitive *beag*.

The comparative and superlative are no longer formally distinguished: *sean* 'old', *sine* 'older, oldest', *ard* 'high', *aoirde* 'higher, highest'. Irregular comparison continues, eg, *maith* 'good', *fearr* 'better, best', *olc* 'bad', *measa* 'worse, worst'.

Numbers

Counting: 1 *a haon*, 2 *a dó*, 3 *a trí*, 4 *a ceathair*, 5 *a cúig*, 6 *a sé*, 7 *a seacht*, 8 *a hocht*, 9 *a naoi*, 10 *a deich*, 11 *a haon déag*, 12 *a dó dhéag*, 13 *a trí déag*, 14 *a ceathair déag*, 15 *a cúig déag*, 16 *a sé déag*, 17 *a seacht déag*, 18 *a hocht déag*, 19 *a naoi déag*, 20 *fiche*, 21 *fiche a haon*, 30 *tríocha*, 40 *daichead*, 50 *caoga*, 60 *seasca*, 70 *seachtó*, 80 *ochtó*, 90 *nócha*, 100 *céad*, 1000 *míle.*

The following are used with nouns: 1 *(aon)* . . . *amháin*, 2 *dhá*, 3 *trí*, 4 *ceithre*, 5 *cúig*, etc., eg, *capall amháin, aon chapall amháin* 'one horse'.

The numbers 30 and 50 to 90 are literary restorations, the living dialects having developed cumbersome compounds: 30 *deich is* ('and') *fiche*, 50 *deich is dá fhichid*, etc., comparable to Scottish and Manx Gaelic, a tendency already visible in Old Irish times.

Definite Article

	Sg. nom. acc. dat. masc.,	fem.,	pl.
	an	*an*	*na*
gen.,		*an*	*na* *na*

The article coalesces with a preposition ending in a vowel: *don luch* 'to the mouse' (*do* 'to'); notice *sa* 'in the', before vowels *san*.

The singular genitive feminine and plural nominative accusative dative prefix *h* to a noun beginning with a vowel: *na hEaglaise* 'of the Church', *na héin* 'the birds'.

The singular nominative accusative masculine prefix *t* to a noun beginning with a vowel: *an t-éan* 'the bird'; singular nominative accusative feminine, genitive masculine and dative prefix eclipsing *t* to a noun beginning with *s* followed by *l, n, r* or a vowel: (nominative accusative) *an tslat* 'the rod', (genitive) *an tseoil* 'of the sail', (dative) *leis an tslait* 'with the rod', *den tseol* 'off the sail'.

The noun is eclipsed in the dative singular in most cases: *leis an gcú* 'with the hound', and always after the genitive plural: *obair na mbard* '(the) work of the poets'. The genitive plural prefixes *n* to a noun beginning with a vowel: *ceol na n-éan* '(the) song of the birds'.

Except when beginning with *d, t* or *s*, the noun is aspirated after the article in the singular nominative accusative feminine, gen. masc., and in a few cases in the dat.: *an bhróg* 'the shoe', *mullach an chnoic* '(the) top of the hill', *don mhac* 'to the son', *sa choill* 'in the wood'.

There is no indefinite article.

Pronouns

The system of incorporated pronouns, characteristic of Old Irish, but declining in the middle period, is now quite obsolete. Only independent pronouns are used, as follows: *mé* 'I, me', *tú* 'thou, thee', *sé* 'he', *sí* 'she', *sinn* 'we, us', *sibh* 'you', *siad* 'they'. When not immediately following a verb (except the copula, p. 110) as its subject – the normal order in Irish – *é, í, iad* correspond to 'he, she, they' or 'him, her, them'. Emphatic forms are common: *mise, tusa, (s)eisean, (s)ise, sinne, sibhse, (s)iadsan*. A neuter *ea* 'it' survives in limited use, eg, *teach nua é, an ea?* 'It's a new house, is it?'. Pronouns are not used with verbal forms which preserve a distinguishing termination, thus *ithim* 'I eat', *ithimid* 'we eat', but *itheann tú* 'thou eatest', *itheann sé* 'he eats'.

Pronouns coalesce with certain prepositions, eg, *ag* 'at': *agam* 'at me', *agat* 'at thee', *aige* 'at him', *aici* 'at her', *againn* 'at us', *agaibh* 'at you', *acu* 'at them', with corresponding emphatic *agamsa, agatsa, aigesean, aicise, againne, agaibhse, acusan*. Other examples include *ar* 'on': *orm* 'on me', *ort* 'on thee', *air* 'on him', *uirthi* 'on her', *orainn* 'on us', *oraibh* 'on you', *orthu* 'on them', emphatic *ormsa*, etc., *le* 'with': *liom* 'with me', *leat* 'with thee', *leis* 'with him', *léi* 'with her', *linn* 'with us', *libh* 'with you', *leo* 'with them', emphatic *liomsa*, etc.

The possessive pronouns today are: *mo*, before vowel sounds *m'* 'my', *do, d'* 'thy', *a* 'his' – all aspirating, *a* 'her' prefixing *h* to vowels, *ár* 'our', *bhur* 'your', *a* 'their' – the plural pronouns all eclipsing. The emphatic particle follows the noun: *mo leabharsa* 'my book' (*leabhar*).

Verbs

The contemporary verb is far less forbidding than that of the old language, thanks in particular to the disappearance of the verbal complexes during the Middle Irish period. Furthermore, the basic conjugational system has been very much reduced. Deponent inflexion as such has been discarded and, although active and passive conjugations flourish in principle as before, many endings have fallen together. It should be noted, however, that the standard paradigms quoted below are considerably more analytic than those used in certain dialects, especially in the south.

The old imperfect is now known as the past habitual. The passive survives in the so-called autonomous form. It cannot take a subject and is felt to be active, hence *ligtear é* lit. 'somebody-or-something-allows him', though a passive translation is commonly apposite: 'he is allowed'. Similarly, *labhraítear Béarla anseo* 'English spoken here'; on the other hand, *táthar ag teacht* 'somebody is coming'.

Two main conjugational classes are recognized today; in our examples – the modern descendants of the Old Irish verbs conjugated on pp. 89–93 – *ligean* and *breith* belong to Class I, *labhairt* to Class II.

Class I

Verbal noun: *ligean* (older spelling *leigean*) 'allowing':

Active

Indicative:
Pres. sg. 1 *ligim*, 2 *ligeann tú*, 3 *ligeann sé*, pl. 1 *ligimid*, 2 *ligeann sibh*, 3 *ligeann siad*.
Fut. sg. 1 *ligfidh mé*, 2 *ligfidh tú*, 3 *ligfidh sé*, pl. 1 *ligfimid*, 2 *ligfidh sibh*, 3 *ligfidh siad*.

Cond. sg. 1 *ligfinn*, 2 *ligfeá*, 3 *ligfeadh sé*, pl. 1 *ligfimis*, 2 *ligfeadh sibh*, 3 *ligfidís*.

Past hab. sg. 1 *liginn*, 2 *ligteá*, 3 *ligeadh sé*, pl. 1 *ligimis*, 2 *ligeadh sibh*, 3 *ligidís*.

Pret. sg 1 *lig mé*, 2 *lig tú*, 3 *lig sé*, pl. 1 *ligeamar*, 2 *lig sibh*, 3 *lig siad*.

Subjunctive:
Pres. sg. 1 *lige mé*, 2 *lige tú*, 3 *lige sé*, pl. 1 *ligimid*, 2 *lige sibh*, 3 *lige siad*.

Imperative:
sg. 1 *ligim*, 2 *lig*, 3 *ligeadh sé*, pl. 1 *ligimis*, 2 *ligigí*, 3 *ligidís*.

We have already noticed (p. 105) that a pronoun is used only when person and number are no longer distinguished by the verbal ending. The morphologically distinct forms may still take an emphasizing particle, eg, present sg. 1 *ligimse* 'I allow', 2 *ligeann tusa*, 3 *ligeann seisean* masculine, *sise* feminine, plural 1 *ligimidne*, 2 *ligeann sibhse*, 3 *ligeann siadsan*.

Periphrastic tenses involving the substantive verb (below) are in common use, as *táim ag ligean* 'I am allowing', lit. 'I am at allowing', *bím ag ligean* 'I allow (habitually)', *bhí mé ag ligean* 'I was allowing', *bhínn ag ligean* 'I used to allow'. A perfect periphrasis may be used: *táim tar éis ligean* 'I have (just) allowed' lit. 'I am after allowing', (pluperfect) *bhí mé tar éis ligean*.

Autonomous

Indicative:
Pres. *ligear*, Fut. *ligfear*, Cond. *ligfí*, Past hab. *ligtí*, Pret. *ligeadh*.

Subjunctive and Imperative as Present Indicative.

Past participle: *ligthe*.

Verbal noun: *breith* 'bearing':

Active

Indicative:
Pres. sg. 1 *beirim*, 2 *beireann tú*, 3 *beireann sé*, pl. 1 *beirimid*, 2 *beireann sibh*, 3 *beireann siad*.
Fut. sg. 1 *béarfaidh mé*, 2 *béarfaidh tú*, 3 *béarfaidh sé*, pl. 1 *béarfaimid*, 2 *béarfaidh sibh*, 3 *béarfaidh siad*.

Irish Celtic

Cond. sg. 1 *bhéarfainn*, 2 *bhéarfá*, 3 *bhéarfadh sé*, pl. 1 *bhéarfaimis*, 2 *bhéarfadh sibh*, 3 *bhéarfaidís*.

Past hab. sg. 1 *bheirinn*, 2 *bheirteá*, 3 *bheireadh sé*, pl. 1 *bheirimis*, 2 *bheireadh sibh*, 3 *bheiridís*.

Pret. sg. 1 *rug mé*, 2 *rug tú*, 3 *rug sé*, pl. 1 *rugamar*, 2 *rug sibh*, 3 *rug siad*.

Subjunctive:

Pres. sg. 1 *beire mé*, 2 *beire tú*, 3 *beire sé*, pl. 1 *beirimid*, 2 *beire sibh*, 3 *beire siad*.

Imperative:

sg. 1 *beirim*, 2 *beir*, 3 *beireadh sé*, pl. 1 *beirimid*, 2 *beirigí*, 3 *beiridís*.

Autonomous

Indicative:

Pres. *beirtear*, Fut. *béarfar*, Cond. *bhéarfaí*, Past hab. *bheirtí*, Pret. *rugadh*.

Subjunctive and Imperative as Pres. Indic.

Past participle: *beirthe*.

Class II

Verbal noun: *labhairt* 'speaking':

Active

Indicative:

Pres. sg. 1 *labhraím*, 2 *labhraíonn tú*, 3 *labhraíonn sé*, pl. 1 *labhraímid*, 2 *labhraíonn sibh*, 3 *labhraíonn siad*.

Fut. sg. 1 *labhróidh mé*, 2 *labhróidh tú*, 3 *labhróidh sé*, pl. 1 *labhróimid*, 2 *labhróidh sibh*, 3 *labhróidh siad*.

Cond. sg. 1 *labhróinn*, 2 *labhrófá*, 3 *labhródh sé*, pl. 1 *labhróimis*, 2 *labhródh sibh*, 3 *labhróidís*.

Past hab. sg. 1 *labhraínn*, 2 *labhraíteá*, 3 *labhraíodh sé*, pl. 1 *labhraímis*, 2 *labhraíodh sibh*, 3 *labhraídís*.

Pret. sg. 1 *labhair mé*, 2 *labhair tú*, 3 *labhair sé*, pl. 1 *labhraíomar*, 2 *labhair sibh*, 3 *labhair siad*.

Subjunctive:

Pres. sg. 1 *labhraí mé*, 2 *labhraí tú*, 3 *labhraí sé*, pl. 1 *labhraímid*, 2 *labhraí sibh*, 3 *labhraí siad*.

Irish

Imperative:
sg. 1 *labhraím*, 2 *labhair*, 3 *labhraíodh sé*, pl. 1 *labhraímis*, 2 *labhraígí*, 3 *labhraídís*.

Autonomous

Indicative:
Pres. *labhraítear*, Fut. *labhrófar*, Cond. *labhrófaí*, Past hab. *labhraítí*, Pret. *labhraíodh*.

Subjunctive and Imperative as Present Indicative

Past participle: *labhartha*.

The Verb 'to be'
The distinction between the substantive verb and the copula, as evolved in Old Irish, survives in the modern language.

(Substantive verb)

Verbal noun: *bheith* 'being':

Active

Indicative:
Pres. sg. 1 *táim*, 2 *tá tú*, 3 *tá sé*, pl. 1 *táimid*, 2 *tá sibh*, 3 *tá siad*; habitual sg. 1 *bím*, 2 *bíonn tú*, 3 *bíonn sé*, pl. 1 *bímid*, 2 *bíonn sibh*, 3 *bíonn siad*.
Fut. sg. 1 *beidh mé*, 2 *beidh tú*, 3 *beidh sé*, pl. 1 *beimid*, 2 *beidh sibh*, 3 *beidh siad*.
Cond. sg. 1 *bheinn*, 2 *bheifeá*, 3 *bheadh sé*, pl. 1 *bheimis*, 2 *bheadh sibh*, 3 *bheidís*.
Past hab. sg. 1 *bhínn*, 2 *bhíteá*, 3 *bhíodh sé*, pl. 1 *bhímis*, 2 *bhíodh sibh*, 3 *bhídís*.
Pret. sg. 1 *bhí mé*, 2 *bhí tú*, 3 *bhí sé*, pl. 1 *bhíomar*, 2 *bhí sibh*, 3 *bhí siad*.
Subjunctive:
Pres. sg. 1 *raibh mé*, 2 *raibh tú*, 3 *raibh sé*, pl. 1 *raibhimid*, 2 *raibh sibh*, 3 *raibh siad*.

Imperative: sg. 1 *bím*, 2 *bí*, 3 *bíodh sé*, pl. 1 *bímis*, 2 *bígí*, 3 *bídís*.

109

Irish Celtic

Autonomous

Indicative:

Pres. *táthar*, habitual *bítear*, Fut. *beifear*, Cond. *bheifí*, Past hab. *bhítí*, Pret. *bhíothas*.

Subjunctive: *rabhthar*.

Imperative: *bítear*.

Special forms are used for the present and preterite when following the negative or other particles, eg, the interrogatives *an*, *nach*:

Pres. neg. sg. 1 *nílim* 'I am not', 2 *níl tú*, 3 *níl sé*, pl. 1 *nílimid*, 2 *níl sibh*, 3 *níl siad*; autonomous *níltear*; the older spelling was sg. 1 *ní fhuilim*, etc. Interrogative sg. 1 *an bhfuilim* 'am I?', *nach bhfuilim* 'am I not?', 2 *bhfuil tú*, 3 *bhfuil sé*, pl. 1 *bhfuilimid*, 2 *bhfuil sibh*, 3 *bhfuil siad*; autonomous *bhfuiltear*.

Pret. sg. 1 *ní raibh mé* 'I was not', *an raibh mé* 'was I?', *nach raibh mé* 'was I not?', 2 *raibh tú*, 3 *raibh sé*, pl. 1 *rabhamar*, 2 *raibh sibh*, 3 *raibh siad*; autonomous *rabhthas*.

(Copula)

Pres. (all persons sg. and pl.): *is*, negative *ní*, interrogative *an?* neg. *nach?* The pronouns are sg. 1 *mé*, 2 *tú*, 3 *é* m., *í* f., also *ea* n. in certain idioms (p. 105), pl. 1 *sinn*, 2 *sibh*, 3 *iad*; since *ní* prefixes *h* to vowels, sg. 3 *ní hé*, etc.

Pret. and Cond.: *ba*, negative *níor*, interrogative *ar?* neg. *nár?* before vowels *níorbh*, *arbh? nárbh?* hence sg. 3 *níorbh é*, etc.

In the absence of a verb 'to have', possession is commonly expressed by the substantive verb with the preposition *ag* 'at', eg, *tá teach againn* 'we have a house' lit. 'is house at-us'.

READINGS

From *Foras Feasa ar Éirinn* (*Foundation of Knowledge about Ireland*, ie, *History of Ireland* by Seathrún Céitinn (Geoffrey Keating), 1570–1644:

(AD 1170. The Anglo-Normans capture Dublin)

Táinig Iarla o' Stranguell   i nÉirinn. Tug
Came Earl of Strangwell (Strongbow) to Ireland. Took

110

Diarmaid Mac Murchadha   *a inghean*
Dermot Son of-Murchadh (MacMurrough) his daughter
leis   i gcoinne an   iarla   an   tráth soin, Aoife a
with-him to meeting of-the earl (at) (the) time that, Aoife her
hainm, agus do pósadh   ris   í, agus ar ndaingniughadh is
name and was-married to-him she and on ratification   and
ar gcríochnughadh an   chleamhnais sin dóibh   da gach
on completion   (of-the) match   that to-them to each
leith,   fágbhais an
side (completion of that match by both sides) left   the
t-iarla bárda   láidir i bPort Lairge is   triallais féin   is
earl garrison strong in Waterford   and marched himself and
a shluagh d'ionnsuighe Átha   Cliath
his host   for attacking of-Ford of-Hurdles (Dublin)
don chur soin; agus ní raibhe ar domhan duine ba lugha ar
forthwith   and not was on world man was less on
lucht Átha Cliath ioná Mac Murchadha is   na   Gaill
people of-Dublin than Mac Murrough and (the) Foreigners
sin   d'fhaicsin chuca,
those for seeing against-them (there was no man on earth whom
the people of Dublin less wished to see than Murchadha with
                    agus do bhí Mac Murchadha lán d'fhíoch is
those foreigners), and was   Mac Murrough full of fury and
d'fhaltanas dóibh-sean mar an gcéadna. Óir is   iad do mharbh
of enmity to-them in-like-manner. For it-is they slew
a athair; agus do adhlaiceadar go heasonórach   anuasal
his father and buried   dishonourably (and) ignobly
é, maille ré   madradh marbh do chur i   n-aon
him, together with dog   dead put   into one (same)
uaigh ris   mar aithis dó.   Ar bhfaicsin na
grave with-him as   insult to-him. On seeing   (of-the)
nGall   soin is neirt Laighean go líonmhar
Foreigners those and strength of-Leinster numerously (in great
        ag teacht   orra,   gabhais uamhan is   imeagla
number) at coming upon-them seized fear   and dread
lucht Átha Cliath, is cuirid   teachta uatha   gus an
people of-Dublin and they-send envoy from-them to the
iarla d'iarraidh síodha is réidhtigh   air
earl for seeking of-peace and of-settlement from-him

.i. (=*iodhón*) *Labhrás Ó   Tuathail*
   to-wit Labhrás Grandson of-Tuathal (O'Toole),
airdeaspog Átha Cliath. An tan iomorro do bhí an réidhteach
archbishop of-Dublin. When, however, was   the settlement
aga dhéanamh eatorro,   do bhí Réamonn de la Grós is
at-its making   between-them was   Raymond de la Gros and
Miles Gogan is   drong do ridiribh óga   mar aon riú
Miles Cogan and party of knights young as   one with-them
        don   taoibh oile don   bhaile, agus fuaradar
(along with them) to-the side   other of-the town   and found
árach   ar bhallaidhibh an   bhaile, gur briseadh   is
opportunity on walls   of-the town that-were-broken and
réabadh   leo   iad; agus lingid féin   san   mbaile
were-torn by-them they and leap themselves into-the town
is   marbhaid gach aon ar a   rugadar   ann.
and slay   each one on whom they-laid-hold there.

From a folk tale about Tomás Láidir Coisdeala (Strong Tom
Costello), said to have lived in the seventeenth century:

(Costello and the Champion Wrestler)

  Is   amhlaidh budh ghnáth   leo   coruigheacht do
  It-is thus   was customary with-them wrestling   to
dheunamh   an   tráth sin, crios leathair   do cheangailt
do   (at) (the) time that belt of-leather to fasten
timchioll cuim an   dá fhear, agus greim do thabhairt do gach
around   waist of-the two men and grip to give   to each
fhear ar chrios an   fhir eile,   agus nuair bheidheadh siad
man on belt   of-the man other, and when would-be   they
réidh agus nuair bhéarfaidhe an focal
ready and when would-carry the word (when the word was given)
dóibh,   thosóchadh siad ag coruigheacht.
to them would-begin they at wrestling.
  Chuaidh an crios air   ann sin, agus fuair an gaisgidheach
  Went   the belt on-him then   and got   the champion
greim daingean air, agus fuair seisean   greim maith ar
grip firm   on-it and got   he (ie, Costello) grip good on
chrios a   námhaid. Tugadh   ordughadh dhóibh ann sin do
belt   of-his opponent was-given order   to-them then   to

thosughadh ar a chéile.   *Nuair fuair sé an focal,*
begin   on his fellow (each other).   When got   he the word,
tharraing Tomás a dhá láimh   *do bhí greamuighthe i*
pulled   Thomas his two hands (which) were   gripped   in
gcrios a   námhaid, asteach chuige féin   go h-obann, acht
belt   of-his opponent in   towards himself suddenly,   but
níor chuir an gaisgidheach cor as   féin.   Fuair
not put   the champion   stir from himself (didn't stir). Got
Tomás   bárróg air   agus thug sé an dara   fásgadh dhó,
Thomas hug   on-him and gave he the second squeeze to-him,
acht níor chorruigh an námhad. Ar   Tomás: 'Cad   tá ar
but not stirred   the opponent. Says Thomas, 'What is on
an   bhfear so   nach   bhfuil sé ag coruigheacht liom?
(the) man   this that-not is   he at wrestling   with-me?
Sgaoil díom   é   go   bhfeicfimid'.   Tháinig na daoine
Untie   from-me him until we-(shall)-see'. Came   the men (every-
        suas ann sin agus sgaoileadar lámha an   ghaisgidhigh
body) up   then   and untied   hands of-the champion
de'n   chrios ann a raibh siad greamuighthe, agus ar an
from the belt   where were they gripped,   and on the
mball do thuit an fear siar,   agus é fuar marbh. Bhí
spot fell   the man backwards, and   he cold dead.   Was
cnámh dhroma briste leis an gceud fhásgadh   thug
bone   of-back broken with the first   squeeze (which) gave
Tomás dó.
Thomas to-him.

Costello's sweetheart was called Una: *Thug Úna grádh dhó-san agus thug seisean ghrádh d'Úna* – 'Una gave love to-him and he gave love to Una'. He made many verses in her honour, like this one:
A Úna, a ainnir, a charaidh, 's a dhéid órdha,
O Una, o maiden, o friend   and o tooth golden,
A bhéilín   meala   nár   chan riamh eugcóra,
O little-mouth of-honey that-not spoke ever   of-wrong,
B'fhearr   liom-sa bheith ar leabaidh léi   'gá
Were better with-me being on bed   with-her at-her
    síor-phógadh
    for-ever-kissing
'Na   mo shuidhe i   bhFlaitheas i gcáthaoir na   Trionóide.
Than my sitting   in Heaven   in chair   of-the Trinity.

Irish Celtic

The texts below appear in the standard spelling and grammar.

'Shule Aroon':
Siúil, siúil, siúil, a rúin,
Walk, walk, walk, o sweetheart,
Siúil go socair agus siúil go ciúin.
Walk quietly and walk calmly.
Siúil go dtí an doras agus éalaigh liom,
Walk up-to the door and flee with-me
Is go dté tú, a mhuirnín, slán.
And may-go you o darling safe (may success attend you).

A prayer before retiring:
A Mhaighdean bheannaithe, a bhanaltra an Rí ghlórmhair,
O Virgin blessed, o nurse of-the King glorious,
bí am' choimhdeacht san oíche agus fair sa ló mé,
be at my protection in-the night and watch in-the day me,
am' shuí dhom, nó mo luí dhom, am' chodla nó am'
at my sitting to-me or my lying to-me at my sleep or at my
shuan, bí am' choimhdeacht, bí am' thíompal, bí am'
slumber, be at my protection be about-me be at my
fhaire gach uair.
watching each hour.

From a reminder issued by the Post Office:

An Dara Fógra — An Fógra Deirí
THE SECOND NOTICE (AND) THE NOTICE FINAL

A Chara,
O Friend,
Maidir le mo litir a cuireadh chugat cheana,
With-reference with my letter which was-sent to-you already,
tá ordú agam a chur i gcuimhne dhuit nach bhfuil
is order at-me to put into memory to-you that-not is (a)
athnuachaint déanta agat go fóill ar do Cheadúnas
renewing done at-you as-yet on your licence
Craol-Ghlacadóireachta a chuaidh in éag an mhí
of-broadcast-receiving which went into expiry (the) month
seo caite agus mura bhfuil athnuachaint déanta
this past (last month) and unless is renewing done

114

agat   ar an gceadúnas ó shin, tá orm   a iarraidh ort
at-you on the licence   since, is on-me to ask   on-you
aire   thabhairt don   scéal gan   a thuilleadh moille.
attention of-giving to-the matter without more   of-delay.
Féadfar ceadúnas a fháil   in aon
Can-be licence   to obtain (a licence can be obtained) in any
Oifig Phoist. Iarrtar   ort   an   Fógra seo nó an   Fógra
office of-post. It-is-asked on-you (the) notice this or (the) notice
roimhe sin a   cuireadh chugat a thíolacadh nuair a bheidh
previous that which was-sent to-you to present   when   will-be
tú ag iarraidh an   cheadúnais.
you at asking of-the licence (when applying for the licence).

Mise, le   meas,
I,   with respect,
Máistir Poist
Master of-Post

The Easter Rising:
Thug Éirí   Amach Sheachtain na   Cásca 1916 (míle, naoi
Gave Rising (Out) of-Week   of-the Easter 1916
gcéad is a sé déag) críoch le   ré amháin i stair   na
end   with era one   in history of-the
hÉireann agus chuir sé tús   le   ré úr.
Ireland   and put it beginning with era new (began a new
Roimh an Éirí Amach ba é dealramh   a   bhí ar an
era). Before the Rising   was it appearance which was on the
scéal gurbh   é a   bhí i ndán d'Éirinn,
matter so-that (it appeared that) it which was in fate for Ireland,
ar a mhéad de, gné   theoranta féinrialtais   faoi   Choróin
at most,   form limited   of-self-government under Crown
na   Breataine a bhaint amach.   Chinntigh an
of-the Britain   to take   out (obtain). Decided the
tÉirí Amach, áfach,   agus an bás   a   fuair na fir   chróga
Rising,   however, and the death which got   the men brave
a   rinne cinnireacht air   go mbeadh   an lá   ar deireadh
who did   leadership on-it that would-be the day at last
leis an idé   phoblachtach agus leis   an éileamh ar Stát
with the idea republican   and with the demand for State
neamhspleách Éireannach. Faoi   Aibreán 1916 ba   dheacair a
independent Irish.   Around April   1916 was difficult to

115

Irish Celtic

shamhlú go   dtarlódh   laistigh de ghearr-achar blianta
imagine that could-happen inside   of short space of-years
tromlach mhuintir na   hÉireann a   gcúl a thabhairt le
majority of-people of-the Ireland   their back to give   with
               páirtí Rialtas Dúchais   chun tacaíocht
(turn their back on) party Rule   of-Home (and) to   support
a dhéanamh le   Sinn Féin   agus le   gluaiseacht
to do   for Sinn Fein (Ourselves) and for movement
na   saoirse náisiúnta. Ba   shin, go fíor, an bua   a
of-the freedom national. Was this truly   the victory which
rug   fir agus mná   Sheachtain na   Cásca sa
bore (won) men and women of-Week   of-the Easter in-the
díomua a   samhlaíodh leo.
defeat which imagined   with-them (in what they imagined was
defeat).

LITERATURE

The forms of the standardized language are set out in Irish in *Gramadach
na Gaeilge: an Caighdeán Oifigiúil – Grammar of Gaelic: the Official
Standard* (1958). Standard forms are also employed in the Christian
Brothers' *New Irish Grammar* (1963, later revised); other primers published in English have generally given preference to Munster forms.

P. S. Dinneen, *Irish–English Dictionary* (1927, often reprinted).
T. de Bhaldraithe, *English–Irish Dictionary* (1959).
Descriptions of living Irish speech include:
E. C. Quiggin, *A Dialect of Donegal* (1906).
T. de Bhaldraithe, *The Irish of Cois Fhairrge*, Co. Galway (1945, revised
edition 1966).
B. Ó Cuív, *The Irish of West Muskerry*, Co. Cork (1944).
Further:
T. F. O'Rahilly, *Irish Dialects Past and Present* (1932, reprinted 1972),
deals also with Scots and Manx Gaelic.
Specimens of folk literature are conveniently accessible in D. Hyde,
Love Songs of Connaught/Amhráin Grádh Chúige Connacht (1893,
reprinted 1969), classical collection, bilingual, containing also tales in
prose and commentaries on the material.
Enquiries regarding works in or about Irish may be made to the Govern-
ment Publications Sales Office, GPO, Dublin, Eire.

CHAPTER SEVEN

Scots Gaelic

🖾🖾🖾🖾🖾🖾

THE Irish were first known to the Roman world as *Hiberni*, but in the fourth century AD a new name, *Scotti* or *Scoti*, becomes prominent. About the middle of the fifth century, *Scoti* from the Ulster Dalriada invaded Argyll, setting up a kingdom there.

Subsequent advances against the Picts have already been outlined (p. 18). Suffice it to recall here that by the middle of the ninth century the newcomers were dominant over the greater part of North Britain. About 843, Scone became their capital and their Gaelic language must have spread rapidly at the expense of Pictish and Pictish Celtic. On the other hand, Gaelic lost some of its gains in the Western Isles as a consequence of Norse immigration from about 800. On the mainland, too, Gaelic advancing from the south eventually came to face Norse which had established itself in the far north. But Gaelic proved the stronger in the long run. It retook the Hebrides and assimilated nearly all the Norse on the mainland, except in the extreme north-west of Caithness (p. 213). Exact datings are not possible, but the replacement of Norse was probably achieved during the twelfth century, that is to say, even before the Norwegians relinquished their suzerainty over the Western Isles by the Treaty of Perth in 1266.

South of the Forth–Clyde line lay two independent kingdoms. The western half was occupied by British-speaking Strathclyde, the eastern half was English-speaking and formed part of Northumbria. On this front the Gaelic advance paused for a while. Independent Strathclyde, however, barely survived into the eleventh century and in 1016 Lothian, that part of Northumbria between the Forth and the Cheviots, was also annexed by the Scots. The gaelicization of Strathclyde had probably begun before the final collapse, and it is likely that by the end of the eleventh century all the western lowlands of Scotland, as the country now came to be called, were Gaelic in speech. But Gaelic could make little impress on the English of

117

Lothian. On the contrary, it was English which now showed itself capable of expansion, and this at a time when Gaelic was the sole language of the rest of the country, apart from the dwindling remnants of Norse in the far west and north. The plain fact is that Lothian was more advanced than the rest of the country, and Edinburgh more important than Scone, which it eventually superseded. And here, of course, was the point of natural contact with the great neighbour to the south.

From the second half of the eleventh century, the Scottish royal house was orientated towards England (p. 198), and Malcolm Canmore (reigned 1058–1093) was the last Scottish king whose native tongue was Gaelic. The new trend aroused resentment in the Celtic parts and the next two centuries are marked by revolts, all apparently futile, against the policies of the central authority. We do not suppose, however, that Gaelic was entirely ignored as long as the direct line of the Dalriadic kings sat on the throne. But by the time the last of these, Alexander III, came to die in 1286, English must have reached an unassailable position as the language of prestige and had certainly spread widely at the expense of Gaelic, though doubtless still a minority language in the country as a whole. The recession of Gaelic naturally began in the Lowlands. By 1300, the greater part appears to have been anglicized, by 1500 only Galloway remaining unaffected, though soon to fall, and meanwhile English had pushed up the east coast as far as Inverness. At the beginning of modern times, therefore, the use of Gaelic was confined to the Highlands and Islands. Here clan society remained intact and the native language continued to be held in honour, encouraged by many of the ruling chiefs, especially the semi-independent Lords of the Isles. But English was in use officially as well and doubtless a familiar tongue in higher circles, though the broad mass of the clansmen understood only Gaelic.

The Scottish Reformation, carried through in 1560, led to a new political confrontation: on the one side the English-speaking Protestant Lowlander, on the other the Highland Catholic Gael. Moreover, the reform movement had brought the extreme pro-English faction to power, whose position was further strengthened by the Union of the Crowns in 1603. The era of inspired assaults on Gaeldom now got under way. But despite official sanctions against their language, the population of the Highlands and Islands generally remained monoglot Gaels. After the defeat of the Young Stuart

Pretender in 1745, however, the systematic destruction of Gaelic society began. During the Highland clearances from 1782 to 1853 large numbers of Gaels were evicted from what had been their hereditary clan-lands. Others left of their own accord to find employment in the English-speaking lowland towns or in the colonies. The depopulation of the Highlands at this time bears comparison with the Gaelic exodus from Ireland in the years of the Famine and afterwards. The percentage of Gaelic speakers in Scotland now fell rapidly. It is estimated to have been 50 per cent or 150,000 Gaels in the sixteenth century; by 1801 it was about 20 per cent or 335,000 Gaels, and though for a time absolute numbers may have increased somewhat, it was down to 10 per cent or 300,000 Gaels in 1861. About this time a knowledge of English spread rapidly and by the end of the century the remaining Gaels had become largely bilingual. The 1901 census returned 231,000 Gaelic speakers, of whom only 28,000 had no English. Official policy is no longer openly hostile to the language and culture of the Highlands, but it is entirely indifferent, in crass contrast to the attitude to Gaelic in Eire. Meanwhile the number of speakers has shrunk to about $1\frac{1}{2}$ per cent of the population. In 1931, 136,000 were returned as Gaelic-speaking; in 1961 the figure was not quite 81,000, of whom less than 1,000 spoke no English and these essentially children under school age. Apart from a few localities along the western seaboard, Gaelic is today predominantly spoken only in the Hebrides. As in the case of Ireland, a substantial number of Gaelic speakers live outside the Gaelic-speaking districts – there are over 10,000 in Glasgow – and we suppose that less than half of those able to speak the language actually use it habitually as the main medium.

It is apparent that the Scottish variety of Gaelic faces a fate not very different from that of Irish, indeed the rate of recession in Scotland is, if anything, swifter than in Ireland. For long denied the recognition which alone could have assured its survival, Scottish Gaelic is surely about to enter its last phase as a living tongue. Numbers are now too small to permit the continuation of the language for much longer. Those children who, in the next decade or two, may yet acquire Gaelic as the language of the home, will, as they grow older, turn more and more to English and will cease to pass on the Gaelic to the next generation. We think that Scots Gaelic will most likely be extinct by about the beginning of the last quarter of the next century.

Emigration from the Highland area led to the loss of Gaelic except on Cape Breton Island, Nova Scotia, where a compact settlement of Gaels took place. Immigration began in 1773, reaching its maximum between 1790 and 1830. Many of the settlers knew only Gaelic and the language was commonly spoken in rural districts until quite recently, though English alone was the sole official language. In 1931, some 30,000 could use Gaelic, mostly people of the oldest generation, the younger ones having generally gone over exclusively to English. Twenty years later the number of speakers had fallen drastically to 6,789, so that Gaelic is now fast disappearing as a living idiom in Nova Scotia.

Scots Gaelic plays hardly any part in education. The formal problems caused by dialect diversity are comparable to those in Ireland. In practice most Gaels are illiterate in their native tongue. The written standard, based on the Bible of 1801, has thus had no appreciable influence on the spoken form. As in Ireland, broad dialect is the necessary rule in Gaelic Scotland, too, where every parish has its shibboleth. Dialect differences can be quite considerable, so much so that speakers from the north have difficulty in understanding the southerners. For these the koine is English.

In the Middle Ages, learned Scottish Gaels, aware of their Irish ancestry, strove to write Irish Gaelic, ie, the standard literary form of that country. There is therefore no medieval literature in Scots Gaelic; indeed, the tradition that Scotland and Ireland shared a common literary language was still fully alive in the sixteenth century. It is noteworthy that the first book to be printed in (Irish) Gaelic was a translation of the prayer-book of the Scottish reformed church by John Carswell, Bishop of the Isles, issued at Edinburgh in 1567, and expressly addressed to Scots and Irish alike. The first considerable document in Scottish Gaelic proper is an early sixteenth-century collection of poems. Here a break was also made with the traditional Irish orthography, but this new departure was not generally followed, though in Scotland only Latin letters are used.

Printed Scots Gaelic literature begins in 1751 with the publication of poems by Alexander MacDonald. Production has necessarily remained modest. Devotional books figure prominently among earlier published works; later poetry and folklore come into their own. Short stories and plays have also been popular. A small supply of school books has left the press, mostly readers, sometimes adapted from Irish.

Scots Gaelic

Until fairly recently Scots Gaelic commonly went under the name of Erse, which is simply a development of the Lowlanders' form of the word 'Irish' (early Sc. dial. *Erische*). Sometimes this term was used for Irish Gaelic, though the Irish themselves have not approved of this usage.

Scots Gaelic has understandably contributed elements to the English as used locally in Scotland, witness eg, *finnock* '(immature) sea trout', *larach* 'site', *sharrow* 'bitter, tart' (Gael. *fionnag* lit. 'whiting', *làrach, searbh*). Standard English, too, has acquired a fair sprinkling of words from this source. Examples include *cairn, clan, fulmar, slogan, whiskey* (Gael. *carn* 'heap of stones', *clann* 'offspring', *fulmair* ultimately of Norse origin, *sluagh ghairm* 'host cry', ie, 'war cry', *uisce* properly *uisce beatha* 'water of-life' (a translation of Lat. *aqua vitae*). Other loans refer chiefly to the local scene, as *clachan, claymore, gillie, ptarmigan, sporan* (Gael. *clachan* 'hamlet', *claidheamh mór* 'great sword', *gille* 'lad, servant', *tarmachan* lit. 'croaker', *sporan* 'purse').

The Gaelic heritage lives on in the names of places and persons. As in Ireland, these are often semantically transparent, eg, *Strathmore*, Gael. *An Strath Mór* 'The Great Valley', *Oban*, Gael. *An t-Òban* 'The Bay'. Surnames usually contain *mac* 'son' followed by the genitive of the name, as *MacIntyre, MacPherson*, Gael. *Mac an tSaoir* (*saor* 'carpenter'), *Mac a' Phearsoin* (*pearson* 'parson'). *Cameron*, Gael. *Camshròn*, was originally a nickname (*cam* 'wry', *sròn* 'nose').

LITERATURE

J. L. Campbell, *Gaelic in Scottish Education and Life* (1945, reprinted 1950).

SKETCH OF SCOTS GAELIC

We are here concerned with the normal practice of the written language. However, even literary Gaelic is not rigorously standardized, so that variants are often met with; in some cases, as in folk literature, the local touch may be quite prominent. In our sample texts, too, items will be found which diverge from the prescriptions of the following grammatical sketch.

121

Phonetics

As explained on p. 20, traditional Gaelic orthography is used in Scotland; it corresponds closely to that of unreformed (pre-1947) Modern Irish.

Since the overall linguistic conditions in Gaelic Scotland are analogous to those in Ireland and as the Scottish phonetic system is no less complicated than the Irish which it largely resembles, we again find ourselves obliged to set up our own working approximation, as follows.

Stress on the first syllable is the general rule.

Vowel Sounds
Reference is to stressed vowels, unless otherwise stated.

[a] is represented by *a, ai,* as *agus* [akəs] 'and', *bainne* [baɲə] 'milk', also in the diminutive suffixes -(*e*)*ag,* -(*e*)*an,* as *caileag* [kal′ak] 'girl', *lochan* [loχan] 'small loch'.

[aː] is represented by *à, ài,* as *làn* [laːn] 'full', *càise* [kaːʃə] 'cheese'.

[e] is represented by *e, ei, ea,* as *le* [l′e] 'with', *leis* [l′eʃ] 'with (the)', *sean* [ʃen] 'old', sometimes by *ai,* as *aig* [ek] 'at', *air* [er] 'on'.

[ɛː] is represented by *è, èa,* as *stèsean* [stɛːʃən] 'station', *gèadh* [g′ɛː] 'goose'.

[eː] is represented by *éi, eu,* as *éisdeachd* [eːʃtʃəχk] 'listening', *beul* [beːl] 'mouth'.

[i] is represented by *i, io,* as *mil* [mil′] 'honey', *fios* [fis] 'knowledge'; often in unstressed syllables by *ai,* as *eaglais* [ekliʃ] 'church'.

[iː] is represented by *ì, ìo,* as *tìr* [tʃiːr] 'land', *sìoda* [ʃiːtə] 'silk'.

[øː] is represented by *ao, aoi,* as *gaoth* [gøː] 'wind', *faoileag* [føːl′ak] 'seagull'.

[o] is represented by *o, oi, eo,* as *bog* [bok] 'soft', *sgoil* [skol′] 'school', *deoch* [dʒoχ] 'drink (noun)', notice *leabhar* [l′o-ər] 'book'.

[ɔː] is represented by *ò, òi, eò, eòi,* as *bròg* [brɔːk] 'shoe', *còir* [kɔːr] 'generous', *ceò* [k′ɔː] 'fog', *feòil* [fjɔːl] 'meat'.

[oː] is represented by *ó, ói,* as *mór* [moːr] 'big', *cóig* [koːk′] 'five'.

[u] is represented by *u, ui, iu,* as *muc* [muk] 'pig', *uisge* [uʃk′ə] 'water', *fliuch* [fl′uχ] 'wet'.

122

Scots Gaelic

[uː] is represented by *ù, ùi, iù, iùi*, as *glùn* [gluːn] 'knee', *cùil* [kuːl']
'nook', *siùcar* [ʃuːkər] 'sugar', *stiùir* [ʃtʃuːr] 'rudder'.

[ə] is represented by unstressed *a, ea, e, u*, see above *passim*, also by
o, as *aotrom* [øːtrəm] 'light (in weight)', further commonly by *ai*
before *r*, as *seòladair* [ʃɔːlətər] 'sailor', occasionally by stressed *a*, as
aghaidh [əɣi] 'face'.

[ai] is represented by *aigh*, as *saighdear* [saitʃər] 'soldier'.

[au] is represented by *a* or *o* before *ll, nn, ng, m* in monosyllables,
as *mall* [maul] 'slow', *anns* [auns] 'in', *long* [lauŋk] 'ship', *trom*
[traum] 'heavy', also by *amh*, especially before consonants, as
samhradh [saurəɣ] 'summer'.

[iə] is represented by *ia, iai*, as *fiadh* [fiəɣ] 'deer (sg.)', *Iain* [iəń] 'John'.

[uə] is represented by *ua, uai*, as *uan* [uən] 'lamb', *fuaim* [fuəm]
'sound'.

Notice also *cruaidh* [krui] 'hard', *an déidh* [ən dʒeːi] 'after', *Gaidheal*
[gai-əl] 'Gael', *oidhche* [øiçə] 'night', *tràigh* [traːi] 'shore'.

An epenthetic vowel may develop between certain consonants, as
ainm [ańəm] 'name', *balbh* [baləv] 'dumb', *airgead* [arək'ət] 'money'.

Consonants

We pronounce as for Irish, except as follows: the contrast between
velar and palatal qualities has been lost in the case of *p, b, m, f, ph,
bh, mh* (the last two [v]), eg, *pian* [piən] 'pain', *peann* [pjaun] 'pen'.
It may thus appear that [j] is represented by *e* in certain cases, as
also initially, as *eòrna* [jɔːrnə] 'barley', further by initial *i*, as *iuchair*
[juχər] 'key'. Except in initial position, *b, d, g* are pronounced like
p, t, c, but without aspiration; palatal *d, t* are [dʒ, tʃ] respectively
when initial, otherwise uniformly [tʃ]; *d* preceded by *ch* is [k], as
luchd [luχk] 'people'. Initial *s* is [s] also in palatal clusters, as *sgian*
[sk'iən] 'knife'. The digraph *th* is sounded [h] in initial position (but
thu [u] 'thou'), also medially between vowels, though here it commonly indicates hiatus, as *rathad* [ra-ət] 'road'; it is otherwise silent,
as *blàth* [blaː] 'warm', *aithne* [ańə] 'knowledge'.

Medial *dh, gh* may merge with vowels to form diphthongs (see
'Vowel Sounds'). They are generally silent between vowels, indicating
hiatus, as *adharc* [ə-ərk] 'horn', *rìoghachd* [riː-əχk] 'kingdom', but
sometimes pronounced, as (velar) *aghaidh* [əɣi] 'face', (palatal)
bòidheach [bɔːjəχ] 'pretty', also the values initially, as *dh'fhàg* [ɣaːk]

'left (preterite)', *a' ghealach* [ə jaləχ] 'the moon'; they are silent medially before consonants, as *Gàidhlig* [gaːlʹikʹ] 'Gaelic (tongue)', *saighdear* [saitʃər] 'soldier'; when final, they are pronounced after *a, à*, as *ruadh* [ruəɣ] 'red', *gràdh* [graːɣ] 'love' (but *ràdh* [raː] 'saying (vb.)', *agh* [əɣ] 'heifer', *bàgh* [baːɣ] 'bay', but are otherwise silent, as *céilidh* [kʹeːlʹi] 'social gathering', *rìgh* [riː] 'king'. Medial *bh, mh* may also merge with vowels to form diphthongs; they are commonly silent between vowels, indicating hiatus, as *gobha* [go-ə] 'blacksmith', *comhairle* [ko-irlʹə] 'advice', but sometimes pronounced as *seabhac* [ʃevək] 'hawk', *Damhar* [davər] 'October'; *bh* is silent when final after *u*, as *dubh* [du] 'black', also *robh* [ro] 'was'.

Initial Mutations

Eclipsis proper, ie, nasalization, though common in some dialects, is not a feature of written Scots Gaelic, but *n* is prefixed to vowels. Aspiration, on the other hand, is as prominent as in Irish, involving the same consonants under comparable conditions. Equally prominent are the other changes affecting the first letter of a word, ie, the eclipsis of *s* by *t* and the prefixing of *h* to words beginning with a vowel.

Nouns

The evolution of the declensional classes has, in general, been comparable to that in Irish Gaelic. A striking feature of Scottish is the prolific use of the plural (nominative vocative accusative dative) ending *-an*, which may also extend to the genitive. Mutations may play a significant part in the declension, as in Irish, and conform by and large to the same patterns. As in Irish, the vocative particle is *a*.

The nouns quoted in the Old Irish section survive in Scotland as follows:

nom. acc. dat. *fear* m. 'man', voc. gen. *fir*, pl. nom. acc. dat. *fir*, voc. *feara*, gen. *fear*.

sgeul f. 'story', gen. *sgeòil*, pl. *sgeulan*, gen. *sgeul*.

dealbh f. 'picture', gen. *dealbha*, pl. *dealbhan*, gen. *dealbh*.

cnàimh m. 'bone', gen. *cnàmha*, pl. *cnàmhan*, gen. *cnàimh*.

sùil f. 'eye', gen. *sùla*, pl. *sùilean*, gen. *sùl*.

muir f. 'sea', gen. *mara*, pl. *marannan*.

cath m. 'battle', gen. *catha*, pl. *cathan*, gen. *cath*.

dorus m. 'door', gen. *doruis*, pl. *dorsan*.

caora f. 'sheep', gen. *caorach*, pl. *caoraich*, gen. *caorach*.
rìgh m. 'king', pl. *rìghrean*.
teanga f. 'tongue', gen. dat. *teangaidh*, pl. *teangan*.
caraid m. 'friend', pl. *càirdean*.
cù m. 'dog', gen. *coin*, pl. *coin*, gen. *con*.
Eirinn f. 'Ireland'.

Alternatives are sometimes acceptable, eg, *sgeòil, deilbh* beside *sgeulan, dealbhan*; genders may vary, thus *sgeul* also masc.

Adjectives

Evolution in Scottish and Irish is again closely comparable. Adjectival inflexion corresponds, in principle, to that of the nouns though a separate pl. gen. has disappeared. Mutations remain a conspicuous feature, conforming by and large to the Irish system. Old Irish *becc* 'small' survives today as *beag*, inflecting as follows:
Sg. masc. nom. acc. dat. *beag*, voc. gen. *big*, fem. all cases *beag*, except gen. *bige*.
Pl. both genders and all cases *beaga*.
The comparative and superlative are not formally distinguished: *sean* 'old', *sine* 'older, oldest', *àrd* 'high', *àirde* 'higher, highest'. Irregular comparison continues, eg, *math* 'good', *feàrr* 'better, best', *olc* 'bad', *miosa* 'worse, worst'.

Numbers

Counting: 1 *a h-aon*, 2 *a dhà*, 3 *a trì*, 4 *a ceithir*, 5 *a cóig*, 6 *a sè*, 7 *a seachd*, 8 *a h-ochd*, 9 *a naoi*, 10 *deich*, 11 *a h-aon deug*, 12 *a dhà dheug*, 13 *a trì deug*, 14 *a ceithir deug*, 15 *a cóig deug*, 16 *a sè deug*, 17 *a seachd deug*, 18 *a h-ochd deug*, 19 *a naoi deug*, 20 *a fichead*, 21 *a h-aon air fhichead*, 30 *deich air fhichead*, 40 *dà fhichead*, 50 *dà fhichead 's a deich*, 60 *trì fichead*, 70 *trì fichead 's a deich*, 80 *ceithir fichead*, 90 *ceithir fichead 's a deich*, 100 *ceud*, 1000 *mìle*.

The following forms are used with nouns: 1 *aon*, 2 *dà*, 3 *trì*, etc., eg, *dà dhuine dheug* '12 men'.

Definite Article

Sg. nom. acc. masc. *an, am* before nouns beginning with a labial consonant: *am feur* 'the grass'.
gen.   *an, a'* when the noun is aspirated, except *fh*:

> *mullach a' chnuic* '(the) top of the hill', but *dath an fheòir* '(the) colour of the grass'.

dat.
   an, a' when the noun is aspirated, except *fh*: *leis a' chù* 'with the dog', but *'n* after a preposition ending in a vowel: *do'n luch* 'to the mouse'.

nom. acc. fem.
   an, a' when the noun is aspirated, except *fh*: *a' bhròg* 'the shoe'.

gen.
   na, prefixing *h* to a noun beginning with a vowel: *na h-eaglaise* 'of the church'.

dat.
   an, a' when the noun is aspirated, except *fh*: *anns a' choille* 'in the wood'.

A noun is aspirated after the article in the nominative accusative feminine, genitive masculine, and dative, except when beginning with *d, t* or *s*.

The nominative accusative masculine prefixes *t* to a noun beginning with a vowel: *an t-eun* 'the bird'; nominative accusative feminine, genitive masculine, dative prefix *t* to a noun beginning with *s* followed by *l, n, r*, or a vowel, thus eclipsing *s*: (nominative accusative) *an t-slat* 'the rod', (genitive) *an t-siùil* 'of the sail', (dative) *leis an t-slait* 'with the rod', *de'n t-seòl* 'off the sail'.

Pl. nom. acc. dat. *na*, prefixing *h* to a noun beginning with a vowel: *na h-eòin* 'the birds'.

gen.
   nan, nam before nouns beginning with a labial consonant: *obair nam bard* '(the) work of the poets'.

There is no indefinite article.

Pronouns

The personal pronouns are as follows: *mi* 'I, me', *thu*, but *tu* after certain verbal forms (as conditional active, copula) 'thou, thee', *e* 'he, him', *i* 'she, her', *sinn* 'we, us', *sibh* 'you', *iad* 'they, them'. Emphatic forms are common: *mise, thusa* or *tusa, esan, ise, sinne, sibhse, iadsan*.

Pronouns are not required with the few verbal forms which preserve a distinguishing termination, thus *bhithinn* 'I would be', *bhitheamaid* 'we would be', but *bhitheadh tu* 'thou wouldst be', *bhitheadh e* 'he would be', etc.

Scots Gaelic

Pronouns coalesce with certain prepositions, eg, *aig* 'at': *agam* 'at me', *agad* 'at thee', *aige* 'at him', *aice* 'at her', *againn* 'at us', *agaibh* 'at you', *aca* 'at them', with corresponding emphatic *agamsa, agadsa, aigesan, aicese, againne, agaibhse, acasan*. Other examples include *air* 'on': *orm* 'on me', *ort* 'on thee', *air* 'on him', *oirre* 'on her', *oirnn* 'on us', *oirbh* 'on you', *orra* 'on them', emphatic *ormsa*, etc., *le* 'with': *leam* 'with me', *leat* 'with thee', *leis* 'with him', *leatha* 'with her', *leinn* 'with us', *leibh* 'with you', *leo* 'with them', emphatic *leamsa*, etc.

The possessives are as follows: *mo*, before vowel sounds *m'* 'my', *do*, before vowel sounds *d'* 'thy', *a* 'his' – all aspirating, *a* 'her' prefixing *h* to vowels, *ar* 'our' prefixing *n* to vowels, *ur* 'your' prefixing *n* to vowels, *an*, before labial consonants *am* 'their'. The emphasizing particle follows the noun: *mo leabhar-sa* 'my book'.

Verbs

The inflexional principle, still prominent in Irish, is much decayed in Scots Gaelic. The synthetic present and imperfect have, in general, been lost and the subjunctive has disappeared, though the term is often used to denote the conditional. In contradistinction to Irish, however, Scottish preserves a passive as such. Periphrastic tenses formed with the substantive verb predominate in the system as a whole. There is only a single class of regular verbs.

The Old Irish verbs conjugated on pp. 89–93 continue essentially as follows:

Verbal noun: *leigeil* 'allowing':

Active

Pres. sg. 1 *tha mi a' leigeil* lit. 'I am at allowing', 2 *tha thu a' leigeil*, etc.

Fut. sg. 1 *leigidh mi*, 2 *leigidh thu*, etc.

Cond. sg. 1 *leiginn*, 2 *leigeadh tu*, 3 *leigeadh e*, pl. 1 *leigeamaid*, 2 *leigeadh sibh*, 3 *leigeadh iad*.

Imperf. sg. 1 *bha mi a' leigeil* lit. 'I was at allowing', 2 *bha thu a' leigeil*, etc.

Pret. sg. 1 *leig mi*, 2 *leig thu*, etc.

Imperative:

sg. 1 *leigeam*, 2 *leig*, 3 *leigeadh e*, pl. 1 *leigeamaid*, 2 *leigibh*, 3 *leigeadh iad*.

Among other periphrastic tenses we note: (perfect) *tha mi air leigeil* lit. 'I am after allowing', (pluperfect) *bha mi air leigeil* lit. 'I was after allowing'.

Passive

Pres. sg. 1 *tha mi leigte* lit. 'I am allowed', 2 *tha thu leigte*, etc., also *tha mi air mo leigeil* lit. 'I am after my allowing', *tha thu air do leigeil*, etc.

Fut. sg. 1 *leigear mi*, 2 *leigear thu*, etc.

Cond. sg. 1 *leigteadh mi*, 2 *leigteadh thu*, etc.

Imperf. sg. 1 *bha mi leigte* lit. 'I was allowed', 2 *bha thu leigte*, etc., also sg. 1 *bha mi air mo leigeil* lit. 'I was after my allowing', *bha thu air do leigeil*, etc.

Pret. sg. 1 *leigeadh mi*, 2 *leigeadh thu*, etc.

Imperative:
sg. 1 *leigtear mi*, 2 *leigtear thu*, etc.

Past participle: *leigte* 'allowed'.

Verbal noun: *breith* 'bearing':

Active

Pres. sg. 1 *tha mi a' breith*, Fut. sg. 1 *beiridh mi*, Cond. sg. 1 *bheirinn*, Imperf. sg. 1 *bha mi a' breith*, Pret. sg. 1 *rug mi*, etc.

Imperative: sg. 1 *beiream*, etc.

Passive

Pres. sg. 1 *tha mi beirte*, Fut. sg. 1 *beirear mi*, Cond. sg. 1 *bheirteadh mi*, Imperf. sg. 1 *bha mi beirte*, Pret. sg. 1 *rugadh mi*, etc.

Imperative:
sg. 1 *beirtear mi*, etc.

Past participle: *beirte*.

Verbal noun: *labhairt* 'speaking':

Active

Pres. sg. 1 *tha mi a' labhairt*, Fut. sg. 1 *labhairidh mi*, Cond. sg. 1 *labhairinn*, Imperf. sg. 1 *bha mi a' labhairt*, Pret. sg. 1 *labhair mi*, etc.

Imperative: sg. 1 *labhaiream*, etc.

128

Passive

Pres. sg. 3 *tha e labhairte*, Fut. sg. 3 *labhairear e*, Cond. sg. 3 *labhairteadh*, Imperf. sg. 3 *bha e labhairte*, Pret. sg 3 *labhaireadh e*.

Imperative:
sg. 3 *labhairtear e*.

Past participle:
labhairte.

The Verb 'to be'
The distinction between the substantive verb and the copula survives much as in Irish; the former has impersonal forms comparable to the Irish autonomous.

(Substantive verb)

Verbal noun: *bith* 'being':

Active

Pres. sg. 1 *tha mi*, 2 *tha thu*, 3 *tha e*, pl. 1 *tha sinn*, 2 *tha sibh*, 3 *tha iad*, negative *chan eil mi*, interrogative *a bheil mi?* neg. *nach eil mi?*
Fut. sg. 1 *bithidh mi*, 2 *bithidh thu*, etc., negative *cha bhi mi*, interrogative *am bi mi?* neg. *nach bi mi?*
Cond. sg. 1 *bhithinn*, 2 *bhitheadh tu*, 3 *bhitheadh e*, pl. 1 *bhitheamaid*, 2 *bhitheadh sibh*, 3 *bhitheadh iad*, negative *cha bhithinn*, interrogative *am bithinn?* neg. *nach bithinn?*
Past. sg. 1 *bha mi*, 2 *bha thu*, 3 *bha e*, pl. 1 *bha sinn*, 2 *bha sibh*, 3 *bha iad*, negative *cha robh mi*, interrogative *an robh mi?* neg. *nach robh mi?*

Imperative:
sg. 1 *bitheam*, 2 *bi*, 3 *bitheadh e*, pl. 1 *bitheamaid*, 2 *bithibh*, 3 *bitheadh iad*.

Impersonal

Present *thatar* 'it is being, there is' (*chan eilear, am beilear? nach eilear?*), Fut. *bitear*, Past *bhatar* (*cha robhar*, etc.).

(Copula)

Present (all persons sg. and pl.): *is*, negative *cha*, interrogative *an?* neg. *nach?* The pronouns are sg. 1 *mi*, 2 *tu*, 3 *e, i*, pl. 1 *sinn*, 2 *sibh*, 3 *iad.* Before vowels *cha* becomes *chan,* hence sg. 3 *chan e,* etc., notice sg. 1 *cha mhi.* Notice interrogative sg. 1 *am mi?*

Past (all persons singular and plural): *bu,* negative *cha bu,* interrogative *am bu?* neg. *nach bu?* Before vowels *bu* becomes *b',* hence sg. 3 *b'e,* etc. Notice sg. 1 *bu mhi.*

In the absence of a verb 'to have', possession is commonly expressed by the substantive verb with the preposition *aig* 'at', eg, *tha taigh againn* 'we have a house' lit. 'is house at-us'.

READINGS

Brosnachadh do na Gaidheil (Incitement to the Gaels), from a Jacobite song of the Forty-Five by Alexander MacDonald:

O! togaibh gu sgairteil grad,
O! rise-up boldly,   speedily,
Sguiribh d'ur   snìomh mar ghad,
Cease   from your twisting like twisted-twig (indecision),
Fògraibh uaibh   fadal 'us lunnachd,
Announce from-you (renounce) delay and sloth,
Ullamh mar pheilear daig',
Ready   like bullet   of-pistol
No fùdar   do theine   snaip,
Or powder to fire (spark) of-trigger,
Tàirnibh 'nur   feachdannan grunndail;
Draw-up-your forces   steadfast;
'S   air Uilleam chinn   chlodaich,
And on William of-head thick,
A   ghineadh   le cocuill,
Who was-begotten by cuckold,
Ur   diùbhaltas cogail   nach bròchd   sibh?
Your revenge   warlike not will-take you?
'S   cuiribh àr   na   sheasas
And put   slaughter what will-stand
De reubalaibh leis-san,
Of rebels   with-him,
'Gan   tolladh, 'gan   leadairt, 's 'gan   strùmpadh.
At-their piercing at-their rending and at-their tearing
(Slaughter the rebels who will support him, piercing them, rending them, tearing them).

Two samples of folk poetry:

Is anmoch chunna mi an dé (It was late yesterday I saw)

   Is anmoch chunna mi an dé
Is late   saw   I   yesterday
Fear earraidh dheirg air a' ghleann;
Man of-habit red   on the glen;
Dh'fhaoiltich mo chridhe r' a cheum,
Rejoiced   my heart   at his step,
   Shaoil mi gur tu féin a bh'ann
Thought I   that thou self who wert in-it (I thought it was you).

   Shaoil   mi gur tu   féin a   bh'ann
Thought I   that thou self who wert in-it,
Sealgair sìthne   nan   damh donn,
Hunter of-venison of-the stags brown,
Siubhlaiche nam frìth 's nam beann,
Traveller   of-the heaths and of-the mountains,
   Gìomanach nam mìle   sonn.
Stalker   of-the thousand heroes (mighty stags).

   Gìomanach nam mìle   sonn,
Stalker   of-the thousand heroes,
Brighde mhìn a bhith dhut   teann,
Brigit   gentle to be   to-thee close (May gentle Brigit be),
Muire mhìn a bhith ri d' chom,
Mary gentle to be   by thy body,
   'S Mìcheal mìngheal   bhith ri d' cheann.
and Michael bright   (to) be   by thy head.

Dh'fhàg mi ann am beul a' bhrugh (I left in the doorway of the fairy mansion)

   Dh'fhàg mi ann am beul a'   bhrugh
Left   I in in mouth of-the fairy-mansion
M' eudail fhéin an donngheal dhubh,
My jewel own the brown-white dark,
A sùil mar reul, a beul mar shubh,
Her eye like star, her mouth like berry,
   A guth mar inneall   theudan.
Her voice like instrument of-string (stringed).

Dh'fhàg mi 'n dé   an innis   nam bó
Left   I   yesterday in meadow of-the cattle
An   cailin   donn   as mìlse   pòg,
The maiden brown of-sweetest kiss,
A   rasg mar reul, a   leac   mar ròs,
Her eye like star her cheek like rose,
   A   pòg air bhlas nam   peuran.
   Her kiss on taste of-the pears.
   (Her kiss has the taste of pears.)

Ròin (Seals):

   Tha dà   threubh ròn   ann: treubh ròn   beag agus
   Are two tribes   of-seals in-it[1]: tribe of-seals small and
   treubh ròn   mór, treubh nan   sìochaire agus treubh nam
   tribe of-seals large, tribe of-the dwarfs   and tribe of-the
   fuamhaire. Nar bheil comann   aig an dà   threubh r'   a
   giants.   Not is   association at the two tribes with his
   chéile. Agus a   bharrachd air a sin: chan e an aon dùthaich
   fellow[2]. And the more   than that is-not it the one region
   is dachaidh daibh.   Tha na ròin bheag a' cumail ris na
   is home   to-them[3]. Are the seals small at keeping to the
   cumhaing agus ris na caolais agus ris na lochan mara
   narrows   and to the straits and to the lochs of-sea (sea lochs)
   ta   dol   a steach dh'an tìr.   Uaidh seo theirear ròn
   which-are going in   to the land. From this is-called seal
   caolais na ròn locha ris an ròn bheag co math ri   ròn
   of-strait or seal of-loch with the seal small as well with seal
   sìochaire. Cha tig   an ròn mór dha na lochan mara na
   of-dwarfs[4]. Not comes the seal great to the lochs of-sea nor
   dha na caolais bheaga chumhang na dha na h-eileanan a staigh.
   to the straits small   narrow   nor to the islands inside.
   Tha e a' cumail ris na h-eileanan a muigh agus ri sgeirean agus
   Is it at keeping to the islands   outside and to skerries and
   ri òbanan a'   chuain mhóir.
   to bays   of-the ocean great.

---

1 'There are two tribes of seals', 2 'With each other', 3 'The same region
is not the home of both', 4 'The small seal is also called the strait or loch
seal as well as the dwarf seal'.

132

Scots Gaelic

Tha diubhair   mhór ann an gnè   agus ann an gnàth
Is   difference great in   in appearance and in   in nature
agus ann am meud an   dà   sheòrsa. Tha an ròn beag a'
and in   in size   of-the two kinds.   Is   the seal small at
breith   a   chuilein ma   mheadhon an   t-samhraidh; tha an
bearing its cubs   about middle   of-the   summer;   is   the
cuilean glas 'ga   bhreith,   agus tha calg   goirid
cub   grey at-its bearing (birth) and is   bristle (bristles) short
cruaidh air   mar tha air a mhàthair. Tha an ròn mór a'
hard   on-it as   is on its mother.   Is   the seal great at
breith   a   chuilean ma   leth a'   gheamhraidh;   tha an
bearing its cubs   about half of-the winter (midwinter); is   the
cuilean geal anns an dath   mar chaora gun   rùsgadh,
cub   white in   the colour as   sheep without (a) fleece
agus le   fionnadh fada mìn   air. Tha an dath   agus am
and with hair   long smooth on-it. Is (the) colour and (the)
fionnadh sin a' fuireach ma   dhà mhìos. Tha an cuilean a'
hair   that at remaining about two months. Is   the cub   at
tilgeil an   fhionnaidh sin agus tha calg   dubhghorm agus
casting of(-the) hair   that and is   bristle dark-blue and
dubhghlas a' tighinn 'na   àite. Is e moineis a   theirear
dark-grey at coming in-its place. Is it *moineis* which is-called
ri   ròn boireann agus briomal ri   ròn fireann.
with seal female   and *briomal* with seal male.

An Cunntas (The Census), 1961:
A réir   a'   Chunntais bha 80,978   bho aois
According-to the Census   were 80,978 (persons) from age
trì   bliadhna agus os cionn sin, comasach air a' Ghàidhlig
of-three years   and above   that able   on the Gaelic
a bhruidheann an 1961. Is   iad na siorrachdan anns a
to speak   in 1961. It-is they the counties   in   which
bheil an àireamh as àirde de luchd-bruidheann   na
are   the number greatest of people-of-speech (speakers) of-the
Gàidhlig Ros is Inbhirnis – còrr air dara   leth na
Gaelic   Ross and Inverness[1] more than second half[2] of-the
h-àireamh. Is   iad na h-Eileanan an   Iar far a bheil trian
number.   It-is they the Islands of-the West where are   third

1 'Ross and Inverness are the counties in which. . . ', 2 'More than half'.

133

de luchd-bruidheann an Albainn na ceàrnaichean far a bheil
of speakers   in Scotland the districts   where is
f ìor neart   na   Gàidhlig. Tha àireamh luchd-bruidheann air
real strength of-the Gaelic.   Is   number of-speakers   after
a dhol   an lughad dìreach mar a tha sluagh nan   eilean a'
its getting less   just   as   is   people of-the islands at
falbh,   agus a nis tha an dà chànain aig a' mhór
going-away[3], and now are the two languages at the great
chuid. Ach an coimeas   ris   an dùthaich air fad   chan eil
part[4]. But the comparison with the country as-a-whole not is
ceàrna eile ann far a bheil a' Ghàidhlig a' cumail a
district other in-it[5] where is   the Gaelic   at holding its
h-àite cho daingeann. Is   ann an sgìreachd Bharabhais agus ann
place so strongly. It-is in in parish   of-Barvas and in
an sgìreachd nan   Loch an Leódhas a   tha an àireamh
in parish   of-the Lochs in Lewis which is the number
as motha de luchd-bruidheann. Am Barabhas tha 4,099 – is e
greatest of speakers.   In Barvas is †4,099 is it
sin   94·6 as   gach ceud –   agus an sgìreachd
that (ie) †94·6 from each hundred (per cent) and in parish
nan   Loch tha 2,329 – is e sin 94·8 as gach ceud – chan eil
of-the Lochs are †2,329 ie,   94·8 per cent   not is
atharrachadh comhairraichte anns na   cunntaisean so   bho
change   significant   in   (the) figures   these since
1891.
1891.

† Today higher numbers are most frequently quoted in English; however, the
Gaelic equivalents of the above are: 80,978 *ceithir fichead mìle, naoi ceud is trì
fichead 's a h-ochd deug*, 1961 *mìle naoi ceud is trì fichead 's a h-aon*, 4,099 *ceithir
mìle is ceithir fichead 's a naoi deug*, 94·6 *ceithir fichead 's a ceithir deug puing a sè*
2,329 *dà mhìle trì cheud is naoi air fhichead*, 94·8 *ceithir fichead 's a ceithir deug deug
puing a h-ochd*, 1891 *mìle ochd ceud is ceithir fichead 's a h-aon deug*.

Anns an Fhasan (In Fashion) – from an advertisement:
   Briogaisean cruachainn   ann an denim cotain
   Trousers   of-hip (hipsters) in in denim of-cotton
soilleir,   siop air a' bheulaidh, crios tana
light(-coloured), zip on the front,   belt narrow

3 'Has declined with the falling population of the islands', 4 'The majority
speak both languages', 5 'There is no other district'.

Scots Gaelic

teann,   dathan: odhar agus gorm, agus leine na
tight(-fitting), colours: fawn and blue, and shirt of-the
fhraoich   a' freagairt air   na briogaisean.
heather (bush shirt) to match   (on) the trousers.

Dreasaichean de dhenim cotain   Frangach le   putanan móra,
Dresses   of denim of-cotton French   with buttons big,
dathan: donn   agus liath. Airson aodach feasgair   gheibh sibh
colours: brown and grey. For   wear of-evening will-get you
na   dreasaichean so   le   sgiortaichean làna no dlùth ris a'
(the) dresses   these with skirts   full or close to the
bhodhaig.
body (close-fitting).

Frocaichean de Dhacron, dathan ciùine le   orainds agus
Frocks   of Dacron, colours quiet with orange and
cyclamen maoth.
cyclamen soft.

Tha an t-uamhas   againn cuideachd de dreasaichean
Is   the great-quantity at-us   also   of dresses
Tricel   striopach is   flùranach. Aodaichean tràghad – tha
of-Tricel striped   and floral.   Wear   of-beach is
roghainn gun   chrìch agaibh an so.
choice   without limit at-you here.

Bithidh sibh anns an fhasan aig   an taigh no anns an
Will-be you in   the fashion about the house or in   the
Roinn-Eòrpa.
Continent-Europe.

Sgrìobhaibh gu Copland agus Lye, Sauchiehall Street,
Write   to Copland and Lye, Sauchiehall Street,
Glaschu, C2.
Glasgow, C2.

LITERATURE

G. Calder, *A Gaelic Grammar* (1923, reprinted 1972).
N. MacAlpine and J. MacKenzie, *Gaelic–English and English–Gaelic Dictionary*, also available in separate volumes as N. MacAlpine, *Pronouncing Gaelic–English Dictionary*, and J. MacKenzie, *English–Gaelic Dictionary*; often reissued, the two parts going back to 1832 and 1845 respectively.
E. Dwelly, *The Illustrated Gaelic–English Dictionary* (1901–11), often reprinted; the most comprehensive dictionary yet compiled.

Irish Celtic

Descriptions of spoken Gaelic include:
M. Oftedal, *The Gaelic of Leurbost, Isle of Lewis* (1956).
N. M. Holmer, *The Gaelic of Kintyre* (1962).

Specimens of folk literature are conveniently accessible in the classic collection by A. Carmichael, *Carmina Gadelica/Ortha nan Gaidheal*, vols. i–v, 1928–54, vol. vi (Glossary and Indexes), 1970 (Bilingual).

Enquiries regarding works in or about Scots Gaelic may be made to Gairm Publications, 29 Waterloo Street, Glasgow, C2, Scotland.

CHAPTER EIGHT

Manx

𝕊𝕊𝕊𝕊𝕊𝕊

MANX is descended from the Gaelic introduced in the fourth century AD into the Isle of Man by its Irish conquerors. The island had been British-speaking. In the ninth century, Man was again invaded, this time by Norsemen, the territory eventually forming a province with the Norse-held Hebrides or *Suðreyjar* 'South Islands', hence the modern bishopric of Sodor and Man. The hegemony of the men of Norway continued under local kings nominally subject to the Norwegian Crown until the death of the last of these in 1265, after which the government of the island passed to Scotland by the Treaty of Perth in 1266. It is more than likely that by this time the Norse element on Man will have been gaelicized, as it appears to have been in the Hebrides also. Scottish rule was short-lived. English nominees soon appear among the Lords of Man, and English suzerainty became permanent in 1333. In 1765 the island was formally taken over by the British Crown. It enjoys, however, a large measure of home rule. It has to this day its own parliament, the Tynwald, which levies taxes and controls expenditure.

Although Scottish and then English overlordship led to the official use of English, there can be little doubt that Manx was universally spoken until the beginning of the eighteenth century at least. However, a knowledge of the foreign tongue as a second language had made appreciable progress in the century before. In 1656, a traveller reported that 'few speak the English tongue', but some forty years later Camden's *Britannia* (1695) states that the town dwellers understood English and could also speak it. The position of English in the towns gained strength and by the end of the eighteenth century a wave of immigration from England, which continued for a generation or so, turned the Manx towns into focal points of anglicization. A writer to the British and Foreign Bible Society in 1817 put the number of English speakers at 7,000 out of a total of 21,000 adults. Shortly afterwards, emigration from the still pretty solidly Manx-

137

speaking northern and southern districts grievously weakened the native language and spelled out its imminent doom. In his preface to Kelly's *Manx Grammar* (1859), the editor writes: 'The decline of the spoken Manx, within the memory of the present generation has been marked. . . . In our churches the language was used by many of the present generation of clergy three Sundays in the month. It was afterwards restricted to every other Sunday; and is now entirely discontinued in most of the churches. In the schools throughout the Island the Manx has ceased to be taught; and the introduction of the Government system of education has done much to displace the language. It is now seldom heard in conversation, except among the peasantry.'

By about 1870 the language had become moribund, as children after this date did not usually acquire Manx. The first census, taken in 1901, returned 4,657 speakers, mostly of the oldest generation, of whom all but 59 spoke English as well. In 1911 the figure was 2,832, all bilingual; in 1921 it was 896; in 1931 a bare 529. A careful enquiry just after the Second World War showed that only a score of native speakers were then left, all aged persons who had used Manx in their childhood with parents or grandparents, though they had scarcely ever spoken it since and had consequently forgotten a great deal. Ten years later these last guardians of the native tongue of Ellan Vannin were no more.

The first known text in Manx is a translation of the 1604 edition of the Book of Common Prayer, thought to have been completed about 1610. The first printed book is a tract on the duties of a Christian and dated 1707. The whole Bible appeared in 1771–73 and its forms are regarded as the literary standard. Altogether a modest literature appeared, mostly in the latter half of the eighteenth, and early decades of the nineteenth century. A considerable amount of both original and translated material, prose and verse, mostly of a religious nature like the printed work, has survived in manuscript. The absence of any amount of traditional matter in Manx is to be attributed to the long period of foreign domination and the indifference of the educated families. As a picturesque relic of ancient democracy, however, the Manx language still plays a part in government ceremonial. Acts of Tynwald were formally promulgated in English and Manx, though the latter was not usually printed. Since 1865, a Manx abstract has sufficed.

Though Manx is extinct, a number of Gaelic expressions have

passed into the English used locally. Some of these are indispensable, as *carval* lit. 'carol', but specifically a ballad on a religious subject, a genre peculiar to the Isle of Man; further the designations of such figures of folk imagination as *buggane* 'hobgoblin' or *phynnodderee* 'satyr'. Needless to say the place names are largely Gaelic – a valley is always *glen* in imitation of Manx *glione* – as are also most traditional personal names, commonly patronymics beginning with *c* (*k*, *qu*), a relic of *mac* 'son', as *Callister* for *Mac Allister*, *Kissack* for *Mac Isaac*, *Quayle* = Sc. Gael. *Mac Phàil* 'son of Paul'.

SKETCH OF MANX

Phonetics

Traditional Gaelic orthography has never been used for Manx. Spellings based on English were employed from the beginning and took final shape, more or less, in the Bible translation of 1771–73. It was no easy matter, however, for the orthoepists to adapt the wayward principles of English spelling to the complex sound patterns of a Gaelic language and numerous inconsistencies could hardly be avoided. The actual pronunciation of Manx was only scientifically recorded during the last seventy-five years or so of its existence and is very often much at variance with the orthography.

Needless to say, living Manx speech was always dialectal, there being no spoken standard. As with other Gaelic, our description is again necessarily a compromise, but enables us to pronounce the written word with acceptable accuracy.

The stress commonly falls on the first syllable, but there are frequent exceptions, as *ordaag* [or'dɛːg] 'thumb', *livrey* [liv'reː] 'deliver'.

Vowel Sounds

Reference is to stressed vowels, unless otherwise stated. Note that *i* in combination with other vowels most commonly has no value of its own, but serves to indicate the palatal quality of the adjacent consonant, thus *nieu* [ńeu] 'poison', *fuill* [fulʼ] 'blood'.

[a] is represented by *a*, also when unstressed, as *arran* [aran] 'bread'.

[aː] is represented by *a*, as *cabbyl* [kaːvəl] 'horse'.

[e] is represented by *e*, sometimes *ea*, as *lesh* [lʼeʃ] 'with', *breac* [brek] 'trout'.

139

[eː] is represented by *e*, sometimes *ea*, *ey*, as *queig* [kweːǵ] 'five', *breag* [breːg] 'lie, falsehood', *keyll* [keːl] 'narrow, slender', also by *ai*, *aiy*, as *mair* [meːr] 'finger', *faiyr* [feːr] 'grass', further by *e* in words with final mute *e*, as *hene* [heːn] 'self'.

[ɛː] is represented by *aa*, as *laa* [lɛː] 'day', also by *ay*, *ea*, as *ayr* [ɛːr] 'father', *nearey* [nɛːrə] 'shame', further by *a* in words with final *e* mute, as *bane* [bɛːn] 'white', and occasionally otherwise, as *dy bragh* [də brɛːχ] 'for ever'; notice *aeg* [ɛːg] 'young', *seihll* [sɛːl] 'world; luck'.

[i] is represented by *i*, as *çhirrym* [ʧirəm] 'dry', occasionally by *ui*, as *cruink* [kriŋk] 'hills', also by *y*, as *nyn* [nin] 'our, your, their'; notice *Gaelg* [gilg] 'Manx (language)'; in unstressed syllables by *i*, as *casherick* [kaʒərik] 'holy'; notice *reeriaght* [ri'riːaχt] 'kingdom'.

[iː] is represented by *ee*, also *eea*, *eey*, as *çheer* [ʧiːr] 'land', *yeean* [jiːn] 'bird', *feeyn* [fiːn] 'wine'; in unstressed syllables by *ee*, as *fuiree* [furiː] 'wait!'.

[o] is represented by *o*, as *bog* [bog] 'soft'; notice *jough* [ʤoχ] 'drink (noun)'.

[oː] is represented by *o* in words with final mute *e*, as *trome* [troːm] 'heavy', also by *oa*, *ow*, *oy*, as *foast* [foːst] 'yet', *towl* [toːl] 'hole', *gloyr* [gloːr] 'glory'.

[ɔː] is represented chiefly by *oa*, *oay*, occasionally by *o*, *au*, as *noa* [nɔː] 'new', *roayrt* [rɔːrt] 'spring tide', *moddey* [mɔːðə] 'dog', *shiaull* [ʃɔːl] 'sail (noun)'.

[œː] is represented by *y*, as *myr* [mœr] 'as'.

[øː] is represented by *eay*, sometimes *aa*, as *geayl* [gøːl] 'coal', *Baarle* [bøːrlə] 'English'; notice *seose* [søːs] 'up'.

[u] is represented by *u*, as *muc* [muk] 'pig', also by *oo*, as *dooinney* [duńə] 'man'; notice *coyrle* [kurl] 'counsel'.

[uː] is represented by *oo*, *ooa*, *ooy*, as *doo* [duː] 'black', *mooar* [muːr] 'big', *shooyl* [ʃuːl] 'walking', by final *eau*, as *slieau* [sl′uː] 'mountain', also by *u* in words with final *e* mute, as *kiune* [k′uːn] 'calm', or when final, as *jiu* [ʤuː] 'today', further by *uy*, as *shuyr* [ʃuːr] 'sister'; notice *briw* [brjuː] 'judge'.

[ə] is represented by unstressed *a*, *e*, *ey*, *y*, see above, *passim*, also eg, *nyn oi* [nən 'ei] 'against us, you, them'.

[ai] is represented by *ie*, also *ai*, *aie*, as *mie* [mai] 'good', *ain* [ain]

'at us', *traie* [trai] 'beach', further by *eigh*, as *leigh* [lai] 'law', and by *i* in words with final *e* mute, as *drine* [drain] 'thorn'; notice *riyr* [rair] 'last night'.

[au] is represented by *au, auy, eau*, as *niau* [ńau] 'heaven', *liauyr* [l′aur] 'long', *blieaun* [bl′aun] 'milking', also by *oau, oauy*, as *loau* [lau] 'rotten', *roauyr* [raur] 'fat; beef', occasionally by *aw*, as *shawk* [ʃauk] 'hawk', further by *ou, ouy, ow*, as *sourey* [saurə] 'summer', *fouyr* [faur] 'autumn', *dow* [dau] 'ox'.

[ei] is represented by *ei, eiy, oi, oie*, as *leih* [lei] 'forgive', *lheiy* [lei] 'calf', *noi* [nei] 'against', *oie* [ei] 'night'.

[eu] is represented by *eu, aue*, as *çheu* [tʃeu] 'side', *laue* [leu] 'hand'; notice *cliwe* [kleuː] 'sword'.

[ui] is represented by *uigh, ooie*, as *buigh* [bui] 'yellow', *mooie* [mui] 'out', also *uy*, as *nuy* [nui] 'nine'; notice *twoaie* [tui] 'north'.

An epenthetic vowel may develop between certain consonants, as *focklyn* [fokələn] 'words'.

Consonants

As in Scottish Gaelic, the contrast between velar and palatal qualities has been lost in the case of labials. In Manx, moreover, palatalization has often been given up in other consonants, too, and the disappearance of true velarization has further greatly modified the inherited Gaelic system.

Consonants are frequently written double, a purely orthographical device having no affect on the pronunciation.

A mute *h* is written in many words after *l, t* (and its eclipsed form *d*), as *lhon* [lon] 'blackbird', *thie*, eclipsed *dhie* 'house', but alternative spellings without *h* are also found, hence *lon*, etc.; rad. *d* and other letters are occasionally treated in this way, notably *n*, as *nhee* [ńiː] 'thing'. Mute *h* is sometimes added after a vowel, especially when final, as *veih* [vei] 'from'.

An *i* is commonly written before or after *l, n, k, g*, often also after *çh, j*, sometimes after *sh*, when these occur before a back vowel: *çheh* [tʃeː] 'hot', but *çhiass* [tʃas] 'heat', *shiaght* [ʃaχt] 'seven', *jiarg* [dʒarg] 'red', *queig* [kweːġ] 'five', *kiune* [k′uːn] 'calm', *ooilley* [ul′ə] 'all', *niart* [ńart] 'strength'.

[j] is represented by *i*, as *bieau* [bjuː] 'swift', *miolaght* [mjɔːlaχt] 'temptation', *iu* [juː] 'drinking', occasionally by *e*, as *Ew* [juː] 'Jew'.

[k] is represented by *c* before *a, o, u*, or before another consonant,

by *k* before *e*, *i*, either letter occasionally replaced by *ck*; [sk] is *sch* in a few words, as *schoill* [skolʹ] 'school'.

The letters *p*, *t*, *k*, (*c*) are pronounced as in other Gaelic, except when occurring between vowels, when *k* is usually voiced, as *fakin* [fagin] 'seeing', while *p*, *t* commonly represent [v, ð] respectively, as *appee* [aːviː] 'ripe', *baatey* [bɛːðə] 'boat'. Medial *b*, *d* also usually represent spirants, again [v, ð] respectively, as *pibbin* [pivin] 'puffin', *coodagh* [kuːðaχ] 'cover (noun)'. Similarly, original palatal *t*, *d* usually become [ʒ], as *aittin* [aʒin] 'gorse', *sheidey* [ʃeːʒə] 'blowing', *maidjey* [maːʒə] 'stick', cf. Ir. *aiteann* [atʹən], *séideadh* [ʃeːdʹə], *maide* [madʹə]. Intervocalic *s*, *ss* are sometimes [z], as *faasaag* [fɛːzɛːg] 'beard', *assyl* [azəl] 'donkey', but very commonly [ð], as *greesagh* [griːðaχ] 'embers', *shassoo* [ʃaːðuː] 'standing'. Medial *sh* is [ʒ], as *toshiagh* [toʒaχ] 'leader'.

The digraph *ch* occurs mostly in initial position, representing [χ] before consonants or back vowels, as *my chree* [mə χriː] 'my heart, my love' (rad. *cree*), *cha* [χa] 'not', and [ç] before front vowels, as *dty chione* [də çoːn] 'thy head' (rad. *kione*); notice *echey* [egə] 'at him'.

The digraph *gh*, when initial, represents [ɣ] before consonants or back vowels, as *dy ghra* [də ɣrɛː] 'to say', *my ghorrys* [mə ɣorəs] 'my door' (rad. *gra*, *dorrys*), and [j] before front vowels, as *dty ghioot* [də juːt] 'thy gift' (rad. *gioot*). It also occurs between (original) back vowels and is pronounced [ɣ], as *claghyn* [klaɣən] 'stones', and before *t* when it is [χ], as *noght* [noχt] 'tonight'. When final, *gh* represents [χ] after back vowels, as *bwaagh* [bwɛːχ] 'pretty', but is silent after front vowels, as *cleigh* [klai] 'hedge'.

The digraph *çh* and the letter *j* represent [tʃ, dʒ] respectively; *g* is occasionally followed by a functionless *u*, as *guilley* [gilʹə] 'lad'; notice *guoiee* [goiː] 'geese'; in a few words, radical *ph* is used for [f], as *phadeyr* [faˈdeːr] 'prophet'.

Initial Mutations

Aspiration (lenition) remains as much a feature of Manx as of other Gaelic, the same consonants being involved under comparable conditions. Only the orthographic representation is necessarily different in most cases, as follows:

p > *ph*; *t*/*th*, *çh* > *h*; *c*/*k* > *ch* (*qu* > *wh*); *b* > *v*; *d*/*dh* > *gh* (*j* > *y*); *g* > *gh*; *f*/*ph* disappear; *s*, *sh* > *h* (disappear before consonant, thus *sl* > *l*).

Eclipsis (nasalization) is found after *nyn* 'our, your, their', and after the gen. pl. article, except in the case of *d/dh* and *g*, which are aspirated: *p>b*; *t/th>d/dh* (*çh>j*); *c/k/q>g*; *b>m*; *d/dh>gh* (*j>y*); *g>gh*; *f/ph>v*.

After the article (p. 144): *s* before vowels >*t* (*sh>çh*), *sl>cl*, *str>tr*.

Words beginning with a vowel take an *h*-prefix under certain conditions as in other Gaelic.

It is necessary to add, however, that the above changes are met with only in careful literary style. In the spoken Manx known to us, the traditional system of initial mutations was much decayed, and in the final stage of the language clearly breaking up. Many texts therefore show numerous irregularities, including the absence of expected mutation.

Nouns

The reduction of inflexions has gone very much further than in Irish or Scots Gaelic. A fair number of common words preserve a distinct singular genitive, but otherwise only the singular and plural are distinguished morphologically, though mutations remain significant, as in the cognate languages. Manx forms a large number of plurals with the ending *-yn*, akin to the Scottish *-an*; the two languages have here shared a common development. The nouns quoted in the Old Irish section survive in Manx as follows:

fer m. 'man', pl. *fir*; *skeeal* m. 'story', gen. *skeealee*, pl. *skeealyn*; *jalloo* m. 'statue', pl. *jallooyn*; *craue* m. 'bone', pl. *craueyn*; *sooill* f. 'eye', gen. *sooilley*, pl. *sooillyn*; *mooir* f. 'sea', gen. *marrey*, pl. *mooiraghyn*; *cah* m. 'battle', pl. *cahnyn*; *dorrys* m. 'door', gen. *dorrysh*, pl. *dorrysyn*; *keyrrey* f. 'sheep', gen. *keyrragh*, pl. *kirree*; *ree* m. 'king', pl. *reeghyn*; *çhengey* f. 'tongue', pl. *çhengaghyn*; *carrey* m. 'friend', pl. *caarjyn*; *coo* m. 'hound', pl. *coyn*; *Nerin* f. 'Ireland'.

Adjectives

There is no declension, but attributive adjectives, especially when monosyllabic, may take a plural ending: *begg* 'small', plural *beggey*.

Comparative and superlative, not formally distinguished, are expressed by adding *s* to the positive which, if monosyllabic, takes the ending *-ey*, thus *aalin* 'beautiful', *s'aalin* 'more, most beautiful',

Irish Celtic

boght 'poor', *s'boghtey* 'poorer, poorest'. There is some irregular comparison, eg, *mie* 'good', *share* 'better, best', *olk* 'bad', *smessey* 'worse, worst'; *shenn* 'old', *ard*, 'high', have comparative-superlative *shinney, syrjey*.

Numbers

Counting: 1 *nane*, 2 *jees*, 3 *three*, 4 *kiare*, 5 *queig*, 6 *shey*, 7 *shiaght*, 8 *hoght*, 9 *nuy*, 10 *jeih*, 11 *nane-jeig*, 12 *ghaa-yeig*, 13 *three-jeig*, 14 *kiare-jeig*, 15 *queig-jeig*, 16 *shey-jeig*, 17 *shiaght-jeig*, 18 *hoght-jeig*, 19 *nuy-jeig*, 20 *feed*, 21 *nane as feed*, 30 *jeih as feed*, 40 *daeed*, 50 *jeih as daeed*, 60 *three feed*, 70 *jeih as three feed*, 80 *kiare feed*, 90 *jeih as kiare feed*, 100 *keead*, 1000 *thousane*.

The following are used with nouns: 1 *un*, 2 *daa*, 12 *daa yeig*, eg, *daa ghooinney yeig* '12 men'.

Definite Article

Sg. nom. acc. dat.	masc.	fem.	pl.
	yn	*yn*	*ny*
gen.	*yn*	*ny*	*ny*

Before consonants *yn* is commonly reduced to *y*, thus *yn* or *y dorrys* 'the door'.

The article coalesces with a preposition ending in a vowel: *da'n lugh* 'to the mouse'.

The form *ny* prefixes *h* to a noun beginning with a vowel: *ny hagglish* 'of the church', *ny hagglishyn* '(of) the churches' (rad. *agglish*, etc.); this aspirate is often omitted in writing.

The singular nominative accusative feminine, genitive masculine, dative eclipse initial *s* followed by *l, r, h*, or a vowel: (nominative accusative) *y clat* 'the rod', *y traid* 'the street', *y tooill* 'the eye', (genitive) *y çhiaull* 'of the sail', (dative) *lesh y clat* 'with the rod', *er y traid* 'on the street', *ayns y tooill* 'in the eye', *jeh'n çhiaull* 'off the sail' (rad. *slat, straid, sooill, shiaull*).

The noun is eclipsed in the genitive plural: *obbyr ny mardyn* '(the) work of the poets' (rad. *bardyn*).

Except when beginning with *d, t, j, çh*, or *s*, the noun is aspirated after the article in the singular nominative accusative feminine, genitive masculine, and dative: *y vraag* 'the shoe', *mullagh y chruink*

144

'(the) top of the hill', *da'n vac* 'to the son', *lesh y choo* 'with the hound', *ayns y cheyll* 'in the wood' (rad. *braag, cruink, mac, coo, keyll*).

There is no indefinite article.

Pronouns

The personal pronouns are as follows: *mee* 'I, me', *oo* 'thou, thee', *eh* 'he, him', *ee* 'she, her', *shin* 'we, us', *shiu* 'you', *ad* 'they, them'. Emphatic forms are common: *mish, uss, eshyn, ish, shinyn, shiuish, adsyn.*

Pronouns are not required with verbal forms which preserve a distinguishing termination, thus *higym* 'I will come', *higmayd* 'we will come', but *hig oo* 'thou wilt come', *hig eh* 'he will come', etc.

Pronouns coalesce with certain prepositions, eg, *ec* 'at': *aym* 'at me', *ayd* 'at thee', *echey* 'at him', *eck* 'at her', *ain* 'at us', *eu* 'at you', *oc* 'at them', with corresponding emphatic *ayms, ayds, echeysyn, ecksh, ainyn, euish, ocsyn*. Other examples include: *er* 'on': *orrym* 'on me', *ort* 'on thee', *er* 'on him', *urree* 'on her', *orrin* 'on us', *erriu* 'on you', *orroo* 'on them', emphatic *orryms*, etc., *lesh* 'with': *lhiam* 'with me', *lhiat* 'with thee', *lesh* 'with him', *lhee* 'with her', *lhien* 'with us', *lhiu* 'with you', *lhieu* 'with them', emphatic *lhiams*, etc.

The possessives are as follows: *my*, before vowels *m'* 'my', *dty*, before vowels *dt'* 'thy', *e* 'his' – all aspirating, *e* 'her' prefixing *h* to vowels, *nyn* 'our, your, their' eclipsing. The preceding are frequently replaced by a circumlocution, thus *y thie aym* lit. 'the house at-me' beside *my hie*; when the plural pronoun would be ambiguous, the circumlocution is usual. The emphasizing particle follows the noun: *my lioar's* 'my book'.

Verbs

The Manx system closely approaches that of Scots Gaelic. The synthetic passive has, however, disappeared, and of the imperative only the second person survives.

The Old Irish verbs conjugated on pp. 89–93 continue as follows:

Verbal noun: *lhiggal* 'allowing'.

Active

Pres. sg. 1 *ta mee lhiggal* lit. 'I am allowing', *t'ou lhiggal*, etc.
Fut. sg. 1 *lhiggeeym*, emphatic *lhiggeeym's*, 2 *lhiggee oo*, 3 *lhiggee eh*, pl. 1 *lhiggeemayd*, 2 *lhiggee shiu*, 3 *lhiggee ad*.
Cond. sg. 1 *lhiggin*, 2 *lhiggagh oo*, 3 *lhiggagh eh*, etc.
Imperf. sg. 1 *va mee lhiggal* lit. 'I was allowing', 2 *v'ou lhiggal*, etc., also sg. 1 *ren mee lhiggal* lit. 'I did allow', 2 *ren oo lhiggal*, etc.
Pret. sg. 1 *lhig mee*, 2 *lhig oo*, etc.

Imperative: sg. *lhig*, pl. *lhigjee*

The synthetic tenses were commonly replaced by periphrases, especially in the spoken language:
Fut. sg. 1 *bee'm lhiggal* lit. 'I shall-be allowing', 2 *bee oo lhiggal*, etc., also sg. 1 *nee'm lhiggal* lit. 'I shall-do allowing', 2 *nee oo lhiggal*, etc.
Cond. sg. 1 *veign lhiggal* lit. '(I) would-be allowing', 2 *veagh oo lhiggal*, 3 *veagh eh lhiggal*, etc., also sg. 1 *yinnin lhiggal* lit. '(I) would-do allowing', 2 *yinnagh oo lhiggal*, 3 *yinnagh eh lhiggal*, etc.
There is further a perfect periphrasis: *ta mee er lhiggal* lit. 'I am after allowing', (pluperfect) *va mee er lhiggal* lit. 'I was after allowing'.

Passive

Pres. sg. 1 *ta mee lhiggit* lit. 'I am allowed', also *ta me er my lhiggal* lit. 'I am after my allowing', etc.
Fut. sg. 1 *bee'm lhiggit* lit. 'I shall-be allowed', etc.
Cond. sg. 1 *veign lhiggit* lit. '(I) would-be allowed', etc.
Past sg. 1 *va mee lhiggit* lit. 'I was allowed', etc.

Past participle: *lhiggit*.

Verbal noun: *breh* 'bearing'.

Active

Pres. sg. 1 *ta mee breh*, Fut. sg. 1 *berym*, Cond. sg. 1 *verin*, Imperf. sg. 1 *va mee breh*, Pret. sg. 1 *ver mee*, etc.

Imperative: sg. *ber*, pl. *berjee*.

Passive

Pres. sg. 1 *ta mee ruggit*, Fut. sg. 1 *bee'm ruggit*, Cond. sg. 1 *veign ruggit*, Past sg. 1 *va mee ruggit*, etc.

Past participle: *ruggit.*

Verbal noun: *loayrt* 'speaking'.

Active

Pres. sg. 1 *ta mee loayrt,* Fut. sg. 1 *loayrteeym,* Cond. sg. 1 *loayrin,* Imperf. sg. 1 *va mee loayrt,* Pret. sg. 1 *loayr mee,* etc.

Imperative: sg. *loayr,* pl. *loayrjee.*

Passive

Pres. sg. 3 *t'eh loayrit,* Fut. sg. 3 *bee eh loayrit,* Cond. sg. 3 *veagh eh loayrit,* Past sg. 3 *v'eh loayrit.*

Past participle: *loayrit.*

The Verb 'to be'
Relics of the copula survive, but only the substantive verb is systematically used, as follows:

Verbal noun: *ve* 'being'
Pres. sg. 1 *ta mee,* 2 *t'ou,* 3 *t'eh,* pl. 1 *ta shin,* 2 *ta shiu,* 3 *t'ad,* negative *cha nel mee,* also literary *cha vel mee,* interrogative *vel mee?* neg. *nagh vel mee?*
Fut. sg. 1 *bee'm,* 2 *bee oo,* 3 *bee eh,* pl. 1 *beemayd,* 2 *bee shiu,* 3 *bee ad,* negative *cha bee'm,* interrogative *bee'm?* neg. *nagh bee'm?*
Cond. sg. 1 *veign,* 2 *veagh oo,* 3 *veagh eh,* etc., negative *cha beign,* interrogative *beign?* neg. *nagh beign?*
Past sg. 1 *va mee,* 2 *v'ou,* 3 *v'eh,* pl. 1 *va shin,* 2 *va shiu,* 3 *v'ad,* negative *cha row mee,* interrogative *row mee?* neg. *nagh row mee?*

Imperative: sg. *bee,* pl. *beejee.*

The surviving forms of the copula are chiefly *she* 'it is' and *cha nee* 'it isn't', used for emphasis; they are often idiomatically 'yes' and 'no'.

In the absence of a verb 'to have', possession is commonly expressed by the substantive verb with the preposition *ec* 'at', eg, *ta thie ain* 'we have a house' lit. 'is house at-us'.

READINGS

Raaghyn creeney lit. *Sayings Wise, ie, Proverbs*:
Leah appee, leah loau.
Soon ripe, soon rotten.
Cha nel sonnys gonnys.
Not-is store soreness.
Caghlaa obbyr   aash.
Change of-work (is) rest.
Eaisht lesh dagh cleaysh, eisht dean briwnys.
Listen with each ear,   then do justice.
Ta aile meeley jannoo bry millish.
Is fire gentle making malt sweet.
Lurg roayrt   hig   contraie.
After spring-tide will-come neap-tide.
Ta drogh hammag ny share na   magher foshlit.
Is mean bush   better   than field   open.
Ta'n aghaue veg shuyr da'n aghaue vooar.
Is the hemlock little sister to the hemlock big.
Cur meer da'n feeagh as hig   eh reesht.
Give scrap to the raven and will-come he again.
Cha ren rieau bangan jeeragh gaase er billey cam.
Not did ever bough straight grow on tree crooked.
Nagh insh dou   cre   va mee, agh insh dou   cre ta mee.
Don't tell to-me what was I,   but tell to-me what am I.

(Mutations: *hammag* radical *tammag*, *veg* r. *beg*, *vooar* r. *mooar*.)

Pishag dy stappal roie folley lit. Charm for stopping of-running
of-blood, *ie*, for staunching blood.
Haink three deiney crauee voish y   Raue – Creest, Peddyr
Came three men   godly from (the) Rome Christ Peter
as Paul. Va Creest er y chrosh, yn uill   Echey shilley,
and Paul. Was Christ on the cross   the blood at-him dripping
as Moirrey er ny glioonyn eck   Liorish.   Ghow fer
and Mary   on the knees   at-her beside-Him. Took one
jeu   yn er-obbee   ayns y laue yesh as
of-them the man-of-sorcery (sorcerer) in (by) the hand right and
hayrn Creest crosh harrish.   Haink three mraane aegey harrish
drew Christ cross over-him. Came three women young over

148

yn ushtey. Dooyrt unnane jeu: *'Seose!' Dooyrt nane elley:*
the water said one of-them, 'Up!' Said another,
'Fuirree!' Dooyrt yn trass unnane: 'Stappym's fuill dooinney
'Wait!' Said the third one, 'I-shall-stop blood of-man
ny ben.   Mish dy ghra eh as   Creest dy yannoo eh ayns ennym
or woman. I to say it and Christ to do it in name
yn   Ayr   as   y   Vac as   y   Spyrryd Noo.'
of-the Father and the Son and the Ghost Holy.'

(Mutations: *chrosh* r. *crosh, uill* r. *fuill, yesh* r. *jesh, ghra* r. *gra,*
yannoo r. *jannoo, Vac* r. *Mac.*)

The Tynwald Ceremony:
Ren yn Chiare as   Feed   cummal yn   veeiteil
Did the Four and Twenty (Keys) holding of-the meeting
oc   ec Tinvaal ec Feaill Eion,   tra   va'd   ceau
at-them at Tynwald at Feast of-John, when were they wearing
yn vollan vane   mygeayrt y mysh y   chione, er yn
the wort white (mugwort) about the head, on the
wheigoo laa jeh'n vee   s'jerree jeh'n touree.   Va   ooilley
fifth day of the month last of the summer. Were all
cooishyn reaghit ec yn   Whaiyl shen liorish ny briwnyn,   as
suits decided at (the) Court that by the deemsters, and
ooilley leighaghyn lhait magh hug yn sleih   three keayrtyn, as
all laws read out to the people three times, and
cha row ad   leigh foast derrey va   shen jeant.
not were they law yet until was that done.
   Ec yn traa   t'ayn   ta shirveish cummit
   At the time (which) is in-it (present time) is service held
ayns Keeill Eoin.   Eisht t'ad   shooyl ayns yn   order
in Church of-John. Then they are walking in (the) order
shoh, jees as jees, voish yn cheeill gys y   Chronk Tinvaal:
this two and two from the church to the Hill of-Tynwald:
kiare sessonee,   ny shey toshee-yoarree, ny captanyn ny
four sergeants, the six coroners, the captains of-the
skeeraghyn, ny saggyrtyn, ny briwnyn beggey,   yn
parishes, the clergy, the deemsters petty (high bailiffs), the
Chiare as   Feed   ny fir-coyrlee,   yn er-cliwe,
Four and Twenty (Keys), the counsellors, the sword bearer,

yn chiannoort, yn daa haggyrt reiltys,   *yn er-lhee*
the governor,   the two chaplain of-government, the surgeon
y   *lught-thie, sidooryn, as*   *eisht as wheesh dy leih*   *as*
of-the household, soldiers, and then as many   of people as
sailliu   *geiyrt*   *orroo*   *shen.*
you-wish following on-them those (as many people as wished
              Ta ny shenn toshee-yoarree livrey   *slattyn*
following them). Are the old   coroners   delivering rods
oc   *da'n chiannoort, as*   *ta'n chied*   *vriw*
at-them to the governor,   and is the first (senior) deemster
loo   *ny feallagh noa stiagh. Eisht ta dy chooilley hoshiagh-*
swearing of-the ones   new in.   Then is every   coroner
jioarrey gliooney sheese roish yn chiannoort, as goaill yn clat
       kneeling down before the governor   and taking the rod
echey veih laueyn yn   *chiannoort.*
at-him from hands of-the governor.

   Ta toshiagh-jioarrey Glenfaba   *lhaih*   *ny slattysyn ayns*
   Is   coroner   of-Glenfaba reading the laws   in
Gaelg.
Manx.

(Mutations: *Chiare* r. *Kiare, veeiteil* r. *meeiteil, vollan* r. *bollan, vane*
r. *bane, chione* r. *kione, wheigoo* r. *queigoo, vee* r. *mee, touree* r.
souree, Whaiyl r. *Quaiyl, cheeill* r. *keeill, Chronk* r. *Cronk, er-cliwe* r.
fer-cliwe, chiannoort r. *kiannoort, haggyrt* r. *saggyrt, leih* r. *sleih,*
er-lhee r. *fer-lhee, vriw* r. *briw, hoshiagh-jioarrey* r. *toshiagh-jioarrey,*
tlat r. *slat.*)

Ny Kirree fo Niaghtey – The Sheep under (the) *Snow,* a traditional
ballad:
   Lurg geurey dy niaghtey as   *arragh dy rio*
   After winter of snow   and spring of frost
   Va   *ny shenn chirree marroo as*   *n'eayin*   *beggey bio.*
   Were the old   sheep dead   and the lambs little   alive.

Chorus:
   Oh! irree shiu guillyn as   *gow shiu da'n*   *clieau,*
   Oh! arise, you lads,   and take you to the hill,
   Ta ny kirree fo   *niaghtey cha dowin as v'ad*   *rieau.*
   Are the sheep under snow   as deep as were they ever.

Shoh dooyrt Nicholas, Raby, as   eh ny   lhie çhing:
This said   Nicholas Raby and he in-his lying sick
(Nicholas of Raby, a farm in Lonan parish).
'*Ta ny kirree fo   niaghtey ayns Braid Farrane Fing*'.
'Are the sheep under snow   in   Braid Farrane Fing.'

Shoh dooyrt Nicholas, Raby, goll   seose er y   lout:
This said   Nicholas Raby, going up   to the loft:
'*Dy row my hiaght bannaght er my ghaa housane   muilt.*
'Be   my seven blessings on my two   thousand wethers.

Kirree t' aym ayns y laggan as goair 'sy   clieau   rea,
Sheep are at-me in   the hollow and goats on-the mountain flat,
Kirree keoi   Coan ny   Chishtey nagh   jig
Sheep wild (in) Valley of-the Chest   that-not will-come
   dy bragh veih.'
   ever   from-it (home)'.

Dirree mooinjer Skeeyll Lonan as   hie   ad   er-y-chooyl;
Arose men   of-Kirk Lonan and went they forthwith;
Hooar ad   ny kirree marroo ayns Laggan Varrule.
Found they the sheep dead   in   Hollow of-Barrule.

Dirree mooinjer Skeeyl Lonan   as   Skeeyll y Chreest neesht;
Arose men   of-Kirk Lonan and of-Kirk   Christ   too;
Hooar ad   ny kirree beggey ayns Laggan Agneash.
Found they the sheep little   in   Hollow of-Agneash.

Ny muilt   ayns y toshiaght, ny reaghyn 'sy   vean,
The wethers in   the front   the rams   in-the middle,
Eisht ny kirree trome-eayin   çheet   geiyrt   orroo
Then the sheep heavy-(with)-lambs coming following on-them
shen.
(those).

Ta   molt   aym son Ollick   as jees son y   Chaisht,
Is (a) wether at-me for Christmas and two for (the) Easter,
As   ghaa ny three elley son yn traa yiowym's baase.
And two or three other for the time I-shall-get death (when I
   die).

(Mutations: *niaghtey* r. *sniaghtey*, *chirree* r. *kirree*, *clieau* r. *slieau*,
hiaght r. *shiaght*, *ghaa* r. *daa*, *housane* r. *thousane*, *Chishtey* r. *Kishtey*,
Chreest r. *Creest*, *vean* r. *mean*, *Chaisht* r. *Caisht*.)

Cre ta Gloyr? – What is Glory? by Rev. T. Stephen, early nineteenth
century:

As   cre   ta gloyr, agh aalid   ennym   vie?
And what is glory, but beauty of-name good?
Ennym!   ta myr y   ghall   ta sheidey   shaghey!
(A) name (which) is as   the *gall* (which) is blowing by!
(*gall*, a mist appearing over the sea in certain weather conditions)
Shoh   moylley'n   pobble, my she moylley shen.
This (is) praise of-the people, if *is* praise that (if indeed
    praise it be),
Son cre   ta'n   pobble, agh yiornage anreaghit,
For what is the people but skein   undone (ravelled),
Earroo neuçhinjagh   ta son jannoo mooar
Crowd inconstant (which) is for making big
Jeh   nheeghyn eddrym nagh   vel toilçhin   scansh
of (values) things   slight   that-not are deserving of-regard
As   coontey   cadjin   reddyn
And of-account common (of small account) things (which)
    ta feeu   arrym?
    are worth respect?
Ta'd   moylley as   ta'd   ooashlagh   shen nagh
They are praising and they are worshipping that that-not
    nhione   daue,
    is-not-known to-them (they know not what),
    As   shen ta'd   gloyragh jiu,   ta'd   jiooldey
And that they are glorifying today, they are rejecting
    mairagh.
    tomorrow.
Cha 's   oc   eer quoi, agh eer myr
Not knowledge at-them just who, but just as
    tadyr   leeidit
    they-are-after led
(they know not whom exactly, but just as they have been led)
Fer er   fer elley geiyrt,   myr guoiee trooid   doarlish.
One after another, following as   geese through gap.
As   cre'n   cooilleen   t'ayns soiagh vooar
And what the satisfaction (which) is in (a) setting great
    nyn   lheid?
    of-their kind (in esteeming such)?

Manx

Dy veaghey er nyn ennal – goo yn sleih,
To live on their breath (the) word of-the people,
marvaanee lheaystagh, myr y gheay neuhickyr!
mortals wavering as the wind unsteady!
Quoi echey ta resoon veagh blakey lurg oc?
Who at-him is reason would-be gaping after at-them
(who has reason to gape after them)?
Lioroo dy ve lheamysit te moylley.
By-them to be tarnished it-is praising (their blame is praise).

(Mutations: *vie* r. *mie, ghall* r. *gall*, *'s* for *ys* r. *fys, vooar* r. *mooar veaghey* r. *beaghey, gheay* r. *geay*.)

From *Ollick Ghennal – Merry Christmas*, anonymous:
Ollick ghennal erriu as blein feer vie,
Christmas merry on-you and year very good,
Seihll as slaynt da'n slane lught-thie.
Luck and health to the whole household.
Bea, gennalys as bioyr eu ry-cheilley,
Life, joy and sprightliness at-you all-together,
Shee as graih eddyr mraane as deiney.
Peace and love between women and men.
Cooid as cowryn, stock as stoyr,
Goods and wealth, stock and store,
Palçhey puddase as skeddan dy-liooar,
Lots of-potatoes and herring enough,
Arran as caashey, eeym as roauyr.
Bread and cheese, butter and beef.

(Mutations: *ghennal* r. *gennal, vie* r. *mie*.)

LITERATURE

E. Goodwin, *First Lessons in Manx* (1901, reprinted 1947).
J. J. Kneen, *A Grammar of the Manx Language* (1931).
J. Kelly, *Manx–English and English–Manx Dictionary* (1866).
J. J. Kneen, *English–Manx Pronouncing Dictionary* (1938, reprinted 1955, with supplement, 1970).
W. Wood, *Short School Dictionary of Manx Gaelic* (1950).
K. H. Jackson, *Contributions to the Study of Manx Phonology* (1955; account of the pronunciation of the last surviving speakers treated in

relation to the sound system of Gaelic generally, to which it incidently forms a most practical introduction).

A. W. Moore, *Manx Ballads and Music* (1896). Manx originals with literal translations into English.

J. Clague, *Manx Reminiscences/Cooinaghtyn Manninagh* (1911) (A collection of bilingual folklore).

Enquiries regarding works in or about Manx may be made to J. B. Caine, Esq., 3 Royal Terrace, Onchan, Isle of Man.

LATER ARRIVALS

🙚🙚🙚🙚🙚

CHAPTER NINE

Latin

🙚🙚🙚🙚🙚🙚

LATIN first comes into our ken as the minor language of the small province of Latium, in particular as that dialect of the language used in its chief town, Rome. But as early as the fifth century BC, Rome had become an aggressive force and the Latin language followed the expansion of Roman power, eventually replacing nearly all the multifarious languages once spoken in ancient Italy and western continental Europe. It was introduced into Britain at the time of the Claudian invasion in 43 AD and remained in official use here until the withdrawal of the Roman garrisons at the beginning of the fifth century, and to a limited extent afterwards.

To what degree Latin replaced British as a vernacular language is a moot point. If events elsewhere in western Europe are any guide, then one may suppose that Latin was widely adopted by the local population with consequent loss of the native dialects. On the other hand, the British Isles, being peripheral, were a special case. To begin with, Ireland remained outside the Roman Empire altogether. Next, and perhaps more significantly, Scotland was unsubdued and unsubduable. The Antonine rampart between the Forth and Clyde had to be abandoned in favour of the more substantial Hadrian's Wall further south, and even this required exceptionally large forces for its defence. Lastly, the British Province itself was divided into a military and a civil zone corresponding approximately to the upland areas of the north-west and the lowland areas of the south-east respectively. It seems unlikely that latinization made much progress in the former. Wales, moreover, appears to have maintained a considerable degree of local autonomy. Certainly the British language was not replaced in the west, for we have Cornish, Welsh and even Cumbric (p. 24) to prove it. But it seems, on balance, that the population in the more accessible and more romanized south-east would be largely Latin-speaking, at any rate in the towns, where there would also be a considerable foreign-born element using Latin either as the native medium or the lingua franca. No doubt there was an appreciable amount of bilingualism in Roman Britain, too. But, in any case, Latin was everywhere the language of prestige. Moreover, it was the only written language. It was indeed the first language ever to be so used in these islands, and the cultivation of Latin by non-native speakers inaugurated a tradition which survived until recent times.

Literary Latin is essentially that form of the language employed in the Classical Period (80 BC to 120 AD). From the evidence of non-literary inscriptions, however, it is seen that the spoken language was even then becoming noticeably different from the literary form, especially during the latter part of the period. The spoken Latin of the first five Christian centuries is termed Vulgar Latin. By the end of this time, the vernacular had become so far removed from the stabilized written norm that the latter was effectively a dead language. Moreover, the dialects of evolving Vulgar Latin were characterized by tangible regional differences, as Italian, Spanish, Gaulish. From the Vulgar Latin of these and other places arose the modern Romance languages.

A comparable development must have taken place in Britain. The Vulgar Latin in use here will also have assumed local features as it evolved towards a distinctive British type of Romance. But spoken Latin was not destined to survive in Britain. It did, however, considerably influence the native British dialects, and this influence is traceable today in the many Latin loan words found in the derivative Welsh, Cornish and Breton. Owing to the advanced phonology of these languages, it is no longer possible, as a rule, to distinguish specifically Romano-British developments as such. But occasionally a regionalism appears plainly enough, as the jocular use of *plantae* lit. 'plants' for human offspring, presupposed by Welsh *plant* 'children'.

After the Roman withdrawal from Britain, the native Celtic element was apparently in the ascendancy (p. 24). We imagine that spoken Latin will have begun to decline, to be finally obliterated by the English flooding into the country from the middle of the fifth century. But whatever the fate of spoken Latin in Britain, it is certain that the language continued to be used for literary purposes, and even when the Anglo-Saxons had introduced the new, illiterate order, the remnant of the British retained some knowledge of Latin as the medium of their Christianity and passed this knowledge on to the Irish. It will be remembered that St Patrick was a fifth-century Briton.

A not inconsiderable amount of Latin literature dealing with Britain during the Roman occupation was produced by contemporary writers, but it is uncertain whether any of it was actually composed in Britain. No native British authors are known from this period, but a large amount of epigraphical material dating back to Roman times has been found – the standard collection, R. G. Collingwood and R. P. Wright, *The Roman Inscriptions of Britain*, I (1965) lists over 2,300 of them, and new discoveries are made from time to time.

The Anglo-Saxons, who by the mid-seventh century occupied most of present-day England and south-east Scotland, had brought with them the runic alphabet, with magical associations (p. 190), but no written literature. When they did begin to practise literacy in the proper sense of the term, it was through the medium of Latin, which first reached them with the coming of Christianity in 597. Latin was the official language of the Roman Church as of the contemporary states in western Europe, and it was soon playing a similar role in Anglo-Saxon England, too. Eventually, though hardly before the eighth century, the Anglo-Saxons took to writing their own language, but Latin continued to be employed as the major literary language throughout the Anglo-Saxon period. The arrival of the Normans in 1066 in no way compromised the position of Latin. The new masters of the country, it is true, cultivated their French mother tongue and produced an extensive literature in it, but they also employed Latin for many official purposes, as well as for pure literature, if anything showing a greater propensity towards it than the Anglo-Saxons. This use of Latin continued throughout the Middle Ages. Domesday Book and Magna Charta were drawn up in Latin, as were most of the historical records of medieval England. Works of learning were chiefly composed in Latin – a truly international medium for much of Europe at the time. Latin likewise dominated in compositions of a religious nature. Poetry flourished as well as prose. Every literary genre is represented in the creations of original writers. Moreover, Latin was also an oral medium and the language of higher education.

But changes came with modern times. By then the main vernaculars had enjoyed a period of literary cultivation and become hallmarks of nationhood. English was no exception. From the beginning of Tudor times, the role of Latin as the traditional medium of the formal document steadily declined. It was fast becoming an anachronism in the seventeenth century and an act of 1650 put an end to its use in domestic records. This measure was repealed at the Restoration, but a similar enactment in 1731, taking effect in 1733, finally established English as the sole official medium. By the mid-seventeenth century Latin had, indeed, been effectively indispensable only in those spheres which had international relevance, as diplomacy and scholarship. John Milton is often remembered as Cromwell's Latin secretary; but Milton stood at the end of an era. In the next generation French became the accepted medium of diplomatic exchanges, thanks to the prestige of the court of Louis XIV. In the field of learning the use of Latin persisted rather longer. Isaac Newton wrote his *Principia* (1687) in that language and works of scholarship in Latin were still quite common in the early years of the next century. But then, as elsewhere in Europe, the vernacular came fully into its own in this last significant area. The Roman Church has been the staunchest upholder of Latin, still its official medium and only recently replaced in the Mass. To a minute extent Latin survives in ceremonial use at certain ancient universities. It provides an international nomenclature for botany, zoology and medicine.

Some knowledge of Latin has been kept alive by school teaching, though its place in the curriculum has much declined in this century and continues to do so. Today only a few people can be said to possess a really comprehensive command of the language. Very occasionally, a book in Latin makes its appearance, usually in connection with Classical studies; among exceptions are the recent translations *Alicia in Terra Mirabili* and *Winnie ille Pu*, a sort of don's delight. But to all intents and purposes, Latin now belongs to history.

As a consequence of its pre-eminent position in our civilization, the Latin language has been of immense significance. It has had considerable influence on the style and syntax of literary English and has provided our language with many thousands of words, essentially terms adopted to express the refinements of advanced knowledge. This element was acquired chiefly during the Renaissance in the fifteenth, and especially the sixteenth, centuries.

It remains to be said, however, that Latin never occupied such a strong position in the Celtic parts of the British Isles as it did in England. The independent Celtic peoples cultivated Latin as a sacral tongue, but for other purposes, as law and administration, the medium was the native Celtic. Hence the extensive legal writings in medieval Irish and Welsh, historiography in Irish, etc.

SKETCH OF LATIN

The following grammatical outline refers to the classical language. Its morphology is equally valid for Medieval Latin, though the pronunciation has changed (see under Orthography below). In stylistic matters, Medieval Latin was influenced by the often unclassical idiom of the Vulgate and the writings of the Fathers of the Church. There was now no native feeling for the medium – there is inevitably something artificial in the cultivation of a dead language – and solecisms often betray the influence of the writer's own vernacular. But though Latin was dead in the sense that it was no longer anyone's mother tongue, it was still very much alive in its own setting. It was variously modified, evolving new expressions to keep pace with changing demands, sometimes borrowing from the vernaculars in the process. Thus Anglo-Latin contains a number of features peculiar to itself, including elements deriving from English and Norman French.

The rich inflexional system of Latin permitted great freedom of word order which, in the spoken language, would reflect emphasis and other idiomatic subtleties. Literary Latin often carried this freedom to remarkable lengths and this, together with certain syntactical constructions, among which we mention the ablative absolute (p. 167), encouraged an involved style employing ponderous periods far removed from any ordinarily spoken language. Though difficult, such style was felt to be elegant and the ability to use it a sign of education. Cicero's diction is considered exemplary in this respect and, after the revival of classical learning at the beginning of modern times, the humanists took him as their model.

Later Arrivals

Phonetics

The Latin alphabet derives via Etruscan from the Greek Chalkidic form used in the Greek colonies in Italy. In the Middle Ages, and later, it was used to write the vernacular languages of Western Europe.

There are five vowels, *a, e, i, o, u,* which occur both short and long, the latter marked in grammar books with a macron, and six diphthongs, *ae, au, oe, ei, eu, ui,* the last three being infrequent.

The consonants *c, g* are always [k, g], *j* and *v* are [j] and [w] respectively; the latter may be written *i, u,* as *jūs, iūs* 'law', *volō, uolō* '(I) wish'.

The stress falls on the penultimate in disyllabic words (*ámō* '(I) love'), in polysyllabic words on the penultimate if this is long by nature (*amắmus* '(we) love') or by position, *ie,* before two consonants (*amántur* '(they) are loved'), otherwise on the prepenultimate (*amắminī* '(you) are loved').

The above outline of classical pronunciation has, in practice, rarely been adhered to since the classical period itself. In particular, the original distinction between short and long vowels has often been ignored, this being partly a reflection of the actual evolution in Vulgar Latin and partly the result of contamination from the various languages native to those who were using Latin as an acquired tongue. It goes without saying that the intonation was that of the native language of the speaker concerned.

Nouns

There are six cases: nominative, vocative, accusative, genitive, dative, ablative, but a distinct vocative occurs only in the singular of one declension (the second), otherwise the nominative is used. Some cases may share the same endings; this is always so with the dative and ablative plural. The nominative and accusative of neuters are identical, whether singular or plural. There are three genders: masculine, feminine, neuter. Sample paradigms:

First declension, chiefly feminine

Sg. nom. *puella* 'girl', acc. *puellam,* gen. dat. *puellae,* abl. *puellā,* pl. nom. *puellae,* acc. *puellās,* gen. *puellārum,* dat. abl. *puellīs.*

Second declension, chiefly masculine and neuter

Sg. nom. *amīcus* m. 'friend', voc. *amīce,* acc. *amīcum,* gen. *amīcī,* dat. abl. *amīcō*, pl. nom. *amīcī*, acc. *amīcōs*, gen. *amīcōrum*, dat. abl. *amīcīs*.

Sg. nom. acc. *bellum* n. 'war', gen. *bellī*, etc., pl. nom. acc. *bella*, gen. *bellōrum*, etc.

Third declension, all genders

Sg. nom. *amor* m. 'love', acc. *amōrem*, gen. *amōris*, dat. *amōrī*, abl. *amōre*, pl. nom. acc. *amōrēs*, gen. *amōrum*, dat. abl. *amōribus*. Similarly *arbor* f. 'tree'.

Sg. nom. acc. *guttur* n. 'throat', gen. *gutturis*, etc., pl. nom. acc. *guttura*, gen. *gutturum*, etc.

In the case of stems ending in *n*, the declensional pattern is as follows: *ōrdō* m. 'row, order', accusative *ōrdinem*, etc., and similarly *virgō* f. 'virgin', *nōmen* n. 'name', genitive *nōminis*, etc.

Many nouns have an *s*-element in the nominative singular, there being numerous different stems, visible in the oblique cases, eg, *prīnceps* m. 'leader, prince', acc. *prīncipem*; *rēx* m. 'king', acc. *rēgem*; *rādīx* f. 'root', acc. *rādīcem*; *pēs* m. 'foot', acc. *pedem*; *virtūs* f. 'strength, virtue', acc. *virtūtem*; *mīles* m. 'soldier', acc. *mīlitem*; *opus* n. 'work', gen. *operis*; *tempus* n. 'time', gen. *temporis*.

Another group (*i*-stems) follows a slightly different declensional pattern, eg, *dēns* m. 'tooth', acc. *dentem*, etc., but pl. gen. *dentium*; *urbs* f. 'city', acc. *urbem*, etc., but pl. gen. *urbium*; *animal* n. 'living creature, animal', gen. *animālis*, etc., but pl. nom. acc. *animālia*, gen. *animālium*; further types: *ignis* m. 'fire', *avis* f. 'bird', acc. *ignem*, *avem*, etc., *mare* n. 'sea', gen. *maris*, etc., but pl. gen. *ignium*, *avium*, *marium* – abl. sg. in -*ī* may also occur, thus more commonly *marī*.

Fourth declension, a small class (*u*-stems), all genders

Sg. nom. *gradus* m. 'step', acc. *gradum*, gen. *gradūs*, dat. *graduī*, abl. *gradū*, pl. nom. acc. *gradūs*, gen. *graduum*, dat. abl. *gradibus*. Similarly *manus* f. 'hand'.

Sg. nom. acc. *cornū* n. 'horn', gen. *cornūs*, etc., pl. nom. acc. *cornua*, gen. *cornuum*, etc.

Fifth declension, a very small class, chiefly feminine

Sg. nom. *rēs* 'thing', acc. *rem*, gen. dat. *reī*, abl. *rē*, pl. nom. acc. *rēs*, gen. *rērum*, dat. abl. *rēbus*.

Adjectives

These follow declensions comparable to those of the first three noun declensions. There are two main patterns, the one to a large extent

Later Arrivals

with distinct endings for all genders, as *altus* 'high', the other distinguishing essentially between animate and inanimate only, as *fortis* 'strong':

Sg. nom. *altus* m., *altum* n., *alta* f., acc. *altum* m. n., *altam* f., etc., ie, according to the second and first declensions respectively.

Sg. nom. *fortis* m. f., *forte* n., acc. *fortem* m. f., *forte* n., etc., ie, according to the third declension, types *ignis, avis, mare*, but sg. abl. always *-ī*.

Some third-declension types do not distinguish gender in the sg. nom., as forms as *fēlīx* m. f. n. 'happy', similarly all present participles, as *amāns* masc. fem. neut. 'loving', acc. *fēlīcem* m. f., *amantem* m. f., etc.

The regular formation of comparative and superlative is as follows: *altior* 'higher', *altissimus* 'highest', *fortior* 'stronger', *fortissimus* 'strongest', *fēlīcior* 'happier', *fēlīcissimus* 'happiest'. There is some irregular comparison, eg, *bonus* 'good', *melior* 'better', *optimus* 'best', *malus* 'bad', *pējor* 'worse', *pessimus* 'worst'.

The superlative declines like *altus*, the comparative according to the third declension (type *amor*), but with neut. sg. nom. acc. *-us*, pl. nom. acc. *-ōra*, thus sg. nom. *altior* masc. fem., *altius* neut., etc.

Numbers

1 *ūnus*, 2 *duo*, 3 *trēs*, 4 *quattuor*, 5 *quīnque*, 6 *sex*, 7 *septem*, 8 *octō*, 9 *novem*, 10 *decem*, 11 *ūndecim*, 12 *duodecim*, 13 *trēdecim*, 14 *quattuordecim*, 15 *quīndecim*, 16 *sēdecim*, 17 *septendecim*, 18 *duodēvīgintī*, 19 *ūndēvīgintī*, 20 *vīgintī*, 21 *ūnus et vīgintī*, 30 *trīgintā*, 40 *quadrāgintā*, 50 *quīnquāgintā*, 60 *sexāgintā*, 70 *septuāgintā*, 80 *octōgintā*, 90 *nōnāgintā*, 100 *centum*, 1000 *mīlle*.

Numbers 1 to 3 inflect: *ūnus* like *altus*; *duo* m. n., *duae* f., acc. *duōs* m., *duo* n., *duās* f., gen. *duōrum* m. n., *duārum* f., dat. abl. *duōbus* masc. neut., *duābus* f.; *trēs* m. f., *tria* n., acc. *do.*, gen. *trium*, dat. abl. *tribus*; 1000 has pl. *mīlia* inflecting like *animālia* (p. 161).

Articles

The classical language does not employ this part of speech to any mentionable extent, though there are rare occurrences of *ille* lit. 'that' and *ūnus* lit. 'one' as definite and indefinite articles respectively.

Medieval Latin sometimes makes a freer use of these, essentially in imitation of the vernaculars.

Pronouns

Paradigms:

Sg. nom.	*ego* 'I'	*tū* 'thou'	*is* 'he'	*ea* 'she'	*id* 'it'	
acc.	*mē*	*tē*	*eum*	*eam*	*id*	
gen.	*meī*	*tuī*	*ēius*	*ēius*	*ēius*	
dat.	*mihi*	*tibi*	*eī*	*eī*	*eī*	
abl.	*mē*	*tē*	*eō*	*eā*	*eō*	
Pl. nom.	*nōs* 'we'	*vōs* 'you'	*eī* m.	*eae* f.	*ea* n. 'they'	
acc.	*nōs*	*vōs*	*eōs*	*eās*	*ea*	
gen.	*nostrum*	*vestrum*	*eōrum*	*eārum*	*eōrum*	
dat. abl.	*nōbīs*	*vōbīs*	*eīs*	*eīs*	*eīs*	

There is a reflexive pronoun, indifferent to gender or number: accusative *sē* 'himself, etc., themselves', genitive *suī*, dative *sibi*, ablative *sē*.

Pronouns are only used as the subject of a verb when special emphasis is required, the verbal terminations themselves being otherwise explicit.

The possessive pronouns for the first two persons are adjectives: *meus* 'my', *tuus* 'thy', *noster* 'our', *vester* 'your'; the third person is expressed by the genitive of the personal pronoun and is therefore invariable: *ēius* 'his, her, its', *eōrum* m. n., *eārum* f. 'their', but the reflexive is an adjective: *suus*.

Verbs

Conjugation is mainly synthetic. There are six tenses of the indicative (present, future, imperfect, perfect, future perfect, pluperfect) and four of the subjunctive (present, imperfect, perfect, pluperfect), three infinitives (present, future, perfect), imperative for second and third persons, and sundry participles and verbal nouns. Verbs fall into four main conjugational classes.

Sample paradigm, first conjugational class:
(Principal parts, ie, indicative present singular 1, infinitive present, indicative perfect singular 1, verbal noun, from which the conjugation can be identified: *amō* '(I) love', *amāre*, *amāvī*, *amātum*).

Later Arrivals

Active

Indicative:

Pres. sg. 1 *amō*, 2 *amās*, 3 *amat*, pl. 1 *amāmus*, 2 *amātis*, 3 *amant*.

Fut. sg. 1 *amābō*, 2 *amābis*, 3 *amābit*, pl. 1 *amābimus*, 2 *amābitis*, 3 *amābunt*.

Imperf. sg. 1 *amābam*, 2 *amābās*, 3 *amābat*, pl. 1 *amābāmus*, 2 *amābātis*, 3 *amābant*.

Perf. sg. 1 *amāvī*, 2 *amāvistī*, 3 *amāvit*, pl. 1 *amāvimus*, 2 *amāvistis*, 3 *amāvērunt*.

Fut. perf. sg. 1 *amāverō*, 2 *amāveris*, 3 *amāverit*, pl. 1 *amāverimus*, 2 *amāveritis*, 3 *amāverint*.

Pluperf. sg. 1 *amāveram*, 2 *amāverās*, 3 *amāverat*, pl. 1 *amāverāmus*, 2 *amāverātis*, 3 *amāverant*.

Subjunctive:

Pres. sg. 1 *amem*, 2 *amēs*, 3 *amet*, pl. 1 *amēmus*, 2 *amētis*, 3 *ament*.

Imperf. sg. 1 *amārem*, 2 *amārēs*, 3 *amāret*, pl. 1 *amārēmus*, 2 *amārētis*, 3 *amārent*.

Perf. sg. 1 *amāverim*, 2 *amāverīs*, 3 *amāverit*, pl. 1 *amāverīmus*, 2 *amāverītis*, 3 *amāverint*.

Pluperf. sg. 1 *amāvissem*, 2 *amāvissēs*, 3 *amāvisset*, pl. 1 *amāvissēmus*, 2 *amāvissētis*, 3 *amāvissent*.

Imperative:

sg. 2 *amā*, 3 *amātō*, pl. 2 *amāte*, 3 *amantō*.

Infinitive:

pres. *amāre*, fut. *amātūrus esse*, perf. *amāvisse*.

Participles:

pres. *amāns*, fut. *amātūrus*.

Verbal nouns:

amandum, amātum, amātū.

Passive

Indicative:

Pres. sg. 1 *amor*, 2 *amāris*, 3 *amātur*, pl. 1 *amāmur*, 2 *amāminī*, 3 *amantur*.

Fut. sg. 1 *amābor*, 2 *amāberis*, 3 *amābitur*, pl. 1 *amābimur*, 2 *amābiminī*, 3 *amābuntur*.

Latin

Imperf. sg. 1 *amābar*, 2 *amābāris*, 3 *amābātur*, pl. 1 *amābāmur*, 2 *amābāminī*, 3 *amābuntur*.

Perf., fut. perf., pluperf. are formed analytically by means of the past participle *amātus* 'loved' and pres., fut., imperf. of the verb 'to be' (see below) respectively, hence perf. sg. 1 *amātus sum* m., *amāta sum* f., etc., fut. perf. sg. 1 *amātus erō*, etc., pluperf. *amātus eram*, etc.

Subjunctive:
Pres. sg. 1 *amer*, 2 *amēris*, 3 *amētur*, pl. 1 *amēmur*, 2 *amēminī*, 3 *amentur*.
Imperf. sg. 1 *amārer*, 2 *amārēris*, 3 *amārētur*, pl. 1 *amārēmur*, 2 *amārēminī*, 3 *amārentur*.

Perf., pluperf. analytic, as in indicative, hence perf. sg. 1 *amātus sim*, etc., pluperf. sg. 1 *amātus essem*, etc.

Imperative:
sg. 2 *amāre*, 3 *amātor*, pl. 2 *amāminī*, 3 *amantor*.

Infinitive:
pres. *amārī*, fut. *amātum īrī*, perf. *amātus esse*.

Participle: *perf. amātus*, further gerundive *amandus* 'lovable'.

One may form some idea of the morphological diversity of the verb by comparing the principal parts of the other classes: Cl. 2 *moneō* 'advise', *monēre*, *monuī*, *monitum*, Cl. 3 *legō* 'read', *legere*, *lēxī*, *lēctum*, Cl. 4 *audiō* 'hear', *audīre*, *audīvī*, *audītum*.

We further illustrate the differences by quoting from the present paradigms of these verbs:

Indic. sg. 1 *moneō*, 2 *monēs*, 3 *monet*, pl. 1 *monēmus*, 2 *monētis*, 3 *monent*; subj. sg. 1 *moneam*, 2 *moneās*, 3 *moneat*, pl. 1 *moneāmus*, 2 *moneātis*, 3 *moneant*.
Indic. sg. 1 *legō*, 2 *legis*, 3 *legit*, pl. 1 *legimus*, 2 *legitis*, 3 *legunt*; subj. sg. 1 *legam*, 2 *legās*, 3 *legat*, pl. 1 *legāmus*, 2 *legātis*, 3 *legant*.
Indic. sg. 1 *audiō*, 2 *audīs*, 3 *audit*, pl. 1 *audīmus*, 2 *audītis*, 3 *audiunt*; subj. sg. 1 *audiam*, 2 *audiās*, 3 *audiat*, pl. 1 *audiāmus*, 2 *audiātis*, 3 *audiant*.

Whereas all regular verbs follow the patterns of the main conjugational classes, the stem formation may vary greatly, especially in the case of verbs belonging to Class 3, as may be seen from the principal parts. Selected examples:

Class 1
(infin. *-āre*):

domō 'tame', *domuī, domitum*; *lavō* 'wash', *lāvī, lautum*; *secō* 'cut', *secuī, sectum*; *stō* 'stand', *stetī, statum*

Class 2
(infin. *-ēre*):

augeō 'increase', *auxī, auctum*; *cieō* 'stir up', *cīvī, citum*; *dēleō* 'blot out', *dēlēvī, dēlētum*; *doceō* 'teach', *docuī, doctum*; *jubeō* 'command', *jussī, jussum*; *moveō* 'move', *mōvī, mōtum*; *prandeō* 'dine', *prandī, prānsum*; *sedeō* 'sit', *sēdī, sessum*; *tondeō* 'shear', *totondī, tōnsum*; *torqueō* 'twist', *torsī, tortum*; *videō* 'see', *vīdī, vīsum*; *voveō* 'vow', *vōvī, vōtum*.

Class 3
(infin. *-ere*):

cadō 'fall', *cecidī, cāsum*; *canō* 'sing', *cecinī, cantum*; *cēdō* 'yield', *cessī, cessum*; *cernō* 'sift', *crēvī, crētum*; *colō* 'till', *coluī, cultum*; *currō* 'run', *cucurrī, cursum*; *emō* 'buy', *ēmī, emptum*; *fingō* 'feign', *fīnxī, fictum*; *flectō* 'bend', *flexī, flexum*; *frangō* 'break', *frēgī, frāctum*; *fundō* 'pour', *fūdī, fūsum*; *gignō* 'beget', *genuī, genitum*; *jungō* 'join', *jūnxī, jūnctum*; *mittō* 'send', *mīsī, missum*; *nōscō* 'know', *nōvī, nōtum*; *pāscō* 'feed', *pāvī, pāstum*; *pellō* 'drive', *pepulī, pulsum*; *petō* 'beseech', *petīvī, petītum*; *pingō* 'paint', *pīnxī, pictum*; *pōnō* 'place', *posuī, positum*; *pungō* 'prick', *pupugī, pūnctum*; *spuō* 'spit', *spuī, spūtum*; *sūmō* 'take', *sūmpsī, sūmptum*; *surgō* 'rise', *surrēxī, surrēctum*; *tangō* 'touch', *tetigī, tāctum*; *terō* 'rub', *trīvī, trītum*; *tollō* 'raise', *sustulī, sublātum*; *trūdō* 'thrust', *trūsī, trūsum*; *ūrō* 'burn', *ussī, ūstum*; *vincō* 'conquer', *vīcī, victum*; *vīvō* 'live', *vīxī, victum*.

Class 4
(infin. *-īre*):

aperiō 'open', *aperuī, apertum*; *fulciō* 'prop', *fulsī, fultum*; *hauriō* 'drain', *hausī, haustum*; *sanciō* 'hallow', *sānxī, sānctum*; *sepeliō* 'bury', *sepelīvī, sepultum*; *veniō* 'come', *vēnī, ventum*; *vinciō* 'bind', *vīnxī, vīnctum*.

Latin

Certain verbs follow a mixed conjugation, as *capiō* 'take', *capere*, *cēpī*, *captum*, similarly *faciō* 'make'. Others show various irregularities, as *dō* 'give', *dare*, *dedī*, *datum*; *edō* 'eat', *ēsse*, *ēdī*, *ēsum*; *eō* 'go', *īre*, *iī*, *itum*; *ferō* 'carry', *ferre*, *tulī*, *lātum*.

A number of verbs active in meaning are nevertheless passive in form; they are termed deponent. Examples are (Class 1) *hortor* 'encourage', (Class 2) *vereor* 'revere', (Class 3) *loquor* 'speak', *ūtor* 'use', perf. part. *locūtus*, *ūsus*, (Class 4) *partior* 'divide'.

The verb 'to be' is irregular in the present: (indic.) sg. 1 *sum* 'am', 2 *es*, 3 *est*, pl. 1 *sumus*, 2 *estis*, 3 *sunt*, (subj.) sg. 1 *sim*, 2 *sīs*, 3 *sit*, pl. 1 *sīmus*, 2 *sītis*, 3 *sint*; also imperf. sg. 2 *es*, 3 *estō*, pl. 2 *este*, 3 *suntō*. The remaining tenses have regular terminations: (indic.) fut. sg. 1 *erō*, imperf. sg. 1 *eram*, perf. sg. 1 *fuī*, fut. perf. sg. 1 *fuerō*, pluperf. sg. 1 *fueram*, (subj.) imperf. sg. 1 *essem*, perf. sg. 1 *fuerim*, pluperf. sg. 1 *fuissem*. Other formations are infin. pres. *esse*, fut. *futūrus esse*, perf. *fuisse*, and fut. part. *futūrus*, also pres. part. *-sēns* (in compounds, as *absēns* 'being away').

The verb *habēre* 'to have' belongs to Class 2 (above).

A note on the ablative absolute construction:

The ablative absolute is a phrase consisting of a noun in the ablative case with an adjective (often a participle) or another noun in agreement with it. The construction describes some circumstance connected with the main sentence, but is syntactically independent of it, eg (p. 168) *dōnante (āream) ... fīliō* 'the son ... donating (the site)', *Gallō et Volusiānō cōnsulibus* 'Gallus and Volusianus being consuls', 'in the consulship of Gallus and Volusianus'.

READINGS

Nine inscriptions from the Romano-British period (restored letters in square brackets, expanded abbreviations in round brackets):

'Cogidubnus inscription', a dedication slab found in 1723 at Chichester. Cogidubnus is believed to be the British king known to have collaborated with the Romans when they landed in 43 AD.

[N]eptuno et Mineruae templum [pr]o salute do[mus]
To-Neptune and Minerva temple for welfare of-house

diuinae   ex auctoritat[e] Ti(beri)   Claud(i)
divine ('Imperial family') by authority   of-Tiberius Claudius
[Co]gidubni regis lega[ti] augusti in Brit(annia) [colle]gium
Cogidubnus king legate   imperial in Britain   guild
fabror(um) et   qui in eo [sunt] d(e) s(uo)
smiths   and (those) who in it are   from their-own
                d(ederunt) donante aream [....]ente Prudentini
(resources) gave   donating site   .... ens of-Prudentinus
fil(io).
son (. . . ens, son of Prudentinus donating the site).

Altar, found in 1822 at Housesteads (Hadrian's Wall), AD 252:
     Deo   Solis   Inuicto   Mitrae Saeculari   Publ(icius)
     To-god of-sun unconquered Mithras lord-of-ages Publicius
Proculinus c(enturio) pro se   et   Proculo fil(io) suo u(otum)
Proculinus centurion for himself and Proculus son   his vow
soluit   l(ibens) m(erito) d(ominis) n(ostris) Gallo et
fulfilled willing rightly   lords   our   Gallus and
Volusi(a)no co(n)s(ulibus).
Volusianus consuls (in the consulship of our lords Gallus and
Volusianus).

Altar, found in 1753 at Bath:
     Locum religiosum per insolentiam   erutum
     Place   sacred   by insolence (insolent hands) wrecked
uirtute et   n(umini) aug(usti)   repurgatum   reddidit
to-virtue and deity   of-emperor cleansed   again restored
G(aius) Seuerius Emeritus c(enturio) reg(ionarius).
Gaius   Severius Emeritus centurion regional.

Altar, found at Bollihope Common, Co. Durham in 1747:
     Siluano   Inuicto sacr(um)   G(aius) Tetius Veturius
     To-Silvanus Invictus holy (altar) Gaius   Tetius Veturius
Micianus pr(ae)f(ectus) alae
Micianus prefect   of-wing (of cavalry detachment)
Sebosiannae ob   aprum   eximiae   formae
Sebosian   on-account-of wild-boar of-exceptional fineness
captum quem multi antecessores eius   praedari   non
caught which many predecessors of-him to-capture not

potuerunt u(oto) s(uscepto) l(ibens) p(osuit)
were-able vow   fulfilled   willing set up (set up this holy altar
in willing fulfilment of his vow).

Milestone, found in 1879 in Lincoln at the intersection of the main
streets of the Roman city, 268–270 AD:
　　Imp(eratori) Caes(ari) Marco Piauonio Victorino P(io)
　　To-emperor Caesar　　Marcus Piavonius Victorinus Pius
F(elici) Inu(icto) Aug(usto) pon[t](ifici) max(imo) tr(ibuniciae)
Felix　Invictus　Augustus　pontifex　　maximus of-tribunician
p(otestatis) p(atri) p(atriae)　　　a　　L(indo)
power　　　father of-(his)-country from Lindum (Lincoln)
S(egelocum)　　　　　　m(ilia)　p(assuum) XIIII
to Segelocum (Littleborough) thousand of-paces   14 (14 miles).

Curse on a leaden plate (pierced with seven nails driven through from
the uninscribed side) found in 1934 in London:
　Tretia(m) Maria(m) defico　et　　illeus (=illius) uita(m) et
　Tretia　Maria　I-curse both her　　　　　　life　　and
me(n)tem et　memoriam (e)t iocinera pulmones intermixta fata
mind　　and memory　and liver(s) lungs　　mixed up　words
cogitata . . .
thoughts . . .

Tombstone, found in 1787 in London, after 197 AD:
　D(is)　　M(anibus)　　　　　　　Fl(auius) Agricola
　To-gods Manes (spirits of the departed): Flavius　Agricola
mil(es) leg(ionis) VI 'sextae' Vict(ricis) u(ixit) an(nos) XLII
soldier of-legion 6th　　　　　Victorious lived　years　42
(*'duos et quadraginta'*) *d(ies) X 'decem' Albia Faustina*
　　　　　　　　　　days 10　　　Albia Faustina
coniugi　　inconparabili f(aciendum) c(urauit)
for-husband incomparable making　　arranged (erected this
memorial).

Tombstone, found about 1815 at Caerleon:
　D(is)　　M(anibus)　　　　　　　Iul(iae)
　To-gods Manes (spirits of the departed) (and) Julia
Nundinae　　　uixit an(nos) XXX ('triginta') Agrius Cimarus
Nundina (who) lived years　30　　　　　　Agrius Cimarus

coniunx   piissimus   f(aciendum) c(uravit)
husband most-devoted making   arranged (erected this
memorial).

Tombstone, found in 1861 at York; a large glass vessel, sealed with
lead, contained the ashes of the deceased:
   D(is)   M(anibus)   *Corellia Optata*
   To-gods Manes (spirits of the departed): Corellia Optata
an(norum) XIII ('tredecim') secreti Manes   qui
of-years   13   hidden spirits of the departed who
regna Acherusia Ditis incolitis   quos parua petunt post
realms Acherusian of-Dis you-inhabit whom small seek   after
lumina uite (=vitae) exiguus cinis et   simulacrum corpo(r)is
lights of-life   meagre ashes and semblance of-body
umbra insontis   gnate (=gnatae) genitor spe   captus
shadow of-innocent daughter   sire   by-hope caught
iniqua supremum hunc nate (=natae, gnatae) miserandus defleo
unjust final   this of-daughter   pitiable   I-bewail
finem Q(uintus) Core(llius) Fortis pat(er) f(aciendum) c(uravit)
end   Quintus   Corellius Fortis father making   arranged
(ye hidden spirits that dwell in Pluto's Underworld, whom the
few ashes and the shadowy semblance of the body seek after
the brief light of life, I, father of an innocent daughter, and
pitiable victim of illusory hopes, bewail this her final end. Her
father, Quintus Corellius Fortis, erected this memorial).

Stanza on the Day of Wrath attributed to St Columba (521–97):
   Regis   regum   rectissimi
   Of-king of-kings most-righteous
   Prope   est dies Domini:
   At-hand is   day of-Lord:
   Dies irae   et   vindictae,
   Day of-wrath and vengeance,
   Tenebrarum et   nebulae,
   Of-darkness and mist,
   Dies mirabilium
   Day of-wondrous
   Tonitruorum   fortium,
   Thunder-claps mighty,

Dies quoque angustiae,
Day also   of-anguish,
Maeroris ac   tristitiae,
Grief   and sorrow,
In quo   cessabit   mulierum
In which will-cease of-women
Amor et   desiderium,
Love and desire,
Hominumque contentio
Of-men-and strife
Mundi   huius et   cupido.
Of-world this   and lust.

From Bede's *Vita sancti Cuthberti* (Life of St Cuthbert), written
between 699 and 705:

   At   ille   egressus   monasterio
   But he (*ie*, Cuthbert) having-gone-out from-monastery
sequente   exploratore descendit   ad mare, cuius ripae
following spy[1]   went-down to sea   whose shores
monasterium idem superpositum erat. Ingressusque
monastery   itself placed-above was[2]. Having-gone-into-and
altitudinem   maris   donec ad collum usque et   brachia
height (depth) of-sea[3] until to neck   up-to and arms
unda tumens assurgeret, pervigiles undisonis   in laudibus
wave swelling surged,   watchful wave-sounding in praises
tenebras noctis   exegit.   Appropinquante autem
darkness of-night he-passed[4]. Approaching,   however,
diluculo   ascendens in   terram denuo coepit   in litore
dawn-twilight[5] going-up onto land   anew he-began on shore
flexis   genibus orare.   Quod dum ageret,   venere
with-bended knees to-pray, which while he-was-doing came
(=*venerunt*) *continuo   duo de   profundo maris quadrupedia*
             straightway two from depth   of-sea four-footed
          quae   vulgo   lutrae vocantur. Haec ante   illum
(animals) which commonly otters are-called. These before him
strata   in arena, anhelitu   suo pedes eius   fovere
prostrate on sand   with-breath their feet   of-him to-warm

1 With a spy following, 2 above the shores of which the monastery itself has
been built, 3 the deep part of the sea, 4 'passed the (watchful) darkness of
night with praises to the sound of the sea', 5 as dawn approached.

coeperunt, ac villo   satagebant extergere. Completoque
began   and with-fur were-trying to-dry.   Completed-and
ministerio, percepta ab   eo   benedictione, patrias sunt relapsa
ministry   received from him blessing,   native   returned
sub   undas.
under waves [6].

From a report of a case in the Hereford Iter, 1292:

Walterus de la Barre et   alii   in brevi nominati attachiati
Walter   de la Barre and others in writ named   attached
fuerunt ad respondendum Johanni Lovet . . . et   unde
were   to answering   of-John Lovet   and whereof
queritur   quod praedictus Walterus et   alii,   die
it-is-complained that aforesaid Walter   and others, on-day
Mercurii   ante   diem dominicum in Ramis
of-Mercury (Wednesday) before day Lord's   in branches
Palmarum   anno   regni   regis   nunc
of-palms (before Palm Sunday) in-year of-reign of-king now
quarto decimo, in ipsum   Johannem Lovet apud
fourteenth,   on himself (the said) John   Lovet at
Hereford vi   et   armis, scilicet gladiis   et   baculis et
Hereford by-force and arms to-wit with-swords and staves and
*   huius   modi, insultum fecerunt, verberaverunt et*
(things) of-this kind onset   made,   beat   and
vulneraverunt, et ibidem inprisonaverunt et   inprisonatum
wounded   and there imprisoned   and (him) imprisoned
decem et octo dies detinuerunt, et bona et   catalla
eighteen   days kept,   and goods and chattels
ipsius   Johannis secum   inventa, scilicet pannos
of-himself (of the said) John   with-him found, to-wit clothes
lecti, robas, arcus et sagittas et alia bona dicti
of-bed robes bows and arrows and other goods of-said
Johannis, ad valentiam viginti   librarum, ceperunt et
John   to value   of-twenty pounds, took   and
asportaverunt, et alia enormia   ei   intulerunt,
carried-away and other grievous (things) to-him did,
contra pacem; et unde   deterioratus est   et damnum
against peace and whereof he-has-suffered loss and damage

6 and their task completed, (and) receiving his blessing, they returned to their
native waves.

habet ad valentiam quadraginta librarum: et   inde   produit
has   to value   of-forty   pounds and thereupon brings
sectam.
suit.

Macaronic verses by James Ryman, second half of fifteenth century:
Ortus est Sol Justitiae ex illibata Virgine (Arisen is the Sun of Justice
from the Virgin undefiled):

Thre kingis on the XIIth daye	
stella micante preuia[1]†	star glittering going-on-ahead
vnto Betheleem they toke theire way	
tria ferentes munera.	bearing three gifts
hym worshyp we now borne so fre	
ex illibata virgine.	from undefiled virgin
They went alle thre that chielde to se	
sequentes lumen syderis[2]	following light of-star
and hym they founde in raggis wounde	
in sinu matris virginis.	in bosom of-mother virgin
hym worshyp, etc.	
For he was king of majeste	
aurum sibi[3] *optulerunt*[4]	gold to-him they-brought
for he was god and ay shal be	
thus devote prebuerunt[5].	frankincense devoutly they-gave
hym worshyp, etc.	
For he was man, they gave hym than	(then)
mirram[6] *que*[7] *sibi placuit*	myrrh which him pleased

† Normalizations (use of *e* for *ae* a feature of later Latin)
1 *praevia*, 2 *sideris*, 3 *ei*, 4 *obtulerunt*, 5 *praebuerunt*, 6 *myrrham*, 7 *quae*.

this infant shone in heven
  trone
qui in presepe[8] *iacuit.*   who in manger lay
hym worshyp, etc.

Warned they were these
  kingis tho
in sompnis[9] *per altissimum*   in dream by most-high
that they ayene no wyse
  shuld go   (gain)
ad Herodem nequissimum.   to Herod most-evil
hym worshyp, etc.

Not by Herode, that wikked
  knyght,
sed per viam aliam   but by another way
they be gone home ageyn full
  right   (went straight back home)
per dei prouidenciam[10].   by God's foresight
hym worshyp, etc.

Ioseph fledde thoo, Mary
  also,
in Egiptum[11] *cum puero*   into Egypt with boy
where they abode till king
  Herode
migrauit ex hoc seculo[12].   departed from this age (*ie*, world)
hym worshyp, etc.

That heuenly king to blis vs
  bringe
quem genuit puerpera   whom bore child-bearer
that was and is and shall not
  mys   (shall be ever)
per infinita secula[13].   through endless ages
hym worshyp, etc.

From Thomas More's *Utopia*, 1516:
    Quae suavitas esse potest, ac   non fastidium potius
    What delight be can   and not revulsion rather (but rather

8 *praesaepe,* 9 *somnis,* 10 *providentiam,* 11 *Aegyptum,* 12 *saeculo,* 13 *saecula.*

      in audiendo latratu atque ululatu canum? Aut qui
revulsion) in hearing barking and howling of-dogs. Or what
major voluptatis sensus est, cum leporem canis insequitur,
greater of-pleasure sense is, when hare   dog chases (a dog
          quam quum canis   canem? Nempe idem
chases a hare) than when dog (chases) dog?   Certainly same
      utrobique   agitur; accurritur   enim,
(thing) in-both-cases is-done; there-is-running for (that is to say)
si te cursus oblectat. At si te   caedis   spes, laniatus
if you running pleases. But if you of-slaughter hope of-butchery
expectatio sub   oculis peragendi retinet,
expectation under eyes being-done holds (if hope of seeing
               misericordiam potius movere
slaughter . . . attracts you), pity   rather to-move
debet, spectare lepusculum a cane, imbecillum a validiore,
it-ought, to-witness little-hare by dog, weak   by stronger
fugacem et timidum a feroce, innoxium denique
fleeing and timid   by fierce, innocent finally (and innocent)
a crudeli discerptum. Itaque   Utopienses totum hoc
by cruel torn-to-pieces. Therefore Utopians all   this
venandi   exercitium, ut rem liberis   indignam, in
of-hunting practice,   as thing to-free (men) shameful to
lanios (quam artem per   servos obire eos supra
butchers which trade through bondmen to-ply them above
diximus)
we-said (we said above that they employ bondmen for that trade),
rejecerunt,   infirmam enim eius
they-have-relegated vilest   for of-it (*ie*, butcher's trade)
partem esse venationem statuunt.
part   to-be hunting   they-consider (for they consider hunting
to be . . .).

Come, all ye Faithful, attributed to John Francis Wade, *c.* 1711–86:
Adeste   fideles
Be-present faithful (ones)
Laeti   triumphantes,
Joyful (ones) triumphing,
Venite, venite in Bethlehem
Come come to Bethlehem

Natum videte regem angelorum
Born behold king of-angels
  Venite adoremus,
  Venite adoremus,
  Venite adoremus   Dominum.
  Come let-us-worship Lord.

Deum de   Deo,
God   from God,
Lumen de   lumine
Light from light
Parturit   virgo mater,
Brings-forth virgin mother,
Deum verum genitum   non factum.
God   true   begotten not made (created).
  Venite adoremus, etc.

Cantet   nunc io
Let-sing now *io*[1]
Chorus angelorum,
Chorus of-angels,
Cantet   nunc aula   caelestium:
Let-sing now court of-heavenly ones:
Gloria in   excelsis Deo!
Glory in (the) highest to-God!
  Venite adoremus, etc.

Ergo   qui   natus
Therefore who born
Die   hodierna,
On-day today's,
Jesu tibi   sit gloria,
Jesu to-thee be glory,
Patris   aeterni verbum caro factum.
Of-Father eternal word   flesh made
(Therefore glory be to Thee, Jesu,
who was born today, the eternal Father's
word made flesh).
  Venite adoremus, etc.

1 A cry of exultation.

176

From the Oxford Degree Ceremony, which is conducted exclusively in Latin.

The Vice-Chancellor opens the Congregation as follows:

Causa   huius   Congregationis est ut   Gratiae concedantur, ut
Reason of-this Congregation is that Graces be-granted, that
gradus conferantur, necnon ut   alia   peragantur
degrees be-conferred, also   that other (things) be-transacted
quae   ad hanc Venerabilem Domum spectant.
which to this Venerable   House   pertain.

The Registrar then testifies:

Ego Registrarius testor omnibus candidatis, quorum nomina
I,   Registrar,   testify to-all   candidates whose   names
Venerabili   Domui a Procuratoribus statim   submittentur,
to-Venerable House by Proctors   forthwith shall-be-sub-
       Gratias a   Collegiis vel Societatibus suis pro Gradibus
mitted, Graces by Colleges or Societies   their for Degrees
quaesitis concessas fuisse,   eosdem   mihi satisfecisse.
requested granted to-have-been the-same me to-have-satisfied
(testify that all candidates . . . have been granted Graces by their Colleges or Societies for the Degrees requested, and that they have satisfied me).

The candidates are presented with the words:

Insignissime   Vice-Cancellarie, vosque   egregii
Most-distinguished Vice-Chancellor, you-and most-excellent
Procuratores, praesento vobis   hos   meos scholares in facultate
Proctors,   I-present to-you these my   scholars in faculty
Artium, ut   admittantur   ad Gradum Baccalaurei in
of-Arts, that they-be-admitted to Degree of-Bachelor in
Artibus.
Arts.

The Vice-Chancellor admits the candidates, saying:

Domini, ego admitto vos ad Gradum Baccalaurei in Artibus;
Sirs,   I   admit you to Degree of-Bachelor in Arts;
insuper auctoritate   mea et   totius   Universitatis, do   vobis
further by-authority my and of-whole University,   I-give you
potestatem legendi   et   reliqua   omnia
power   of-reading (lecturing) and remaining all (things)
faciendi,   quae   ad eundem
of-doing (and of doing all other things), which to the-same

177

Later Arrivals

Gradum spectant.
Degree pertain.

LITERATURE

There are a considerable number of primers and dictionaries available for the study of Latin, of which B. H. Kennedy, *The Revised Latin Primer*, and Cassell's *Latin–English, English–Latin Dictionary*, are well-known, often reprinted examples. M. D. Gray and T. Jenkins, *Latin for Today*, 4 vols., likewise often reprinted, is a general textbook for beginners.
A convenient account of post-classical writing (from the middle of the fourth to the end of the seventeenth century) is to be found in F. A. Wright and T. A. Sinclair, *A History of Later Latin Literature* (1931).
W. Ripman, *A Handbook of the Latin Language* (1930), frequently reprinted, is both an admirable textbook and a useful book of reference. Lewis and Short, *A Latin Dictionary*, is a comprehensive work, frequently revised since its first appearance in 1879. H. Waddell, *A Book of Medieval Latin* (1931) includes famous examples of Anglo-Latin Poetry and Prose.

178

CHAPTER TEN

English

🕸🕸🕸🕸🕸🕸

IN the light of its linguistic consequences, the coming of the Angles, Saxons and Jutes to Britain must appear not only as the greatest event in our history, but as one of the most momentous ever to have happened anywhere. The unwritten speech of the tribesmen who then took possession of this land was destined to develop into a cultured medium which, in the fullness of time, would not merely dominate the British Isles as no language had ever done before, but would become without dispute the world's leading language.

The dialects of the newcomers belonged to the western division of Germanic, at that time spread over Jutland, the Low Countries and Germany. On the Continent, West Germanic survives today as Dutch–Flemish, Frisian and German. It was distinct from North Germanic, commonly called Norse, spoken in Scandinavia and continuing in the modern languages of that area, but the common origin of the two divisions is evident at a glance (p. 201).

The traditional date for the first wintering in Britain is 449 AD, and though archaeologists now believe they have finds pointing to settlements perhaps a couple of decades earlier, we may conveniently take the mid-fifth-century date for the beginning of an invasion comparable in its scale to that of the Celts a thousand years before. The details of the conquest itself are largely lost, but by 650 the newcomers were firmly established everywhere south of the present Scottish border with the exception of the north-west, Wales and the Devon peninsula, while north of that border they had occupied Lothian (p. 117). The gains of their language were made at the expense of Latin, in so far as it may have survived, but chiefly in any event at the expense of British. Such native inhabitants as remained within the area of conquest were to all appearances promptly assimilated. By the middle of the seventh century, the age of mass migrations was over, but Celtic continued to retreat as described in previous chapters.

The earliest records of the new language are simply the names of persons and places occurring in charters from the end of the seventh century. Continuous texts follow, but are not numerous until the tenth century. A considerable literature came into being, but political developments curtailed its further expansion. The advent of the Normans in 1066 meant that French superseded English as the language of government and influential society. With the Normans, too, came an increased use of Latin in administration. The native language, now without prestige and deprived of official recognition, was consequently neglected and fell more and more into disuse as a literary medium. One may say that the year 1100 marks the end of the first period in the history of English.

Only a small amount of English was being written in the twelfth century, but towards 1200 there are signs of change and from that date production quickly increases, though French retained its leading position until the fourteenth century. Now English was coming into its own again; it acquired full official status, and in 1363 parliament was for the first time since the Norman Conquest formally opened in English. The language as written from 1100 to 1400 – or, as some prefer, to 1500 – is termed Middle English.

The language after the medieval period is appropriately known as Modern or New English. It is within this period that English has made its greatest territorial advances. In 1600 the Celtic languages in Britain were still of considerable significance. True, the area of Cornish speech was rapidly contracting, but almost the whole of Wales remained purely Welsh-speaking. The Islands and Highlands of Scotland, the Isle of Man, and all Ireland outside Dublin and the Pale were as solidly Gaelic. But today, barely one fifth of the population of Wales can employ the Welsh language, while Gaelic has fared even worse and faces extinction in the not too distant future. Until 1600, English remained a local language, confined to Britain. But since then it has spread far and wide over all the globe and is now the mother tongue of two hundred millions and more who have never seen its island home. At the same time, it has become the unchallenged lingua franca of peoples throughout the world, the first and so far only language to have won such universal acceptance.

MEDIEVAL ENGLISH

In the following, we offer summary descriptions and illustrations of the language in its Old and Middle stages.

180

English

SKETCH OF OLD ENGLISH

Two chief dialect groupings may be traced in Old English: Anglian and West-Saxon, corresponding to the usage of the districts north and south of the Thames respectively, hence the term Anglo-Saxon, often used as a synonym for Old English. Anglian is further subdivided into Northumbrian (north of the Humber) and Southumbrian or Mercian (Midlands), while in the south a few documents with distinctive Kentish features reflect the influence of Canterbury. The materials in Mercian and West-Saxon are by far the most numerous. After the time of Alfred (d. 899), whose capital was Winchester, West-Saxon became something of a standard language and nearly all Old English literature proper has survived in manuscripts written in West-Saxon, though very often forms from other dialects occur in these texts, particularly in poetry.

Phonetics

For monumental purposes, Old English was sometimes written in the runic alphabet (p. 190), but otherwise Irish-style Latin letters (p. 81) were used, commonly supplemented by the rune þ called 'thorn', interchangeable with the letter ð called 'eth' or 'crossed d'; and also by the rune p called 'wyn' (joy) generally (but not always) transliterated today as w.

In addition to the familiar five vowels *a, e, i, o, u*, Old English possessed *y* [y] and the ligature *æ* [æ] called 'ash'. The macron marks long vowels.

Between voiced sounds *f, s, þ* were themselves voiced, *ie*, [v, z, ð]. The letter *h* was an aspirate at the beginning of a word, but in other positions was pronounced [χ] after back vowels, [ç] after front vowels. The letter *c* represented [k] or [tʃ], the latter distinguished here as *ċ*. The letter *g* was an occlusive at the beginning of a word before a back vowel and in the combination *ng*, but otherwise [ɣ] or [j], the latter distinguished here as *ġ*. The digraphs *sċ* and *ċġ* were [ʃ] and [dʒ] respectively. Double consonants were so pronounced.

Prefixes may be unstressed, as *ġe-*.

Nouns

These fall into several classes, conventionally designated *a*-stems, *ō*-stems, etc. The relevance of such designations is not, in most cases,

181

immediately apparent from the actual forms of the Old English words, but the terms are justified historically. For instance, OE *fisċ* 'fish' is called an *a*-stem since it descends from a prehistoric form **fiskaz*, analysable as comprising a stem *fiska-* and a case termination *-z*, the former then further divisible into a root *fisk-* with a stem vowel *-a-*.

Nouns have four cases: nominative, accusative, genitive, dative. The first two are identical in most classes in the singular and always so in the plural. There are three genders. Sample paradigms:

a-stems, masc. and neut.

Sg. nom. acc. *fisċ* m. 'fish', gen. *fisċes*, dat. *fisċe*, pl. nom. acc. *fisċas*, gen. *fisċa*, dat. *fisċum*.

Similarly *word* n. 'word' except that pl. nom. acc. are uninflected.

ō-stems, fem.

Sg. nom. *sāwol* 'soul', acc. gen. dat. *sāwle*, pl. nom. acc. gen. *sāwla*, dat. *sāwlum*.

i-stems, masc. and fem.

Sg. nom. acc. *wine* m. 'friend', gen. *wines*, dat. *wine*, pl. nom. acc. *wine*, gen. *wina*, dat. *winum*.

Sg. nom. acc. *hӯd* f. 'hide', gen. dat. *hӯde*, pl. nom. acc. *hӯde*, gen. *hӯda*, dat. *hӯdum*.

u-stems, chiefly masc.

Sg. nom. acc. *sunu* 'son', gen. dat. *suna*, pl. nom. acc. gen. *suna*, dat. *sunum*.

n-stems, all genders

Sg. nom. *boga* m. 'bow', acc. gen. dat. *bogan*, pl. nom. acc. *bogan*, gen. *bogena*, dat. *bogum*.

Sg. nom. *tunge* f. 'tongue', acc. gen. dat. *tungan*, pl. nom. acc. *tungan*, gen. *tungena*, dat. *tungum*.

Sg. nom. acc. *ēare* n. 'ear', gen. dat. *ēaran*, pl. nom. acc. *ēaran*, gen. *ēarena*, dat. *ēarum*.

Further, various minor declensions including:

Sg. nom. acc. *fōt* m. 'foot', gen. *fōtes*, dat. *fēt*, pl. nom. acc. *fēt*, gen. *fōta*, dat. *fōtum*.

Sg. nom. acc. *bōc* f. 'book', gen. dat. *bēċ*, pl. nom. acc. *bēċ*, gen. *bōca*, dat. *bōcum*.

Adjectives

Adjectives may be declined 'strong' or 'weak'; in the latter case reference is to a definite entity: (strong) *sēoc ćild* '(a) sick child', (weak) *þæt sēoce ćild* 'the sick child', the article being a secondary development, often absent in poetic texts.

The strong declension is as follows:

Sg. nom. masc.	*sēoc* 'sick'	fem. *sēoc*	neut. *sēoc*
acc.	*sēocne*	*sēoce*	*sēoc*
gen.	*sēoces*	*sēocre*	*sēoces*
dat.	*sēocum*	*sēocre*	*sēocum*
Pl. nom. acc.	*sēoce*	*sēoce*	*sēoce*
gen.		*sēocra*	
dat.		*sēocum*	

The weak declension corresponds to that of nouns with *n*-stems, except that the genitive plural has much more commonly the ending *-ra* (from the strong declension) than the historically correct *-ena*, hence Sg. nom. *sēoca* m., *sēoce* f. n., etc.

The comparative and superlative are usually formed by adding *-ra* and *-ost* to the positive stem: *sēocra* 'sicker', *sēocost* 'sickest'. Examples of irregular comparison: *gōd* 'good', *betera* 'better', *betest* 'best', *yfel* 'evil', *wyrsa* 'worse', *wyrrest* 'worst'.

Numbers

1 *ān*, 2 *twēġen*, 3 *þrī*, 4 *fēower*, 5 *fīf*, 6 *siex*, 7 *seofon*, 8 *eahta*, 9 *nigon*, 10 *tīen*, 11 *enlefan*, 12 *twelf*, 13 *þrēotīene*, 14 *fēowertīene*, 15 *fīftīene*, 16 *siextīene*, 17 *seofontīene*, 18 *eahtatīene*, 19 *nigontīene*, 20 *twentiġ*, 21 *ān and twentiġ*, 30 *þrītiġ*, 40 *fēowertiġ*, 50 *fīftiġ*, 60 *siextiġ*, 70 *hundseofontiġ*, 80 *hundeahtatiġ*, 90 *hundnigontiġ*, 100 *hundtēoniġ*, also *hund*, *hundred*, 1000 *þūsend*.

Numbers 1–19 variously inflect: *ān* is strong or weak; 2 and 3 are irregular: nom. acc. masc. *twēġen*, *þrī*, fem. neut. *twā*, *þrīo*, gen. *twēġ(r)a*, *þrīora*, dat. *twǣm*, *þrim*; 4 and above take endings when used independently, thus nom. acc. masc. fem. *fēowere*, neut. *-o*, gen. *-a*, dat. *-um*.

To a very limited extent, *ān* functions as an indefinite article.

Definite article

Sg.	nom.	masc. *sē*	fem. *sēo*	neut. *þæt*	Pl. *þā*
	acc.	*þone*	*þā*	*þæt*	*þā*
	gen.	*þæs*	*þǣre*	*þæs*	*þāra*
	dat.	*þǣm*	*þǣre*	*þǣm*	*þǣm*

Pronouns

In addition to singular and plural, the pronouns of the first and second person also have a dual number. Paradigms:

Sg.	nom.	*iċ* 'I'	*þū* 'thou'	*hē* 'he'	*hēo* 'she'	*hit* 'it'
	acc.	*mē*	*þē*	*hine*	*hīe*	*hit*
	gen.	*mīn*	*þīn*	*his*	*hire*	*his*
	dat.	*mē*	*þē*	*him*	*hire*	*him*

Pl.	nom.	*wē* 'we'	*ġē* 'you'	*hīe* 'they'
	acc.	*ūs*	*ēow*	*hīe*
	gen.	*ūre*	*ēower*	*hira*
	dat.	*ūs*	*ēow*	*him*

Du.	nom.	*wit* 'we'	*ġit* 'you'
	acc.	*unc*	*inċ*
	gen.	*uncer*	*inċer*
	dat.	*unc*	*inċ*

The genitive of the pronoun functions as a possessive, in the case of the first two persons following the strong declension of adjectives: *mīn* 'my', etc., in the case of the third person remaining invariable: *his* 'his, its'.

Verbs

As in the modern language, Old English verbs fall into two main categories: strong and weak. The latter are by far the more numerous, but the former are among the most commonly used. Strong verbs are characterized by internal vowel change, eg, *drive, drove*, whereas weak verbs employ a dental suffix, eg, *hear, heard*.

The inflected forms of a strong verb may be illustrated as follows:

Infinitive: *drīfan* 'drive', *tō drīfanne* 'to drive'.

English

Indicative: pres. sg. 1 *drīfe*, 2 *drīfst*, 3 *drīfþ*, pl. *drīfaþ*; past sg. 1 *drāf*, 2 *drife*, 3 *drāf*, pl. *drifon*.

Imperative: sg. *drīf*, pl. *drīfaþ*.

Subjunctive: pres. sg. *drīfe*, pl. *drīfen*; past sg. *drife*, pl. *drifen*.

Participles: pres. *drīfende*, past *ġedrifen*.

There are a number of other patterns of vowel change, seen in the principal parts: infin., past sg. 1, past pl., past part.: *sċēotan* 'shoot', *sċēat*, *sċuton*, *ġesċoten*; *berstan* 'burst', *bærst*, *burston*, *ġeborsten*; *stelan* 'steal', *stæl*, *stǣlon*, *ġestolen*; *ġiefan* 'give', *ġeaf*, *ġēafon*, *ġeġiefen*; *faran* 'go, fare', *fōr*, *fōron*, *ġefaren*; *lǣtan* 'let, allow', *lēt*, *lēton*, *ġelǣten*.

An example of the weak conjugation:

Infinitive: *hīeran* 'hear', *tō hīeranne* 'to hear'.

Indicative: pres. sg. 1 *hīere*, 2 *hīerest*, 3 *hīereþ*, pl. *hīeraþ*; past sg. 1 *hīerde*, 2 *hīerdest*, 3 *hīerde*, pl. *hīerdon*.

Imperative: sg. *hīer*, pl. *hīeraþ*.

Subjunctive: pres. sg. *hīere*, pl. *hīeren*; past sg. *hīerde*, pl. *hīerden*.

Participles: pres. *hīerende*, past *ġehīered*.

The auxiliaries 'to be' and 'to have':

Infinitive: *wesan* or *bēon* 'be', etc.

Indicative: pres. sg. 1 *eom*, 2 *eart*, 3 *is*, pl. *sindon*, or sg. 1 *bēo*, 2 *bist*, 3 *biþ*, pl. *bēoþ*; past sg. 1 *wæs*, 2 *wǣre*, 3 *wæs*, pl. *wǣron*.

Imperative: sg. *wes*, pl. *wesaþ*, or sg. *bēo*, pl. *bēoþ*.

Subjunctive: pres. sg. *sīe*, pl. *sīen*, or sg. *bēo*, pl. *bēon*; past sg. *wǣre*, pl. *wǣren*.

Participles: pres. *wesende bēonde*, past (wanting).

Infinitive: *habban* 'have', etc.

Indicative:
pres. sg. 1 *hæbbe*, 2 *hæfst* or *hafast*, 3 *hæfþ* or *hafaþ*, pl. *habbaþ*; past sg. 1 *hæfde*, 2 *hæfdest*, 3 *hæfde*, pl. *hæfdon*.

Imperative:
sg. *hafa*, pl. *habbaþ*.

Subjunctive:
pres. sg. *hæbbe*, pl. *hæbben*; past sg. *hæfde*, pl. *hæfden*.

Participles:
pres. *hæbbende*, past *ġehæfd*.

READINGS

Cædmon's Hymn, composed *c.* 670, the earliest example of religious verse, in its West Saxon version:

1 *Nū wē sċulon herian heofonrīċes Weard,*
 Now we shall praise heaven-kingdom's Guardian,

2 *Metodes mihte and His mōdġeþanc,*
 Creator's might and His mind-thought (=intention, design?),

3 *weorc Wuldorfæder, swā Hē wundra ġehwæs,*
 work Glory-Father's how He of-wonders of-each,

4 *ēċe Dryhten, ōr onstealde.*
 eternal Lord, (the) beginning established.

5 *Hē ǣrest sċōp eorþan bearnum,*
 He first created earth for-men,

6 *heofon tō hrōfe, hāliġ Sċieppend.*
 heaven to (as) roof holy Creator.

7 *þā middanġeard mancynnes Weard,*
 Then middle-yard (earth) mankind's Guardian,

8 *ēċe Dryhten, æfter tēode*
 eternal Lord, afterwards fashioned

9 *fīrum foldan, Frēa ælmihtiġ.*
 for-men earth, Lord almighty.

There follows a Latin note: 'Primo cantavit *Cædmon* istud carmen' – 'First sang Cædmon (*ie*, Cadman composed) this hymn.'

The poetic line is characterized by alliteration, as *herian* . . . *heofonrīċe* (1) or *Metodes mihte* . . . *mōdġeþanc* (2), the first stressed word after the caesura being thus linked to the preceding half-line; vowels alliterate, as *ēċe* . . . *ōr* (4).

Variation is a prominent feature of the style. In the concluding sentence the subject, first mentioned as *mancynnes Weard*, is variously repeated: *ēċe Dryhten* (8) and *Frēa ælmihtiġ* (9). By the same token *Hē* (3, 5) anticipates the main subjects *ēċe Dryhten* (4) and *hālig Sċieppend* (6) respectively.

From the *Charm*, sometimes called *Field Ceremonies*, date of composition unknown:

Hēr is sēo bōt   hū   þū   meaht þīne æceras bētan   ġif
Here is the remedy how thou canst thy fields improve if
hīe nyllaþ wel weaxan oþþe þær hwilċ unġedēfe þing
they not-will well grow   or   wherever unseemly thing
onġedōn biþ   on   drȳ   oþþe on lyblāce.
done   is (to them) on (by) sorcery or   by witchcraft.

Hwonne man   þā sulh   forþ drīfe and þā forman
When man (one) the plough forth drives and the first
furh   onsċēote,   cweþ þonne:
furrow in-shoots (cuts) say then:

Hāl wes þū,   folde,   fīra   mōdor,
Hale be thou (hail) earth,   of-men mother,
bēo þū   grōwende   on Godes fæþme,
be thou growing   in God's embrace,
fōdre   ġefylled   fīrum tō   nytte.
with-food filled   to-men as a benefit (noun)[1].

Nim þonne ælċes   cynnes melu, and ābace man   inneweardre
Take then of-each kind   meal[2], and bake man[3] of-inward
handa brādne hlāf, and ġecned hine mid meolce and mid
hand broad loaf[4], and knead it   with milk and with
hāliġwætere, and leġe   under þā forman furh.
holy water and lay (it) under the first   furrow.

Three extracts from the *Anglo-Saxon Chronicle*:
(The coming of the English) AD 449:

Hēr   Martianus and Valentinus onfēngon
Here (*ie*, in the year 449) Martianus and Valentinus obtained
rīċe   and rīxodon seofon winter. And on hira dagum ġelaþode
empire and ruled   seven winters. And in their days invited
Wyrtġeorn Angelcynn hider. And hīe   cōmon on þrim ċēolum
Vortigern Angle-kin hither. And they came in three ships

1 For men's use or enjoyment, 2 meal of every kind, 3 let one bake, 4 a loaf as broad as the palm of the hand.

hider tō Bretene, on þǣm stede þe   is ġenemned Ypwines flēot.
hither to Britain, to the   place which is called   Ebbsfleet.
Sē cyning Wyrtġeorn ġeaf him land on sūþan-ēastan þissum
The king Vortigern gave them land in south-east(-of) this
lande, wiþ þǣm þe   hīe sċeoldon feohtan wiþ
land, with that that (provided that) they should fight with
Peohtas. Hīe þā fuhton wiþ Peohtas, and sige   hæfdon
Picts.   They then fought with Picts,   and victory had
swā hwǣr swā hīe   cōmon. Þā   cōmon men of þrim mǣgþum
wherever   they came.   Then came men of three tribes
Germanie,   of Eald-Seaxum, of Anglum, of Iutum. Hira
of-Germany, of Old Saxons, of Angles, of Jutes. Their
heretogan   wǣron tweġen ġebrōþru, Hengest and Horsa.
army-leaders were two   brothers Hengist and Horsa.

(The annal for the year in question is the following poem which
celebrates King Edmund as liberator of that part of the Danelaw
known as the Five Boroughs) AD 942:
   Hēr Ēadmund cyning,   Engla þēoden,
   Here Edmund king,   Angles' ruler,
   māga   mundbora,   Mierċe ġeēode,
   kinsmen's protection-bearer, Mercians conquered,
   dīere dǣdfruma,   swā Dor sċādeþ,
   dear deed-performer, as Dore divides,
   Hwītanwielles ġeat   and Humbran ēa
   Whitwell's gate   and Humber's river
   brāda brimstrēam.   Burga   fīfe,
   broad sea-stream.   Of-boroughs five,
   Ligoraċeaster   and Lindcylene
   Leicester   and Lincoln
   and Snotingahām,   swilċe Stānford ēac
   and Nottingham   and   Stamford also
   and Dēorabȳ,   Dene wǣron ǣr,
   and Derby,   Danes were formerly (had been)
   under Norþmannum,   nīede   ġebēġde,
   under Northmen   by-force bowed-down
   on hǣþenra   hǣfteclommum
   in heathens'   binding-fetters
   lange þrāge,   oþ hīe ālīesde eft
   long time,   until them freed   afterwards

for his weorþscipe   *wīgendra hlēo,*
for his honour   warriors' protector,
eafora Ēadweardes,   *Ēadmund cyning.*
son   of Edward,   Edmund king[1].

1 (Christian) Danes for a long time had been forcibly subjugated by (pagan) Northmen, in the binding fetters of those heathen, until King Edmund, son of Edward (the Elder), protector of warriors, afterwards liberated them for his honour (to his great credit).

(William the Conqueror lands in England) AD 1066:

On þisum ġēare cōm   Willelm eorl of Normandie in tō
In this   year   came William earl of Normandy in to
Pefenes ēa on sancte Michaeles mæsseǣfen and worhton
Pevensey   on St   Michael's mass-eve   and built
castel   æt Hæstinga porte. Þis   wearþ   þā
fortification at Hastings' port. This became (was) then
Harolde   cyninge ġecȳdd,   and he gaderode þā   miċelne here,
to-Harold king   reported and he gathered then great   army
and cōm   him tōġēanes æt þǣre hāran apuldran.   And Willelm
and came him against   at the   old   apple-tree. And William
him cōm   onġēan on unwær   ǣr his folc ġefylċed
him came against one unaware (unawares) ere his army drawn-up
wǣre. Ac sē   cyning þēah   him swīþe heardliċe wiþ   feaht
was. But the king   though him very   boldly   with fought[1]
mid þǣm mannum þe   him ġelǣstan woldon. And þǣr   wearþ
with those men   who him assist   would. And there was
miċel wæl   ġeslæġen on ǣġþre healfe: þǣr   wearþ ofslæġen
great carnage struck   on either half[2]   there was   slain
Harold cyning, and Lēofwine eorl his brōþor, and Gyrþ   eorl his
Harold king   and Leofwine earl his brother and Gyrth earl his
brōþor, and fela   gōdra   manna. And þā Frenċisċan āhton
brother and much of-good men.   And the French   obtained
wælstōwe   ġeweald, eallswā him   God ūþe   for folces
of-carnage-place control[3], just-as them God granted for people's
synnum.
sins.

1 Fought very resolutely against him, 2 caused on each side, 3 possession of the field of battle.

Runes

The runes may be called the national script of the Germanic peoples. They are known from inscriptions going back to the third century AD and form a distinctive alphabet called the fuþark after its first six letters. However, the number of letters used as well as their shapes were subject to a great deal of local variation as they were repeatedly modified to follow the evolution of the emergent Germanic languages. The question of origins has been much debated, but it is now generally agreed that the prototype is to be sought among the north Italian alphabets employed in the Alpine area in the second century BC. It was long ago realized that the script was adopted in the first place for occult purposes, as the very name *rune* (lit. 'secret') at once confirms. Later, it became a monumental script, but the old magico-religious associations doubtless persisted to some extent.

The surviving specimens of Old English written in runes are not numerous and all belong to the earlier period; it appears that the use of runes among the Anglo-Saxons died out in the tenth century. In the Scandinavian parts of the country, on the other hand, the practice continued for quite two centuries longer (p. 211). As chance would have it, nearly all the known Old English runic texts are written in the Northumbrian dialect, as in the samples which follow. In our transliteration vowel quantities, undistinguished in the original, have been added.

Lines of verse carved on the Franks Casket, apparently in allusion to the casket's being made of whalebone; early eighth century:

ᚠᛁᛋᚳ	ᚠᛚᚩᛞᚢ	ᚪᚻᚩᚠ	ᚩᚾ	ᚠᛖᚱᚷᛖᚾᛒᛖᚱᛁᚷ			
fisc	*flōdu*	*āhōf*	*on*	*fergenberig*			
fish	flood	lifted	onto	cliff-bank			

ᚹᚪᚱᚦ	ᚷᚪᛋᚱᛁᚳ		ᚷᚱᚩᚱᚾ	ᚦᚫᚱ	ᚻᛖ	ᚩᚾ	ᚷᚱᛖᚢᛏ	ᚷᛁᛋᚹᚩᛗ
warþ	*gāsrīc*		*grorn*	*þǣr*	*hē*	*on*	*greut*	*giswom*
became	savage-creature		dejected	where	he	onto	sand	swam

ᚻᚱᚩᚾᚫᛋ	ᛒᚪᚾ
hronæs	*bān*
whale's	bone

Two fragments of the poem 'The Dream of the Rood' engraved on the Ruthwell [rivl] Cross, Dumfriesshire; early eighth century.

(a)

> ᛣᚱᛁᛋᛏ ᛈᚠᚻ ᛗ ᚱᚯᛈᛁ
> *krist wæs on rōdi*
> Christ was on rood (cross)

ᚻᛈᛗᛈᚱᚪ	ᚦᛗᚱ	ᚠᚢᚻᚠ	ᚠᛤᚱᚱᛈᛁ ᛆᛈᛈᛈᛁᚾ
hweþræ	*þer*	*fūsæ*	*fēarran kwōmu*
howbeit	thither	hastening	from-afar came

ᚠᚦᚦᛁᚠᚠ	ᛏᛁᚱ	ᛗᛁᚾᛈᛁ
æþþilæ	*til*	*ānum*
nobles	to	him-alone

ᛁᚻ	ᚦᚻᛁ	ᛗᛏ	ᛒᛁᚻ...
ic	*þæt*	*al*	*bih(ēald)*
I	that	all	beheld

ᚻ...	ᛁᚻ	ᛈᚠᚻ	ᛗᛁ.	ᚻᛈᚱᛤᚾᛈᛁ ᛪᛁᛗᚱᛦ..ᛗ
s(āræ)	*ic*	*wæs*	*mi(þ)*	*sorḡum gidræ(fi)d*
sorely	I	was	with	sorrows troubled

(b)

> ᛗᛁᚦ ᚻᛏᚱᛗᛏᚾᛁ ᛪᛁᛈᚾᚻᛈᛈᚻ
> *miþ   strēlum   giwundad*
> with   spears (?)   wounded

ᛈᛏᛉᛈᛈᚾᛦ	ᚾᛁᚠ	ᚾᛁᚾᚠ	ᛚᛁᛗᛈᛦᚱᛁᛉᚠᛈ
ālegdun	*hiæ*	*hinæ*	*limwærignæ*
laid-down	they	him	limb-weary

ᛪᛁᚻᛏᛈᛈᛈᛈᚾᛦ	ᚾᛁᛁ	.....	ᛚᛁᚾᚠᚻ	.. ᚠ .. ᛗ
gistōddun	*him*	*(æt)*	*līcæs*	*(hēa)f(du)m*
stood	him	(at)	body's head†

Epitaph on a cross fragment from Thornhill, West Riding. *c.* 800.

ᛉᛁᚦᚾᚾᛁᚦ	ᛗᚱᚠᚱᛈᛗ	ᚠᚠᛏᛗ	ᛒᛗᚱᚾᛏᚻᚾᛁᚦᛗ	ᛒᛗᛈᚾᛦ
jilsuiþ	*arærde*	*æfte*	*berhtsuiþe*	*bekun*
Ġilswïþ	raised	after	Berhtswïþ	beacon[1]

	ᛗ	ᛒᛗᚱᛉᛁ	ᛪᛗᛒᛁᚦᛈᛈᚦ	ᚦᚠᚱ ᚻᛗᚾᛚᛗ
	on	*bergi*	*gebiddaþ*	*þær saule*
	on	barrow[2]	pray-for	her soul

† Stood at his head.
1 Monument, 2 mound, *ie,* tomb.

Later Arrivals

LITERATURE

P. S. Ardern, *First Readings in Old English* (1951).
R. W. V. Elliott, *Runes* (1959).
B. Mitchell, *A Guide to Old English* (1964).
Sweet's Anglo-Saxon Reader, revised by D. Whitelock (1967).
R. I. Page, *An Introduction to English Runes* (1973).

SKETCH OF MIDDLE ENGLISH

The pre-Conquest tradition of writing English was greatly modified in the course of the twelfth century. Not only were the grammatical forms of the West Saxon standard forgotten, but also its orthographical system. When, from 1200, texts again become frequent, authors are seen to be writing more or less as they spoke, revealing dialect features and following various spelling conventions partly adopted from contemporary Norman French practice. During the fifteenth century, the East Midland dialect became the generally accepted literary standard. This was the dialect of Oxford and Cambridge and, more importantly, also of London, with Chaucer as its first great exponent. On the position in Scotland, see p. 99.

Middle English seems qualitatively different from the Old English which preceded it. The breakdown in the inflexional system of the old period and the loss of its specifically literary vocabulary left a language recognizably like the English we use today, while Old English remains largely unintelligible without special study.

To illustrate the character of the language in the Old English period, the standard forms of later West Saxon are conveniently to hand. But there is no comparable yardstick for Middle English, where dialect writing is the rule. For our grammatical section we therefore offer forms selected to give an idea of the position around 1300 in the more conservative south and Midlands. It may be said that in the north inflexional decay was even more marked. To the north, incidently, the modern language owes the third singular ending of the present tense verb, as northern *drīves* 'drives', otherwise *drīveþ* 'driveth'.

Phonetics

A notable innovation is the frequent use of the (French) digraph *ou* in place of *ū*. Similarly, *o* may replace *u*, which in turn may now represent OE *y* (here distinguished as *ü*); *y* henceforth takes the value of *i* and is freely interchangeable with it. Length is sometimes shown by doubling the vowel, but is most often unmarked.

The letter *k* was introduced before front vowels, but *c* was retained before back vowels; *ck* has the same value. The digraph *ch* (of French provenance) commonly represents [ʧ], *gh* [χ] and [ç], the latter values also rendered by *h*. Thorn remains in use, but may be replaced by *th*.

Length is marked in the accidence and first four extracts below, but only in the case of vowels traditionally long. During the middle period, however, changes took place in the system of quantities, notably the lengthening of short vowels in stressed open syllables, thus OE *hara* 'hare', *beran* 'bear', *smocu* 'smoke', ME *hāre*, *bēren*, *smōke*, the vowels *i* and *u* changing their quality also: OE *wicu* 'week', *lufu* 'love', ME *wēke*, *lōve*. Though the evidence is often inconclusive – the orthography of most Middle English texts is disturbingly erratic – it appears that the changes were not uniform and subject to regional variation, which may account for many of the irregularities observed. For example, while the postulated lengthening in ME *wēke* is confirmed by the modern *week*, it is contradicted in the case of ME *lōve* since the vowel is now short. Further, in forms like the modern *driven*, the short vowel has apparently survived unchanged in quality or quantity since the earliest times. The lengthening in question is dated to the thirteenth century. While our first passage is earlier than this development, the position of the two mid-thirteenth century pieces is ambiguous, there being no evidence either way. For this reason, traditional length only is marked as such.

The Irish-style insular hand used in writing Old English yielded, about 1500, to the continental Carolingian minuscule. The Chancery hand, the precursor of modern handwriting, appears about 1400.

Nouns

The case system and declensional categories of Old English were drastically reduced, so that there is effectively a single inflexional type, as sg. nom. acc. dat. *fish*, gen. *fishes*, pl. all cases *fishes*. Only in the dialects of the south was a plural ending -*en* common for a time as well. A few traditional forms remain as exceptions, thus *fōt* 'foot', pl. *fēt*.

Later Arrivals

Adjectives

These are invariable, except for monosyllables ending in a consonant which distinguish strong and weak declensions in the singular, as follows: strong singular *sēk* 'sick', weak singular *sēke*, but plural uniformly *sēke*. Comparison: *sēker* 'sicker', *sēkest* 'sickest'. Examples of irregular comparison: *gōd* 'good', *betere* 'better', *best* 'best', *evel* 'bad', *werse* 'worse', *werst* 'worst'.

Numbers

1 *ōn*, 2 *twēyn* or *twō*, 3 *þrē*, 4 *four*, 5 *fīf*, 6 *six*, 7 *seven*, 8 *eghte*, 9 *niyen*, 10 *ten*, 11 *enleven*, 12 *twelf*, 13 *þrettēne*, 14 *fourtēne*, 15 *fiftēne*, 16 *sixtēne*, 17 *seventēne*, 18 *eghttēne*, 19 *niyentēne*, 20 *twentī*, 21 *ōn and twentī*, 30 *þrittī*, 40 *fourtī*, 50 *fiftī*, 60 *sixtī*, 70 *seventī*, 80 *eghttī*, 90 *niyentī*, 100 *hundred*, 1000 *þūsend*.

A form of the numeral 'one', *an*, *a*, functions as the indefinite article.

Definite Article

þe (uninflected).

Pronouns

Sg. nom.	*ich* 'I'	*þū* 'thou'	*hē* 'he'	*heo, she* 'she'	*hit* 'it'
acc. dat.	*mē*	*þē*	*him*	*hire*	*him*
Pl. nom.	*wē* 'we'	*yē* 'ye'		*hī, þey* 'they'	
	ūs	*you*		*hem, þem*	

Possessive pronouns for the first two persons decline like adjectives: singular *mīn*, before consonants *mī*, plural *mīne* 'my', *þīn*, before consonants *þī*, plural *þīne* 'thy', *our*, plural *oure* 'our', *your*, plural *youre* 'your'; the third person is invariable: *his* 'his, its', *hire* 'her', *hire, þeire* 'their'.

Verbs

Strong conjugation:

Infinitive: *tō drīven* 'to drive'.

Indicative: pres. sg. 1 *drīve*, 2 *drīvest*, 3 *drīveþ*, pl. *drīveþ*; past sg. 1 *drōf*, 2 *drive*, 3 *drōf*, pl. *driven*.

194

Imperative: sg. *drīf*, pl. *drīveþ*.

Subjunctive: pres. sg. *drīve*, pl. *drīven*; past sg. *drive*, pl. *driven*,

Participles: pres. *drīvende* or *drīving*, past *idriven*.

Other patterns of vowel change (infin., past sg. 1, past pl., past part.): *shēten* 'shoot', *shēt, shuten, ishoten*; *bersten* 'burst', *barst, borsten, iborsten*; *stelen* 'steal', *stal, stēlen, istolen*; *yeven* 'give', *yaf, yāven, iyeven*, also partly through Scandinavian influence *given, gaf, gēven, igiven*; *faren* 'go, fare', *fōr, fōren, ifaren*; *lēten* 'let, allow', *lēt, lēten, ilēten*.

Weak Conjugation:

Infinitive: *tō hēren* 'to hear'.

Indicative: pres. sg. 1 *hēre*, 2 *hērest*, 3 *hēreþ*, pl. *hēreþ*; past sg. 1 *hērde*, 2 *hērdest*, 3 *hērde*, pl. *hērden*.

Imperative: sg. *hēr*, pl. *hēreþ*.

Subjunctive: pres. sg. *hēre*, pl. *hēren*; past sg. *hērde*, pl. *hērden*.

Participles: pres. *hērende* or *hēring*, past *ihēred*.

The auxiliaries 'to be' and 'to have':

Infinitive: *tō bēn* 'to be'.

Indicative: pres. sg. 1 *am*, 2 *art*, 3 *is*, pl. *aren*, or sg. 1 *bē*, 2 *bēst*, 3 *bēþ*. pl. *bēþ*; past sg. 1 *was*, 2 *wēre*, 3 was, pl. *wēren*.

Imperative: sg. *bē*, pl. *bēþ*.

Subjunctive: pres. sg. *bē*. pl. *bēn*, past sg. *wēre*, pl. *wēren*.

Participles: pres. *bēnde* or *bēing*, past *ibēn*.

Infinitive: *tō haven* 'to have'.

Indicative: pres. sg. 1 *have*, 2 *hast* or *havest*, 3 *haþ* or *haveþ*, pl. *haveþ*; past sg. 1 *hadde*, 2 *haddest*, 3 *hadde*, pl. *hadden*.

Imperative: sg. *have*, pl. *haveþ*.

Subjunctive: sg. *have*, pl. *haven*; past sg. *hadde*, pl. *hadden*.

Participles: pres. *havende* or *having*, past *ihad*.

From the *Peterborough Chronicle*, for the year 1137:
(Old English orthographical principles partly retained. Note *u* before
vowel = *w*).

> *Þā   þe King Stephne tō Englalande cōm, þā   macod hē*
> When the King Stephen to England   came, then made he
> *his gadering   æt Oxene ford and þār   hē nam þe*
> his gathering (Assembly) at Oxford   and there he took the
> *bisĉop Roger of Sereberi and Alexander Bisĉop of Lincol and*
> bishop Roger of Salisbury and Alexander Bishop of Lincoln and
> *te Canceler Roger, hise neves,   and dide ælle in prisun til*
> the Chancellor Roger, his nephews, and put all in prison till
> *hī   iāfen up here castles. Þā   þe suīkes underǵǣton ðat*
> they gave up their castles. When the traitors perceived that
> *hē   milde man was and sōfte and gōd,   and nā*
> he (a) mild man was and soft and good (easy-going) and no
> *jüstice ne dide,   þā   diden hī   alle*
> justice not did (did not prosecute them), then did   they all
>   *wunder. Hī   hadden him manrēd   maked and suōren*
> (sorts of) horrors. They had   him homage done and sworn
> *āthes, ac hī   nān   trēuthe ne² hēolden; alle*
> oaths, but they none (none of them) pledge not kept   all
> *hī   wǣron forsworen and here trēothes forloren,*
> they (all of them) were forsworn and their pledges lost
>   *for ævriĉ rīĉe man his castles makede and āǵǣnes*
> (broken), for every rich man his castles made   and against
> *him   hēolden and fylden þe land ful of castles. Hī*
> him (they) held   and filled the land full of castles. They
> *suenĉten suȳðe þe wreĉĉe men of þe land mid castelweorces.*
> oppressed much the poor   men of the land with castle-works
> (with the making of castles).

Sunset on Calvary, early thirteenth century:

> *Nou gōth sonne under wode;*   Now goes sun under wood¹;
> *Mē rēwes², Marie, þī faire rode.*   I pity, Mary, thy fair face.

---

1 Judging from similar expressions in other languages, *eg*, Old Norse, the
phrase 'sun goes under wood' will have been a (stylistically lofty) euphemism for
'the sun sets', 2 Northern form, otherwise *rēweþ*.

Nou gōth sonne under trē;	Now goes sun under tree (cross);
Mē rēwes[2], Marie, þī sone and þē.	I pity, Mary, thy son and thee.

Sing, Cuckoo, about 1240:
(Note *lh* with redundant *h*)

Sumer is icumen in.	Summer has come.
Lhūde sing, cuccū!	Sing loudly, cuckoo!
Grōweþ sēd and blōweþ mēd	Seed grows and meadow blossoms
And springþ þe wude nū.	And sprouts the forest now.
Awe blēteþ after lomb,	Ewe bleats to lamb,
Lhōuþ after calve cū,	Cow calls (lows) to calf,
Bulluc sterteþ, bucke verteþ,	Bullock jumps, billy goat farts,
Mürie sing, cuccū!	Sing merrily, cuckoo!
Cuccū, cuccū!	Cuckoo, cuckoo!
Wel singes þū, cuccū.	Well singest thou, cuckoo.
Ne swīk þū naver nū.	Not cease thou never now.

Lenten is come with Love to Town, mid-thirteenth century:
(*u*=*v* in *loue, woderoue; üe*=*ü* in *hüere*)

Lenten ys come wiþ loue tō toune	Spring is come with love to town (homes of men)
wiþ blosmen and wiþ briddes roune	with flowers and bird's song
þat al þis blisse bryngeþ:	that brings all this pleasure:
dayes ēyes in þis dales,	daisies in these valleys,
notes suēte of nyhtegales,	sweet notes of nightingales,
üch foul song singeþ.	each bird sings a song.
þe þrestelcoc him þrēteþ oo;	The cock thrush threatens (grows restive) aye;
away is hüere wynter woo	their winter woe vanishes
when woderoue springeþ.	when woodruff sprouts.
þis foules singeþ ferly fele,	These birds sing, wonderfully many,
ant wrytleþ on hüere wynne wele.	and warble in their joy's wealth.

Later Arrivals

From the *General Prologue of the Canterbury Tales*, by Geoffrey Chaucer (*c.* 1340–1400):

> Ther was also a nonne, a Prioresse,
> That[1] of hir smylyng[2] was ful symple and coy[3];
> Hire grettest ooth was but 'By seint Loy'.
> And she was cleped[4] madame Eglentyne,
> Ful weel she soong the service dyvyne,
> Entuned[5] in hir nose ful semely[6];
> And Frenssh she spak ful faire[7] and fetisly[8] –
> After the scole of Stratford-atte-Bowe,
> For Frenssh of Parys was to hire unknowe.

LITERATURE

F. Mossé, *A Handbook of Middle English* (1952).
K. Sisam, *Fourteenth Century Verse and Prose* (1921).
B. Dickins and R. M. Wilson, *Early Middle English Texts* (1951).
J. A. W. Bennett and G. V. Smithers, *Early Middle English Verse and Prose* (1966).
M. L. Samuels, *Linguistic Evolution with special reference to English* (1972).

ENGLISH IN SCOTLAND

The land between the Tweed and the Forth was settled by Angles in the closing decades of the Anglo-Saxon Conquest. Known as Lothian, it formed part of Northumbria and the English speech of the newcomers doubtless soon displaced the earlier British Celtic. In 1018, this district was lost by Northumbria and incorporated into the aggressive, essentially Gaelic, kingdom of Scotland which had been formed about 843 with its royal centre at Scone. The new territory, however, resisted gaelicization. The English element was then strengthened by the arrival of numbers of Anglo-Saxon refugees after the Norman invasion of England in 1066. Prominent among these was Margaret, a grand-niece of Edward the Confessor, who married Malcolm Canmore, the Scottish king. Canmore's native tongue was Gaelic, but he had taken refuge in England during the reign of Macbeth and spoke the language. It is significant that all the

1 'Who', 2 'when she smiled', 3 'quiet', 4 'called', 5 'intoned', 6 'fittingly', 7 'beautifully', 8 'charmingly'.

eight children of the royal pair bore English names, thus making a
conscious break with Gaelic tradition. Lothian, with Edinburgh as its
chief town, was now the most influential part of the kingdom and
English became expansive. Within the next two centuries it had
wrested most of the Lowlands from Gaelic to become without
question the leading language in the country. It goes without saying
that English in Scotland, written as well as spoken, was the local
(Lothian) variety of the Northumbrian dialect.

In England, dialect writing virtually ceased during the fifteenth
century (p. 192). In Scotland, however, Northumbrian continued in
use for another hundred years or so, a clear reflection of Scottish
political independence. This literary Scottish (or Scots), as it may be
called, held its own until the Reformation when the growth of Pro-
testantism had created a pro-English party which encouraged the
adoption of the London standard for Scotland also. Nevertheless,
Scottish particularism persisted to a degree in the linguistic sphere
as in others. Literary Scots was not entirely eclipsed, though inevitably much modified by the southern standard. It remained as a
familiar poetic medium, to be raised to immortal heights in the
eighteenth century by the genius of Robert Burns.

The all-pervading influence of the standard language has levelled
the dialects in England to the point of extinction. But not so yet in
Scotland, where indeed the colloquial may be so far removed from
other English as not to be immediately comprehensible to a Sassenach
at all. It is therefore not surprising that Modern Scots, today often
called Lallans (Lowlands), lives on in song and verse. A contemporary sample illustrates its vitality:

From the ballad *The Highland Division's Farewell to Sicily* (1943),
by Hamish Henderson:

The pipie is dozie, the pipie is fey,
He wullna come roon' for his *vino* the day,
The sky ow'r Messina is unco an' grey,
An' a' the bricht chaumers are eerie.

Then fareweel, ye banks of Sicily,
Fare ye weel, ye valley and shaw,
There's nae Jock wull mourn the kyles o' ye,
Puir bliddy swaddies are weary.

The drummie is polished, the drummie is braw,
He canna be seen for his webbin' ava,
He's beezed himsel' up for a photie an' a'
Tae leave wi' his Lola, his dearie.

Sae fareweel, ye dives o' Sicily,
Fare ye weel, ye shieling an' ha',
We'll a' mind shebeens an' bothies
Whaur kind *signorinas* were cheery.

Then tune the pipes an' drub the tenor drum,
Leave your kit this side o' the wa',
Then tune the pipes an' drub the tenor drum,
A' the bricht chaumers are eerie.

pipie 'piper', here 'pipe-major', *fey* 'acting strangely as if under
doom', *wullna* (=will no) 'will not', *roon*=round, *the day* 'today',
ow'r=over, *unco an'* (=uncouth and) 'ominously', *a'*=all, *bricht*=
bright, *chaumers* (=chambers) '(barrack) rooms', *weel* 'well', *shaw*
'wood', *nae*=no, *kyles* 'straights' (Gael. *caol*), *drummie* 'drummer',
here 'drum-major', *braw* (=brave) 'smart', *canna* 'cannot', *ava*
(=of all) 'at all', *beezed* 'smartened', *photie* 'photo', *shieling*
(properly a shelter of stones or sods for the accommodation of
shepherds or dairymaids in remote areas used for summer grazing)
'hut', *ha'* (=hall) 'farmhouse', *mind* 'remember', *shebeens* 'taverns'
(an Irish term, Gael. *sibín*), *bothies* (properly hillside shelters, huts
for farm labourers) 'lodging houses', *wa'*=wall.

LITERATURE

W. Grant and J. M. Dixon, *Manual of Modern Scots* (1921).

CHAPTER ELEVEN

Norse and Norn

𝕨𝕨𝕨𝕨𝕨𝕨

THE ethnic composition of our population was again modified by the arrival in the Viking Age of large numbers of Scandinavians. They settled extensively in both the English and Celtic parts of the country, where they managed to preserve their national identity and Norse speech for several generations. In Orkney and Shetland the language proved exceptionally durable and here, under the name of Norn, continued in use down to recent times.

NORSE

Norse, or more technically Old Norse, established itself in the British Isles at the very outset of the Viking Age, ie, just before 800 AD, and at once became a most important language here as the settlements of the Norsemen rapidly increased, reaching its zenith in the tenth century. But linguistic assimilation soon set in over much of the area and, except in the far north (see Norn below) Norse had apparently everywhere died out, or at least become moribund, by the beginning of the thirteenth century.

The first invaders were Norwegians who colonized Orkney and Shetland in the last decade or so of the eighth century. They next quickly took possession of the Hebrides and large tracts of the Northern Scottish mainland, especially Sutherland and Caithness. From such strongholds, the newcomers mounted attacks on Ireland which were soon to lead to permanent settlement at points around the coast, out of which developed the earliest towns in that country, foremost among them Dublin. These centres were still in Norse hands when the Anglo-Norman invaders landed in 1169.

In 851, a Danish Viking element made its appearance in Ireland. After initial friction with the Norwegians already present, differences between the two were generally resolved, so that all Norsemen tended to make common cause together. Meanwhile the Isle of Man had been occupied and now considerable settlements were made in Galloway and even larger ones in Cumberland, Westmorland and north Lancashire. The foreigners also set themselves up further south, notably in the Wirral and here and there around the Welsh coast. It goes without saying that the Vikings dominated the Irish Sea, and their domination continued into the first half of the twelfth century. They interfered in local politics and their assistance to the Welsh princes in North Wales helped the latter to remain independent in spite of Norman pressure. The Norse-controlled Hebrides and Man were closely linked down to 1266, their rulers being known as kings of Man and the Isles.

In these circumstances, it is not surprising that the Norse language was still in living use locally in the twelfth century, as is amply proved by datable inscriptions (p. 212). But afterwards, total assimilation to the neighbouring languages will have become the order of the day, ie, to Gaelic (Ireland, Scotland, Man), to English and in a few cases to Welsh. In general, the demise of Norse in these areas meant a return to the status quo, but not entirely so. In the north, Pictish had by now vanished completely, so that Norse in Scotland was everywhere replaced by Gaelic. It is not known for certain what language was current in Galloway when the Norse colonies were founded in the ninth century. Gaelic may already have established itself, but it seems equally likely that there was at least some British remaining. Judging from place names, British still survived in the Lake District at this time. It thus appears that British here, and possibly also in Galloway, owes its extinction to the intrusion of Norse.

The Norwegians who colonized Orkney and Shetland were doubtless responsible for the infamous raid on Lindisfarne in 793, but England generally remained free from Viking incursions until 835. From that year on, Danish Vikings made continual assaults, after 855 increasing in severity and assuming more and more the character of invasions. Settlement proper began in 876 with large-scale landtaking in Northumbria. Within two or three years, equally impressive allotments were being made in North Mercia and East Anglia. In this way, the Danelaw came into being. But early in the next century, the English began to reconquer the lost territories. Attempts to set up an independent Norse kingdom in Northumbria failed, and by 954 the authority of English rulers was everywhere acknowledged.

The Anglo-Norse of the Danelaw was essentially Norse as spoken in Denmark, though on the evidence of place names a Norwegian element has been detected in Yorkshire. Since an occasional Celtic name occurs in the nomenclature in question, it has been concluded that the settlements concerned were the result of a migration from the Lake District, where the Norse colonizers were predominantly Norwegians who had been living in a Celtic environment (above).

It is impossible to say how long Norse survived in the former Danelaw. The assumption is, of course, that the language increasingly fell into disuse as the English reconquest progressed. On the other hand, certain areas had become predominantly Scandinavian, in some cases almost exclusively so. Such an area is Cleveland, where indeed three villages with the Norse name *Ingleby* (lit. Angles' village) still bear their quaint testimony to a time when this district was so thoroughly Scandinavian that a place inhabited by Englishmen was remarkable enough to lead to its being so named. The continuing influence of the Danes in English affairs may also be taken into consideration, for although there was no further Scandinavian colonization in England, at least not to an appreciable extent, the country did suffer a second period of invasion from 980 to 1016, and was then ruled by Danish kings until 1042. Not until the Norman Conquest was England effectively barred to Scandinavian influence.

We would hazard the guess that in the compact Scandinavian-speaking districts of the old Danelaw, Norse was still a living reality in the first half of the eleventh century. In more remote places, such as Cleveland, the language most likely continued longer. Perhaps it was William's Harrying of the North which brought about its final collapse there. We know that Norse was still in use in the Lake District in the twelfth century (p. 212).

The assimilation of Norse speakers was doubtless facilitated by the similarity between Old Norse and Old English. It seems likely that over wide areas a compromise colloquial arose, a Scandinavian–English dialect which concentrated on basic comprehension without undue regard for grammatical niceties. It is well known that a large number of Norse words, several hundred in fact, have passed into English. Certainly Norse influence hastened that loss of inflections which proceeded slowly from north to south during the next three centuries.

SKETCH OF OLD NORSE

The one-time presence of Viking settlers in the British Isles is attested by the considerable number of runic inscriptions found in those parts where Old Norse was formerly spoken. But there are no surviving manuscript materials. However, the language is well known from the abundant literature of the age which was written down chiefly in Iceland. Some of this literature was actually composed in Britain (see selections below). In our grammatical outline and literary samples we therefore reproduce the form of the language as standardized in Iceland. This classical form is, in all essentials, thoroughly representative of the language once used in these islands also.

In its general structure Old Norse was very similar to Old English, the two languages representing the northern and western divisions of Germanic at a comparable stage of their evolution. Morphologically, however, Old Norse was in some respects more archaic; for example, the verb retained the distinctive endings for all persons of the plural, whereas Old English had reduced these to a single term.

Phonetics

The acute accent marks long vowels; *ǫ* is open in contrast to closed *o*: the vowels *y*, *ø* and *æ* are pronounced [y], [ø] and [ɛː] respectively.

Intervocalic *g* is [ɣ] after a back vowel, [j] after a front vowel; *þ* is the voiceless, *ð* the voiced dental spirant; *z* is [ts].

Nouns

a-stems, masc. and neut.

Sg. nom. *fiskr* m. 'fish', acc. *fisk*, gen. *fisks*, dat. *fiski*, pl. nom. *fiskar*, acc. gen. *fiska*, dat. *fiskum*.

Similarly *orð* n. 'word' except that pl. nom. acc. are uninflected.

ō-stems, fem.

Sg. nom. acc. *sál* 'soul', gen. *sálar*, dat. *sál*, pl. nom. acc. *sálar*, gen. *sála*, dat. *sálum*.

i-stems, masc. and fem.

Sg. nom. *vinr* m. 'friend', acc. *vin*, gen. *vinar*, dat. *vini*, pl. nom. *vinir*, acc. *vini*, gen. *vina*, dat. *vinum*.

Sg. nom. acc. *húð* f. 'hide', gen. *húðar*, dat. *húð*, pl. nom. acc. *húðir*, gen. *húða*, dat. *húðum*.

u-stems, masc.

Sg. nom. *sonr* 'son', acc. *son*, gen. *sonar*, dat. *syni*, pl. nom. *synir*, acc. *sonu*, gen. *sona*, dat. *sonum*.

n-stems, all genders

Sg. nom. *bogi* m. 'bow', acc. gen. dat. *boga*, pl. nom. *bogar*, acc. *boga*, gen. *bogna*, dat. *bogum*.

Sg. nom. *tunga* f. 'tongue', acc. gen. dat. *tungu*, pl. nom. acc. *tungur*, gen. *tungna*, dat. *tungum*.

Sg. (all cases) *eyra* n. 'ear', pl. nom. acc. *eyru*, gen. *eyrna*, dat. *eyrum*.

Minor declensions include:

Sg. nom. *fótr* m. 'foot', acc. *fót*, gen. *fótar*, dat. *føti*, pl. nom. acc. *føtr*, gen. *fóta*, dat. *fótum*.

Sg. nom. acc. *bók* f. 'book', gen. *bókar*, dat. *bók*, pl. nom. acc. *bøkr*, gen. *bóka*, dat. *bókum*.

Adjectives

Strong declension:

Sg. nom. masc.	*sjúkr* 'sick'	fem. *sjúk*	neut. *sjúkt*
acc.	*sjúkan*	*sjúka*	*sjúkt*
gen.	*sjúks*	*sjúkrar*	*sjúks*
dat.	*sjúkum*	*sjúkri*	*sjúku*
Pl. nom.	*sjúkir*	*sjúkar*	*sjúk*
acc.	*sjúka*	*sjúkar*	*sjúk*
gen.		*sjúkra*	
dat.		*sjúkum*	

Weak declension:

In the singular as for the *n*-declension of nouns: sg. nom. *sjúki* m. *sjúka*, fem. neut. etc.; (all genders) pl. nom. acc. gen. *sjúku*, dat. *sjúkum*.

The comparative and superlative are usually formed by adding -*ari* and -*astr* to the stem: *sjúkari* 'sicker', *sjúkastr* 'sickest'. Examples of irregular comparison: *góðr* 'good', *betri* 'better', *beztr* 'best', *illr* 'bad', *verri* 'worse', *verstr* 'worst'.

Numbers

1 *einn*, 2 *tveir*, 3 *þrír*, 4 *fjórir*, 5 *fimm*, 6 *sex*, 7 *sjau*, 8 *átta*, 9 *níu*, 10 *tíu*, 11 *ellifu*, 12 *tólf*, 13 *þrettán*, 14 *fjórtán*, 15 *fimtán*, 16 *sextán*, 17 *sjaután*, 18 *átján*, 19 *nítján*, 20 *tuttugu*, 21 *tuttugu ok einn*, 30 *þrír tigir*, 40 *fjórir tigir*, 50 *fimm tigir*, 60 *sex tigir*, 70 *sjau tigir*, 80 *átta tigir*, 90 *níu tigir*, 100 *tíu tigir*, *hundrað* usually 120, *þúsund* 1200.

The first four numbers inflect irregularly, as nom. *einn* masc., *ein* fem., *eitt* neut., acc. *einn* masc., *eina* fem., *eitt* neut., etc.

Occasionally, *einn* functions as an indefinite article.

Definite Article

	masc.	fem.	neut.		masc.	fem.	neut.
Sg. nom.	*inn*	*in*	*it*	Pl.	*inir*	*inar*	*in*
acc.	*inn*	*ina*	*it*		*ina*	*inar*	*in*
gen.	*ins*	*innar*	*ins*			*inna*	
dat.	*inum*	*inni*	*inu*			*inum*	

When used with a noun, the article is suffixed, in which position the stem vowel may be suppressed, eg, *fiskrinn* 'the fish', but *boginn* 'the bow', *tungan* 'the tongue'.

Pronouns

Dual forms are present, as in Old English. Paradigms:

Sg. nom.	*ek* 'I'	*þú* 'thou'	*hann* 'he'	*hon* 'she'	*þat* 'it'
acc.	*mik*	*þik*	*hann*	*hana*	*þat*
gen.	*mín*	*þín*	*hans*	*hennar*	*þess*
dat.	*mér*	*þér*	*honum*	*henni*	*því*

Pl. nom.	*vér* 'we'	*þér* 'you'	*þeir*	*þær*	*þau* 'they'
acc.	*oss*	*yðr*	*þá*	*þær*	*þau*
gen.	*vár*	*yðar*		*þeira*	
dat.	*oss*	*yðr*		*þeim*	

Du. nom.	*vit* 'we'	*þit* 'you'
acc.	*okkr*	*ykkr*
gen.	*okkar*	*ykkar*
dat.	*okkr*	*ykkr*

There is a third-person reflexive pronoun, the same for singular and plural: acc. *sik*, gen. *sín*, dat. *sér*.

The possessive pronouns for the first two persons decline, in principle like the strong adjective illustrated above: *minn* 'my', *þinn* 'thy', *várr* 'our', *yðarr* 'your', *okkarr* 'our two', *ykkarr* 'your two'; the third person is expressed by the genitive of the personal pronoun unchanged: *hans* 'his', etc., but the reflexive is an adjective: *sinn*.

Verbs

Paradigm of a strong verb:

Infinitive: *drífa* 'drive, throng, rush', *at drífa* 'to drive, etc.'

Indicative: pres. sg. 1 *dríf*, 2, 3 *drífr*, pl. 1 *drífum*, 2 *drífið*, 3 *drífa*; past sg. 1 *dreif*, 2 *dreift*, 3 *dreif*, pl. 1 *drifum*, 2 *drifuð*, 3 *drifu*.

Subjunctive: pres. sg. 1 *drífa*, 2 *drífir*, 3 *drífi*, pl. 1 *drífim*, 2 *drífið*, 3 *drífi*; past sg. 1 *drifa*, 2 *drifir*, 3 *drifi*, pl. 1 *drifim*, 2 *drifið*, 3 *drifi*.

Imperative: sg. *dríf*, pl. *drífið*.

Participles: pres. *drífandi*, past *drifinn*.

Other patterns of vowel change (infin., past sg. 1, past pl. 1, past part.): *skjóta* 'shoot', *skaut*, *skutum*, *skotinn*; *bresta* 'burst', *brast*, *brustum*, *brostinn*; *stela* 'steal', *stal*, *stálum*, *stolinn*; *gefa* 'give', *gaf*, *gáfum*, *gefinn*; *fara* 'go, fare', *fór*, *fórum*, *farinn*; *láta* 'let, allow', *lét*, *létum*, *latinn*.

An example of the weak conjugation:

Infinitive: *heyra* 'hear', *at heyra* 'to hear'.

Indicative: pres. sg. 1 *heyri*, 2, 3 *heyrir*, pl. 1 *heyrum*, 2 *heyrið*, 3 *heyra*; past sg. 1 *heyrða*, 2 *heyrðir*, 3 *heyrði*, pl. 1 *heyrðum*, 2 *heyrðuð*, 3 *heyrðu*.

Imperative: sg. *heyr*, pl. *heyrið*

Subjunctive: pres. sg. 1 *heyra*, 2 *heyrir*, 3 *heyri*, pl. 1 *heyrim*, 2 *heyrið*, *heyri*; past sg. 1 *heyrða*, 2 *heyrðir*, 3 *heyrði*, pl. 1 *heyrðim*, 2 *heyrðið*, 3 *heyrði*.

Participles: pres. *heyrandi*, past *heyrðr.*

The auxiliaries 'to be' and 'to have':

Infinitive: *vera* 'be', etc.

Indicative: pres. sg. 1 *em*, 2 *ert*, 3 *er*[1], pl. 1 *erum*, 2 *eruð*, 3 *eru*; past sg. 1 *var*, 2 *vart*, 3 *var*, pl. 1 *várum*, 2 *váruð*, 3 *váru.*

Imperative: sg. *ver*, pl. *verið.*

Subjunctive: pres. sg. 1 *sé*, 2 *sér*, 3 *sé*, pl. 1 *sém*, 2 *séð*, 3 *sé*; past sg. 1 *væra*, 2 *værir*, 3 *væri*, pl. 1 *værim*, 2 *værið*, 3 *væri.*

Participles: pres. *verandi*, past (neuter) *verit.*

Infinitive: *hafa* 'have', etc.

Indicative: pres. sg. 1 *hefi*, 2, 3 *hefir*, pl. 1 *hafum*, 2 *hafið*, 3 *hafa;* past sg. 1 *hafða*, 2 *hafðir*, 3 *hafði*, pl. 1 *hafðum*, 2 *hofðuð*, 3 *hofðu.*

Imperative: sg. *haf*, pl. *hafið.*

Subjunctive: pres. sg. 1 *hafa*, 2 *hafir*, 3 *hafi*, pl. 1 *hafim*, 2 *hafið*, 3 *hafi*; past sg. 1 *hefða*, 2 *hefðir*, 3 *hefði*, pl. 1 *hefðim*, 2 *hefðið*, 3 *hefði.*

Participles: pres. *hafandi*, past *hafðr.*

READINGS

From *Ragnars saga Loðbrókar* – Saga of Ragnar Shaggy-Breeches:
(Ælla, king of Northumbria, has captured in battle (*c.* 865) a marauding Viking chief, who refuses to disclose his identity; he is in fact the redoubtable Ragnarr Loðbrók).

Þá   mælti Ella konungr: 'Sjá   maðr man verða at koma í
Then said Ælla king: 'This man will have to come into
meiri   mannraun, ef hann vill eigi segja oss,   hverr hann er;
greater ordeal,   if he   will not say to-us who he   is;
nú   skal   kasta honum í   einn ormgarð ok láta hann
now shall (one) cast him   into a snake-pit and let him
þar   sitja mjǫk lengi.' Nú   er honum þangat fylgt, ok   hann sitr
there sit   very long.' Now is he   thither led, and he   sits

---

1 Archaic *es*, elided to *'s*, occurs in the poetic readings below.

208

þar   mjǫk lengi, svá at   hvergi   festask
there very long, so that (yet even so) nowhere fasten-themselves
ormar við   hann. Þá   mæltu menn: 'Þessi maðr er mikill
snakes with (onto) him. Then said   men: 'This man is great
fyrir sér   Hann bitu eigi vápn   í dag,
indeed (lit. 'for himself'). Him bit not weapons today,
enn   nú   granda honum eigi ormar.' Þá   mælti
moreover now harm   him   not snakes.' Then said
         Ella konungr, at   hann væri flettr   af klæði
(commanded) Ælla king   that he be stripped of clothing
því, er   hann hafði yzt,   ok var svá gǫrt, ok hengu
that which he   had outermost, and was so done, and hung
ormar ǫllum   megin á honum. Þá   mælti Ragnarr: 'Gnyðja
snakes with-all might on him.   Then said Ragnar: 'Grunt
mundu nú   grísir,   ef þeir vissi, hvat inn gamli
would now young-boars[1], if they knew what the old (one)
þyldi.'   Nú   lætr   hann líf sitt, enn Ella þykkisk   vita,
suffered.' Now leaves he   life his, but Ælla seems   (to) know
at   Ragnarr hefir líf sitt látit.
that Ragnar has life his left (*ie*, feels sure that it must have
been Ragnar).

From *Egils Saga Skallagrímssonar*:
(The hero of the saga, the skald Egil Skallagrímsson, finds himself
in the realm of his mortal enemy, Eric Blood-Axe, then king of
Northumbria. But Egil boldly went into the king's presence at York,
where he composed a poem in praise of Eric's warlike career. This
encomium *Hǫfuðlausn* – Head Ransom – from which we quote the
opening stanzas, saved his life. The encounter between the skald and
the king took place towards the middle of the tenth century.)

Þá   gekk Egill fyrir Eirík konung ok   hóf upp kvæðit,
Then went Egil before Eric king   and began the-poem,
kvað   hátt ok fekk   þegar hljóð:
declaimed loudly and obtained at-once hearing:

  Vestr fórk   of   ver,   en ek Viðris ber
  West fared-I over ocean,   and I Vidrir's bear

---

1 The young boars are Ragnar's sons.

```
munstrandar mar;      svá's  mitt of      far.
mind-shore's sea¹;    so  is my  around going².
Drók   eik á flot     við  ísabrot,
Drew-I oak afloat     with ice-breaking,
(ie, set sail when the ice broke,)
hlóðk   mærðar hlut       munknarrar skut.
loaded-I praise's portion   mind-ship's hold³.

Buðumk  hilmi   lǫð;      ák    hróðrs of kvǫð;
I-bade-me to-prince invitation;   have-I praise's – duty⁴;
berk   Óðins mjǫð   á    Engla  bjǫð.
bear-I Odin's mead⁵  onto Angles' fields.

Lofat   vísa    vann,    víst  mærik  þann,
Extolled ruler (I) got⁶,   truly praise-I that-one,
hljóðs  biðjum   hann,  þvít hróðr of  fann...
of-hearing I-ask-for-myself him,   since praise – (I) found⁷...
```

```
Eiríkr konungr sat uppréttr meðan Egill kvað    kvæðit,  ok
Eric  king    sat upright while Egil declaimed the-poem, and
hvesti   augun á hann. Ok er    lokit   var drápunni, þá
fastened eyes  on him. And when finished was the-ode,  then
mælti konungr: 'Bezta er kvæðit    fram flutt.'
said  king:   'Best  is the-poem recited⁸.'
```

1 'Sea of Vidrir's (=Odin's) mind-shore', kenning for poetry, 2 'So it is with me', 3 'Mind-ship's hold', kenning for mind: 'I loaded my mind with a portion of praise', 4 'I invited myself to the prince; I owe him duty', 5 'Odin's mead', kenning for poetry, 6 'I extolled the ruler', 7 'A hearing I beg of him, for I contrived his praise', 8 'The poem was recited excellently'.

From *Eiríksmál – Eric's Lay*:
(Eric Blood-Axe fell in battle at Stainmore, in the Yorkshire–Westmorland border country in 954. His widow Gunnhild commissioned the lay in his memory. Our selection describes the scene in Valhalla.)

```
Óðinn kvað:
Odin spake:
  Hvat's þat drauma?     Hugðumk  fyr   dag   rísa,
  What is that of-dreams¹   me-thought before day (to) rise²,
  Valhǫll  at ryðja      fyr vegnu folki;
  Valhalla to prepare   for slain folk;
```

1 'What have I been dreaming?', 2 'I thought I rose before day'.

210

vakðak	*Einherja,*	*baðk*	*upp rísa,*
awakened-I	Einherjar[3],	bade-I (them)	up rise,

bekki	*at stráa,*	*bjórker*	*at leyðra,*
benches	to strew,	beer-goblets	to wash,

Valkyrjur vín	*bera,*	*sem vísi kømi . . .*
Valkyries wine	(to) bear,	as-if ruler came[4] . . .

Sigmundr ok Sinfjǫtli!	*rísið snarliga*
Sigmund and Sinfjǫtli!	rise speedily

ok gangið í gǫgn grami . . .
and go towards king . . .

inn þú bjóð,	*ef Eiríkr sé;*
in thou invite (him)	if Eric (it) be

hans es mér nú ván	*vituð . . .*[5]
of-him is to-me now expectancy	known . . .

Sigmundr:
Sigmund:

Heill nú Eiríkr!	*vel skalt hér kominn*
Hail now, Eric!	Well shall here (be) come[6]

ok gakk í hǫll, horskr!
and go into hall, brave (man)!

Hins vilk fregna	*hvat fylgir þér*
Of-that will-I enquire	what (who) follows thee

jǫfra frá	*eggþrimu?*
of-kings from	(sword-)edge-clash[7]?

Eiríkr:
Eric:

Konungar 'ru fimm,	*kennik þér nafn allra;*
Kings are five,	teach-I thee name of-all;

ek em inn sétti sjalfr.
I am the sixth (my)self.

Four runic inscriptions (in transliteration)
Kirkmichael, Isle of Man, c. 1100:

MALLUMKUN RAISTI KRUS ÞENA EFTER MALMURU FUSTRU SIN(A)

---

3 Odin's chosen warriors, 4 'As would befit a ruler', 5 'I am expecting him now', 6 'Thou shalt be welcome here', 7 'Battle'.

E(N) TOTIR TUFKALS KONA AÞISL ATI (B)ETRA ES LAIFA FUSTRA
KUÞAN ÞAN SON ILAN

(normalized) *Mallumkun   reisti kros þenna eptir Malmuru*
          Maollomchon raised cross this   after Maolmhuire,
fóstru   sína, en dóttir   Dufgals,   kona er   Aðils
foster-mother his, and daughter Dubhghall's wife whom Aðils
átti. Betra er   leifa fóstra   góðan en   son illan.
had[1]. Better is (to) leave fosterling good than son bad.

1 'Maollomchon and Dubhghall's (Doughal's) daughter, whom Aðils had to
wife, together raised ...'.

Maeshowe, Orkney, 1152–53:

UT NORÞR ER FE FOLGIT MIKIT ÞAT ER LO EFTIR SÆL ER SA IR
FINA MA ÞAN ØUÞ HIN MIKLA

(normalized) *Útnorðr   er fé   fólgit mikit þat er   lá*
          Out-north[1] is treasure hidden great that which lay
eptir. Sæll   er sá   er finna má þann auð   inn mikla!
after[2]. Lucky is that (one) who find can that wealth the great!

1 'North-west', 2 'which was left after death'.

Pennington, Furness, Lancashire, *c.* 1150:

(KA)MIAL SETI ÞESA KIRK HUBERT MASUN UAN

(normalized) *Gamall setti   þessa kirkju.   Hubert   masun*
          Gamal endowed this   church. Hubert (the) mason
vann.
built (it).

Greenmount, Co. Louth, twelfth century:

TOMNAL SELSHOFOÞ A SOERÞ (Þ)ETA

(normalized) *Domnal   Selshofuð   á   sverð þetta.*
          Domhnall (Donald) Seal's-Head owns sword this.

LITERATURE

E. V. Gordon, *An Introduction to Old Norse*, 2nd edition, revised by
A. R. Taylor (1957).

NORN

We have referred to Shetland and Orkney as the first landfall of the invading Norwegians in the closing years of the eighth century, and here their language was destined to continue longest. It survived, in fact, until recent times and is known by the name of Norn. To judge from the place names, which are almost exclusively Scandinavian, the native Picts must have been overwhelmed by the newcomers. That there were, however, survivors is proved by (Scandinavian) place names containing *Pett-* 'Pict' and also by the continuation of Pictish sculpture (p. 20) until about 900, and their language may be supposed to have survived at least as late as this.

By the end of the ninth century, at the latest, Orkney together with Shetland formed a Norse state under native earls which lasted until 1231, owing allegiance to Norway. When the Norse earls were succeeded by Scottish earls, the latter continued this allegiance until the political connexion was broken in 1468/69. Norwegian rights were then transferred to Scotland as part of the dowry of Margaret of Denmark on her marriage to James III of Scotland – it will be remembered that Norway itself had been dominated by Denmark since the union of the crowns in 1380.

The Orkney earldom originally included Caithness, and Norn apparently survived there as late as the fifteenth century. In the earlier phase it had yielded to Gaelic which had elsewhere absorbed the Norse enclaves in Scotland, but possibly it was English moving up the coast which finally dislodged it from its last stronghold in the north-east corner.

In the islands themselves, the language survived even better. Although a degree of scotticization, linguistically the equivalent of anglicization, inevitably followed the accession of the Scottish earls, the native language persisted as the ordinary medium until the transference to Scotland. A few samples of the written language from the fourteenth and fifteenth centuries have come down to us and show that the islanders traditionally shared the literary language of Norway, but in the period of Danish ascendancy they followed the Norwegians in employing Danish also. The use of literary Scandinavian ceased after 1468/69 and Norn was henceforth no more than a patois, doomed to extinction in the face of competition from English, the only official medium and the language of prestige. Contemporary writers bear witness to the decline and extinction of

Norn. The Orcadian dialect was the first to be lost. In 1596 we hear that 'of the Iles of Orchnay, sum ar Inglese, sum of the language of Norway'. Less than a century later, Norn survived only in three or four parishes, and then chiefly as the language of the home, Scots English having otherwise become universal. Norn must have become moribund shortly afterwards, for in 1750 Murdoch MacKenzie could write: 'Thirty or Forty years ago this (Norn) was the Language of two Parishes in Pomona Island; since which, by the Means of Charity-Schools, it is so much wore out, as to be understood by none but old People; and in thirty years more, it is probable, will not be understood there at all.' That prediction was certainly correct, and regrettably nobody appears to have attempted to record the dialect before it vanished for ever. The only surviving text in recent Orkney Norn is a paternoster taken down in the eighteenth century.

From Shetland the story is the same but, being more remote, Norn survived for two or three generations longer than the sister dialect in Orkney, finding a last refuge in the more northerly islands. A paternoster and a specimen of oral literature were collected in the eighteenth century and when, towards the end of the last century, philologists began to take an interest in Norn, a few corrupt, half-forgotten verses and sayings could still be recorded. In the first half of the last century the English style of the Shetland Islanders was still quite exotic. A London taxidermist, Robert Dunn, wrote in his *Ornithologist's Guide*, 1837, that 'the English language is commonly spoken . . . they have introduced into it a great many words from the Norwegian, Danish and Dutch languages, and this medley uttered by a native of the country is exceedingly unpleasant to the ear and very difficult to understand'. This means, in more objective terms, that the natives in the country districts, though English-speaking, nevertheless continued to employ a large number of expressions deriving from the indigenous Norn, which, after all, had only lately passed out of use as a living tongue. Indeed, when Dunn was writing, there were still a few old people alive who had themselves spoken Norn in their childhood.

Although so poorly represented in actual texts, a fair amount of Norn lexical material survives in the English as spoken locally in the islands. This is particularly true of Shetland. Naturally enough, Norn has contributed but little to Standard English. But one item at least is fairly prominent, namely *vole*, abbreviated from *vole-mouse* 'field-mouse'. Occasionally local bird names have gained some currency, as *bonxie* and *ember-goose*, more officially termed *great skua* and *great northern diver* respectively.

READINGS

Shetland

A legal document dated November 9, 1405. Norwegian:

> *Øllum mønnum þeim, sem þetta bréf séa edur heyra, senda*
> To-all men   those as   this letter see or   hear   send
> *Gudbrandr Magnusson, sóknarprestr í Jala í Hjaltlandi, Svein*
> Gudbrand Magnus'son parish-priest in Yell in Shetland, Svein
> *Markusson, løgman   í sama landi, Jón   Haraldsson,*
> Mark's son lawman (sheriff) in same land, John Harold's son,
> *løgrettuman   í Hjaltlandi, Kvøðu   Guds ok*
> lawrightman (assizeman) in Shetland, Greeting God's and
> *sína,   kunnigt gerandi at þat er os   viturligt, at   Ragnild*
> theirs[1], known making that it   is to-us evident that Ragnhild
> *Havardsdóttir   var ei fletgingin   ok sjálf   réd*
> Havard's daughter was not floor-gone[2] and (her-)self managed
> *hon sínum peningum, þá   þróndr Dagfinnson   kom til*
> she her moneys,   when Thrond Dagfinn's son came to
> *Vindas ok sat þar   til hús,   ok til sannenda hér um settum*
> Windas and sat there to house[3], and to truth   hereof set
> *vér vár insigli fyr   þetta bréf, er   gørt var í Papiliu*
> we our seal   before this letter, which done was in Papil
> *mánadagin fyr   Marteins messu A.D. 1405.*
> Monday   before Martinmas   A.D. 1405.

From the Hildina Ballad:
(A unique record of the otherwise lost oral literature in Norn are the thirty-five verses of a traditional ballad taken down in Foula in 1774 by the scholar George Low from the recitation of William Henry, then an elderly man. Our text is from the critical edition of the corrupt original by M. Hægstad, *Hildinakvadet* (1900). Verse translation of the first twelve stanzas in N. Kershaw, *Stories and Ballads of the Far Past* (1921).

1 God's greeting and their own, 2 had not surrendered her estate, 3 took his abode there.

1   *Da var Jarlin   or   Orkneyar*
     It was the-Earl from Orkney
     for frienda   sin spirde ro,
     of kinsman his asked advice,
     whirdi   an skilde   meun
     whether he should the-maiden
     or   vannaro ednar fo,
     from plight-her   rescue,
     or   glasburyon   burt taga?
     from the-glass-castle away take?

2   '*Tega du   meun   or   glasburyon,*
     'Take thou (if thou takest) the maiden from the-glass-castle,
     kere friende   min,
     dear kinsman mine,
     yamna-men eso vrildan   stiende
     as-long-as   this the-world stands
     gede   min vara to din.'
     spoken shall be   of thee.'

3   *Yom   keimir eullingin*
     Home comes the-king
     fro   liene;
     from war (lit. 'from leading')
     burt a   sta var fruen   Hildina;
     away from place was the-lady Hildina;
     hemi   stumer   stiene.
     at-home step-mother stands.

4   '*Whar   an yaar e   londen,*
     'Where he is   in lands (in whatever land he is),
     ita   kan sadnast   wo,
     this can hold-true on (this you can take as true),
     an skal   vara heinde wo osta   tre
     he shall be   hanged on highest tree
     sin reitin ridna dar   fro.'
     as roots run   (there) from (that ever ran 'grew' from roots).

Original Norse apparently:

1   *Þat var jarlinn ór Orkneyum | fyrir frænda sinn spurði ráð |*

Norse and Norn

*hvert hann skyldi meyna | ór vandaráði hennar fá | ór glasborginni
burt taka?*

2 '*Tekr þú meyna ór glasborginni | kæri frændi minn | jafnan
meðan þessur verǫldin stendr | getit mun vera til þín.*'

3 *Heim kemr ǫðlingrinn | frá leiðinni | burt af stað var frúin
Hildina | heima stjúpmóðir stendr.*

4 *Hvar hann er í lǫndum | þetta kann sannast á | hann skal vera
hengdr á hæsta tré | sem rótum rennr (þar) frá.*

At the end of the last century, fragments of corrupt Norn were still
remembered by a few people in Shetland. Here is a relatively well-
preserved riddle:

Føre honga, føre gonga, føre stad apo skø;
Twa vistre vegebi, and en comes ate drilandi.

Original form presumably:

Fjórir hanga, fjórir ganga, fjórir standa upp á ský;
Four hang, four walk, four stand up to clouds;
(tveir) vísa veg í bý, (ok) einn (kemr) aftan drollandi.
two   show way to farm, and one comes after dangling.

(Answer: a cow)

Orkney

The beginning of a complaint by the Orkney people to the Danish
king against David Menzies of Weem, about 1425. Danish:

Thætta   ære the articuli *ther   alt landit   i Ørknø*
That (these) are the items   which all the-country in Orkney
kære   ower David Menies oc hava storliga til hulpit
complains-of about David Menies and have greatly contributed
at   landit   ær fordarvat.   Først æpter thet landit
that the-country is impoverished. First after that the-country
war plagat   thet kornit   wæxte ekke tha war alt landit
was afflicted that the-corn grew not then was all the-country
oc David Menies owereens thet eynte korn sculde utføras
and David Menies agreed   that no   corn should be-taken-out

217

af landit   uthan thet sculde sciptas   oc sælias
of the-country but   that should be-divided and be-sold in
landit   for møghelige pæninge, oc   ower thet   tha   loot
the-country for possible   moneys, and over that   then let
forsagde David føra af   landit   iiii   schip med korn oc
aforesaid David take from the-country four ships with corn and
til Scotland i   thet sama aar, oc   for   the forsagde
to Scotland in the same year, and before the aforesaid
endrakt   war giord, tha   loot forsagde David føra ut   v
agreement was made, then let   aforesaid David take out five
schip æller vi, oc   ther med ward   landit   mæst
ships or   six and therewith became the-country most
fordarvat.
impoverished.

LITERATURE

F. T. Wainwright (editor), *The Northern Isles* (1962).
J. Jakobsen, *An Etymological Dictionary of the Norn Language in Shetland* (1928–32).
H. Marwick, *The Orkney Norn* (1929).

CHAPTER TWELVE

Norman French

𝔊𝔊𝔊𝔊𝔊

THE outcome of the Battle of Hastings was as shattering in the linguistic history of these islands as it was in any other sphere of the national life. The new situation was summed up in lines written a century later:

> Li reis amat mult ses Normanz;
> Les Engleis enveia as chans.
> The king loves much his Normans;
> The English (he) sent to the dogs.

An alien ruler and his followers imposed themselves absolutely on the country and their Norman French language at once became the medium of government and business, in this respect supplanting entirely the language of the conquered. Influential society spoke only French and cultivated a literature written in that tongue, with fatal consequences for the Old English literary language, as explained on p. 180. It may be added that French expressed not only the domination of the Norman, but also reflected the prestige of all France, at that time the most advanced part of Europe. It will be remembered, too, that Norman England was but an overseas province of a larger realm – the French possessions remained the heartland of the state. The Angevins, indeed, added new French territories. Henry II, who reigned from 1154 to 1189, ruled the whole of western France as well as England, so that his kingdom stretched from the Cheviots to the Pyrenees. His queen, Eleanor, was celebrated for her patronage of courtly French literature.

The French language remained the native medium of the ruling classes, and often the only one, for quite a century and a half. Any business with monoglot Saxons could be conducted through bilingual bailiffs. If analogical situations elsewhere be any guide, it is more than likely that large numbers of the native English swiftly acquired a knowledge of French as a second language and a social asset.

No doubt some of those who managed to join the establishment would actually go over to French as the habitual medium and pass it on to their children. But these would be exceptions. The mass of the indigenous inhabitants remained faithful to their English mother tongue. The native French speakers never formed more than a tiny fraction of the total – perhaps five per cent – and virtually all were of foreign race, but thanks to their status in the society of the time, they exercised an influence quite out of proportion to their relative numerical strength.

The loss of Normandy to France in 1204, however, marked a turning point. England was again essentially an island kingdom. The barons had now to choose between their English and French estates. Those who remained in England threw in their lot with the native English and the gradual assimilation of the Norman followed inevitably. In the next two or three generations the French language had so much declined as a spoken medium that a contemporary, writing towards the end of the thirteenth century, could report that he had seen many a nobleman who knew not a word of French. We may assume that by this time native French in England was rapidly becoming a thing of the past. The royal court, however, remained a great stronghold of the language until the accession in 1399 of Henry IV, who was born in 1367, the first king after the Conquest to speak English as his mother tongue.

Although French had largely fallen into disuse as a naturally spoken tongue, it retained its hold on education until the middle of the fourteenth century and also had considerable snob value, as a witness, Ranulph Higden (died *c.* 1364) confirms in his *Polychronicon*. Here he states that the school children of his day *derelicto proprio vulgari construere Gallice compelluntur* – 'neglecting their own vernacular are obliged to construe in French'. John of Trevisa translated Higden's work in 1387 and continues as follows (here as printed by Caxton in 1482): 'Also gentilmens childeren ben lerned and taught from theyr yougthe to speke frenssh. And uplondyssh ("rural, country") men will counterfete and likene hem self to gentilmen and arn besy ("are keen") to speke frensshe for to be more sette by'. And now the translator inserts some information of his own: 'Wherfor it is sayd by a comyn proverbe "Jack wold be a gentilman if he coulde speke frensshe". This maner was moche used to fore the grete deth ("before the Black Death which reached Britain in 1348"). But syth it is somdele ("since it has partly") chaunged For sir Johan cornuayl

(John Cornwall, who taught at Merton College, Oxford) a master of gramer chaunged the techyng in gramer scole and construction of Frenssh in to englyssche. and other Scoolmaysters use the same way now . . . and leve all frenssh in scoles and use al construction in englissh.'

The vogue of French literature continued rather longer than the use of French in schools. In pure literature, its last notable representative was John Gower, who also wrote in Latin as well as in his native English; he died in 1408. Polite letter writing about this time still seems to have been done mainly in French.

French appears to have been dominant in parliamentary business in the first half of the fourteenth century, though petitions were sometimes presented in English. The first reference to a parliamentary speech in English is dated 1337, when the member is described as speaking in that language so as to be clearly understood by all. Parliament was first opened in English in 1363, but its proceedings were recorded in French until 1483.

Official French survived longest in the law courts. The Statute of Pleading of October 1362 had provided for the replacement of French by English on the grounds that the former was too little known, but this dispensation could only tardily be obeyed, since (as a later authority put it) the law was 'scarcely expressible properly in English', and Law French in fact remained in common use until Henry viii's time. Set aside entirely in 1650, it was restored in 1660, to be finally abolished, along with Latin, in 1733.

It goes without saying that French was also employed in Wales, though chiefly in the south, wrested from the Welsh in the closing years of the eleventh century. In 1169, French was carried to Ireland, where it maintained itself more or less as in England; it was in use as a judicial language until 1508. French also reached Scotland. Norman immigrants were permitted to settle in that country from 1124 and their language is found to a limited extent in official documents until the early fourteenth century.

SKETCH OF NORMAN FRENCH

The following outline of accidence gives an idea of the type of French introduced into England in 1066. For the next century and a half, the language kept pace with the evolution of Norman French on the

Continent and was indistinguishable from it. But after 1204 the language in this country began here and there to develop insular peculiarities. It has been noticed, for instance, that *ch* and *j* apparently retained their old values on English soil long after they had changed to [ʃ] and [ʒ] respectively in France. The language was taking on a distinctive character which justifies its technical name, Anglo-Norman. But as long as Anglo-Norman remained a living tongue, it was always very close to contemporary French which exercised a continuous, if variable, influence upon it. It acquired something of a composite character. Beside *feit* 'faith' (p. 223) there occurs the form *fei* with loss of final spirant as in later Continental French, cf. Modern French *foi*. The term *roche* 'rock' has a variant *roque* – English has taken over the latter alternative, so contrasting with Modern French *roche*. In the closing stages, the dialect of Paris and the Ile de France, which had meantime become the leading type of literary French on the Continent, considerably affected Anglo-Norman. It is seen, for instance, that the Continental pronunciation of *ch* and *j*, referred to above, now had some currency in England as well. Indeed, those English writers who continued to employ French for literature towards the end of the fourteenth century, were actually striving to write *francien*, ie, Parisian French. In this connexion, we note Chaucer's remarks on the French spoken by his prioress (p. 198). By this time, however, French had ceased to be a truly living tongue in this country. The traditional Anglo-Norman was still, indeed, to do service for many centuries to come as the parlance of the jurists. But their so-called Law French was no longer a language in the full sense of the word and, wide open to the corrupting influence of English, grew more and more degenerate, a 'barbarous tong and old French', as it was described in Henry VIII's time.

The position of French in England was peculiar in that it was a class language; it had no dialects.

As a consequence of the long-standing employment of French in these islands, an extraordinary number of French words were borrowed into English. The main period of borrowing appears to have been after 1250, about the time when French as a spoken language was dropping out of use. It seems that when the upper classes went over to English they continued to employ a large number of French words. In view of their education and social status, their frenchified style would be widely imitated and eventually generalized, reshaping average English to the exclusion of many traditional Germanic words. Celtic, too, borrowed considerably from French.

Phonetics

Old French evolved a complex vocalic system. Length was not phonemic, but there were varieties of *e* and *o*, not normally distinguished in the script; *u* commonly represents [y] as *lunsdi* ['lynzdi] 'Monday', on the other hand *luve* ['luvə] 'she-wolf'. There were numerous diphthongs and even triphthongs. There was a tendency to nasalize vowels and some diphthongs when followed by a nasal consonant.

Of the consonants, *c* was [ts] before front vowels: *cire* ['tsirə] 'wax', otherwise [k]: *cors* [kɔrs] 'body', but *garcon* [gar'tsõn] oblique case of *garz* [garts] 'boy'; *q(u)=k*, as *q(u)i=ki* 'who'. In a few words, *d* stands for [ð]: *pedre* ['peðrə] 'father', similarly *t* may represent [θ]: *parlet* ['parləθ] 'speaks', *feit* [feiθ] 'faith'. Before front vowels *g* is [ʤ]: *argent* [ar'dʒɛnt] 'silver', otherwise [g]: *gote* ['gotə] 'drop', *ch* and *j* are respectively [ʧ, ʤ]: *chief* [tʃief] 'head', *jambe* ['dʒãmbə] 'leg', *s* may be [z]: *chose* ['tʃɔzə] 'thing', otherwise [s]: *set* [sɛt] 'seven', *z* may be [dz]: *doze* ['dodzə] 'twelve', otherwise [ts]: *fi(l)z* [fi(l)ts] 'son'. Palatalized *l* and *n* occur, as in the modern language: *fille* ['fiʎə] 'daughter', *ligne* ['liɲə] 'line'. It will be noticed that several of these values are preserved in Norman loan words still current in English, as *faith*, *chief*, *jamb*, *Fitz-*, where Continental French has innovated, cf. *foi* [fwa], *chef* [ʃɛf], *jambe* [ʒãb], *fils* [fis].

The running together of words to make the phrase the unit of utterance, rather than the single word, is a feature of later French which separates it from the sister languages, eg, Italian, Spanish. But in eleventh-century French, the word was still the most significant factor in the intonation system and the accent still predominantly one of stress, as today in Italian or Spanish – or English. The position of the accent in any given word was generally that of the Latin prototype, thus *ami* [a'mi] 'friend' < Lat. *amícus*, further *chanter* [tʃãn'ter] 'to sing', *chantet* ['tʃãntəθ] 'sings' < Lat. *cantắre, cắntat* (cf. p. 160).

Nouns

There are two cases, nominative and oblique, the latter historically the accusative. The nominative is the case of the subject (and also

223

functions as a vocative), the oblique is used for all other purposes, including the genitive: *la fille le rei* 'the king's daughter'. There are two genders, masculine and feminine. Most feminine nouns, however, do not distinguish morphologically between nominative and oblique, even in the oldest language, and the two-case system finally broke down in the fourteenth century, when the oblique forms regularly replaced the nominative to give a single-case system as found in French today. Classification is by gender in the first instance.

Masculine
Main class:
Sg. nom. *chiens* 'dog', obl. *chien*, pl. nom. *chien*, obl. *chiens*, thus *dis* 'day', *murs* 'wall', *nons* 'name', *pains* 'bread', *reis* 'king', *vins* 'wine', also *fruiz* 'fruit', *monz* 'mountain', *piez* 'foot', sg. obl. *fruit*, etc., further *anz* 'year', *filz* > *fiz* 'son', sg. obl. *an*, *fil*, etc.

Two minor classes:
Sg. nom. obl. *coltre* 'knife', pl. nom. *coltre*, obl. *coltres*, thus *fredre* 'brother', *maistre* 'master', *pedre* 'father'.
Sg. nom. *ber* 'baron', obl. *baron*, pl. nom. *baron*, obl. *barons*, similarly *garz* 'boy', *ledre* 'robber', *on* 'man', *pastre* 'shepherd', *sire* 'lord', sg. obl. *garcon*, *ladron*, *ome*, *pastour*, *seignour*, etc.; further sg. nom. *enfes* 'child', obl. *enfant*, pl. nom. *enfant*, obl. *enfanz*, similarly *nies* 'grandson, nephew', obl. *nevou*, etc. The nom. sg. occasionally survived in the later language in some special function, giving doublets, cf. Mod. Fr. *gars*, *on*, *pâtre*, *sire*, beside *garçon*, *homme*, *pasteur*, *seigneur*.

Feminine
Main class:
Sg. nom. obl. *chambre* 'room', pl. nom. obl. *chambres*, thus *corne* 'horn', *fueille* 'leaf', *geline* 'hen', *levre* 'lip', *rose* 'rose', *tere* 'land'.

Two minor classes:
Sg. nom. *flours* 'flower', obl. *flour*, pl. nom. obl. *flours*, thus *amors* 'love', *mains* 'hand', *nefs* 'ship', similarly *vertuz* 'virtue', obl. *vertut*, etc. Nouns in this class early showed a tendency to generalize the

224

s-less form in the singular, ie, sg. nom. obl. *flour*, so effectively following the main class.

Sg. nom. *ante* 'aunt', obl. *antain*, pl. nom. obl. *antains*, similarly *none* 'nun', further *suer* 'sister', obl. *sorour*, etc. Mod. Fr. *nonne* beside *nonnain* is an instance of the exceptional survival of the nom. sg., cf. above *garz*, etc., as also *sœur* 'sister'. Mod. Fr. *tante* 'aunt' derives from a childish **ant-ante*.

Adjectives

The inflexions are in principle comparable to those for nouns, but relics of a neuter singular are also present. Three main classes are distinguished:

Sg. nom. masc. *bons* 'good', fem. *bone*, neut. *bon*, obl. masc. *bon*, fem. *bone*, neut. *bon*; pl. nom. masc. *bon*, fem. *bones*, obl. masc. *bons*, fem. *bones*.

Sg. nom. masc. *granz* 'big', fem. neut. *grant*, obl. masc. fem. neut. *grant*; pl. nom. masc. *grant*, fem. *granz*, obl. masc. fem. *granz*.

Sg. (invariable) *altre* 'other', pl. nom. masc. *altre*, fem. *altres*, obl. masc. fem. *altres*.

Comparison was reduced to two terms, positive and comparative, the latter also doing duty for the lost superlative. Comparison is usually analytic: *durs* 'hard', *plus durs* 'harder' lit. 'more hard', but a few common adjectives retain a traditional synthetic form, as *granz* 'big', *graindre* 'bigger', declining as follows: sg. nom. *graindre*, obl. *graignour*, pl. nom. obl. *graignours*, and similarly *bons* 'good', *mieildre* 'better', *mals* 'bad', *pire* 'worse', obl. *meillour*, *peiour*, etc., the latter also having a sg. nom. neut. *pis*.

Numbers

1 *uns*, 2 *dui*, 3 *treis*, 4 *quatre*, 5 *cinc*, 6 *sis*, 7 *set*, 8 *uit*, 9 *nuef*, 10 *diz*, 11 *onze*, 12 *doze*, 13 *treze*, 14 *quatorze*, 15 *quinze*, 16 *seze*, 17 *diz et set*, 18 *diz et uit*, 19 *diz et nuef*, 20 *vint*, 21 *vint et uns*, 30 *trente*, 40 *quarante*, 50 *cinquante*, 60 *seisante*, 70 *setante*, 80 *oitante*, 90 *nonante*, 100 *cent*, 1000 *mil*.

The first two retain traditional inflexions: 1 *uns* (like *bons*), 2 *dui* masc., *dous* fem., oblique *dous* masc. fem.

The numeral *uns* also functions as an indefinite article, though this part of speech was not so common in the old language as it is today.

Later Arrivals
Definite Article

Masculine: sg. nom. *li*, obl. *le*, pl. nom. *li*, obl. *les*.
Feminine: sg. nom. obl. *la*, pl. nom. obl. *les*.

There is an enclitic inflexion in conjunction with the prepositions *a* 'to', *de* 'of', *en* 'in', as follows:

	sg. m.	f.	pl.
	al,	*a la,*	*als*
	del	*de la*	*dels*
	enl	*en la*	*els*

Pronouns

Certain pronouns have (grammatically significant) unstressed forms, here printed second. The pronouns of the third person often retain a traditional difference between the accusative and dative, otherwise merged in the oblique. There are relics of a neuter pronoun.

Sg. nom. *jo, je* 'I' *tu* 'thou' *il* 'he' *ele* 'she' *el* 'it'
acc.⎫
  ⎬ obl. *mei, me* *tei, te* *le* *la* *le*
dat.⎭ *lui,* *li,* —,
  li *li*
Pl. nom. *nos* 'we' *vos* 'you' *ils* m. *eles* f. 'they'
acc.⎫
  ⎬ obl. *nos* *vos* *els, les* *eles, les*
dat.⎭ *lor* *lor*

There is a reflexive pronoun of the third person, indifferent to number: acc. dat. *sei* 'himself, etc.; themselves'.

The possessives also distinguish stressed and unstressed forms: (stressed) sg. masc. nom. *miens* 'my', obl. and neut. *mien*, fem. *meie*, pl. masc. nom. *mien*, obl. *miens*, fem. *meies*, and similarly sg. masc. nom. *tuens*, etc. 'thy', sg. fem. *toe*, pl. *toes*, also *suens* 'his, her, its'; sg. *nostre* 'our', pl. masc. nom. *nostre*, obl. and fem. *nostres*, also *vostre* 'your'; *lor* 'their' indeclinable; (unstressed) sg. masc. nom. *mis* 'my', obl. *mon*, fem. *ma*, pl. masc. nom. *mi*, obl. and fem. *mes*, also *tis* 'thy', *sis* 'his, etc.'; sg. *nostre* 'our', pl. masc. nom. *nostre*, obl. *noz*, fem. *nostres*, also *vostre* 'your'; *lor* 'their' indeclinable.

Verbs

In marked contrast to the decayed case system, the synthetic character of the verb is well preserved. Nevertheless, there have been numerous changes, notably the introduction of periphrastic tenses unknown in the parent Latin. These involve the use of the auxiliaries *aveir* 'to have' to form a new perfect periphrasis, eg, *ai amet* '(I) have loved', and *estre* 'to be' which replaced the synthetic passive of the ancestral language, eg, *sui amet* 'am loved'.

There were five synthetic tenses of the indicative (present, future, imperfect, preterite, conditional) and two of the subjunctive (present, imperfect), further an infinitive, imperative, two participles and a gerund, the last falling together with the present participle.

The synthetic paradigm of *amer* 'to love' is as follows:

Indicative:
Pres. sg. 1 *aim*, 2 *aimes*, 3 *aimet*, pl. 1 *amons*, 2 *amez*, 3 *aiment*.
Fut. sg. 1 *amerai*, 2 *ameras*, 3 *amerat*, pl. 1 *amerons*, 2 *amereiz*, 3 *ameront*.
Imperf. sg. 1 *amoue*, 2 *amoues*, 3 *amouet*, pl. 1 *amiiens*, 2 *amiiez*, 3 *amouent*.
Pret. sg. 1 *amai*, 2 *amas*, 3 *amat*, pl. 1 *amames*, 2 *amastes*, 3 *amerent*.
Cond. sg. 1 *amereie*, 2 *amereies*, 3 *amereiet*, pl. 1 *ameriiens*, 2 *ameriiez*, 3 *amereient*.

Subjunctive:
Pres. sg. 1 *aim*, 2 *aims*, 3 *aint*, pl. 1 *amiens*, 2 *amiez*, 3 *aiment*.
Imperf. sg. 1 *amasse*, 2 *amasses*, 3 *amast*, pl. 1 *amassiens*, 2 *amassiez*, 3 *amassent*.

Imperative: sg. *aime*, pl. *amez*.

Participles: pres. *amanz*, past *amet*.
Gerund: *amant*.

One notes the change in the stem vowel which is *a* in most forms, but *ai* in the present singular and third plural and in the imperative sg., ie, in those parts of the verb where the accent falls on the stem. Changes of this sort occur in many verbs, arising from different treatment of stressed and unstressed vowels. In the present case, the stem vowel *a* of the parent language (p. 164), when stressed, became *ai* in Old French.

The descendants of the other Latin conjugations (p. 165) are largely present in Old French, though variously modified. Some typical differences may be illustrated from the present-tense forms of *veeir* 'to see' < Lat. *vidēre* (Lat. *monēre* not surviving), *lire* 'to read' < Lat. *legere*, and *oir* 'to hear' < Lat. *audīre*:

(indic.) sg. 1 *vei*, 2 *veiz*, 3 *veit*, pl. 1 *veons*, 2 *veez*, 3 *veient*; (subj.) sg. 1 *veie*, 2 *veies*, 3 *veiet*, pl. 1 *veiiens*, 2 *veiiez*, 3 *veient*.

(indic.) sg. 1 *li*, 2 *lis*, 3 *lit*, pl. 1 *lisons*, 2 *lisez*, 3 *lisent*; (subj.) sg. 1 *lise*, 2 *lises*, 3 *liset*, pl. 1 *lisiens*, 2 *lisiez*, 3 *lisent*.

(indic.) sg. 1 *oi*, 2 *oz*, 3 *ot*, pl. 1 *oons*, 2 *oez*, 3 *oent*; (subj.) sg. 1 *oie*, 2 *oies*, 3 *oiet*, pl. 1 *oiiens*, 2 *oiiez*, 3 *oient*.

Irregular stem formation, common in Latin (p. 166), sometimes survives in French, eg, *vivre* 'to live', *vif* '(I) live', *vesqui* '(I) lived' < Lat. *vīvere, vīvō, vīxī*, but analogical and other changes have generally removed the French verb very far from its Latin prototype in these cases.

The auxiliaries conjugate as follows:

estre 'to be'

Indicative:
Pres. sg. 1 *sui*, 2 *ies*, 3 *est*, pl. 1 *somes*, 2 *estes*, 3 *sont*.
Fut. sg. 1 *ier*, 2 *iers*, 3 *iert*, pl. 1 *ermes*, 2 *ertes*, 3 *ierent*, or sg. 1 *serai*, 2 *seras*, 3 *serat*, pl. 1 *serons*, 2 *sereiz*, 3 *seront*.
Imperf. sg. 1 *iere*, 2 *ieres*, 3 *ieret*, pl. 1 *eriiens*, 2 *eriiez*, 3 *ierent*.
Pret. sg. 1 *fui*, 2 *fus*, 3 *fut*, pl. 1 *fumes*, 2 *fustes*, 3 *furent*.
Cond. sg. 1 *sereie*, 2 *sereies*, 3 *sereiet*, pl. 1 *seriiens*, 2 *seriiez*, 3 *sereient*.

Subjunctive:
Pres. sg. 1 *seie*, 2 *seies*, 3 *seiet*, pl. 1 *seiiens*, 2 *seiiez*, 3 *seient*.
Imperf. sg. 1 *fusse*, 2 *fusses*, 3 *fust*, pl. 1 *fussiens*, 2 *fussiez*, 3 *fussent*.

Imperative: sg. *seies*, pl. *seiiez*,

Participles: pres. *estanz*, past *estet*.

aveir 'to have'

Indicative:
Pres. sg. 1 *ai*, 2 *as*, 3 *at*, pl. 1 *avons*, 2 *avez*, 3 *ont*.
Fut. sg. 1 *avrai*, 2 *avras*, 3 *avrat*, pl. 1 *avrons*, 2 *avreiz*, 3 *avront*.
Imperf. sg. 1 *avoue*, 2 *avoues*, 3 *avouet*, pl. 1 *aviiens*, 2 *aviiez*, 3 *avouent*.
Pret. sg. 1 *oi*, 2 *oüs*, 3 *oüt*, pl. 1 *oümes*, 2 *oüstes*, 3 *oürent*.
Cond. sg. 1 *avreie*, 2 *avreies*, 3 *avreiet*, pl. 1 *avriiens*, 2 *avriiez*, 3 *avreient*.

Subjunctive: Pres. sg. 1 *aie*, 2 *aies*, 3 *aiet*, pl. 1 *aiiens*, 2 *aiiez*, 3 *aient*.
   Imperf. sg. 1 *oüsse*, 2 *oüsses*, 3 *oüst*, pl. 1 *oüssiens*,
   2 *oüssiez*, 3 *oüssent*.

Imperative: sg. *aies*, pl. *aiiez*.

Participles: pres. *avanz*, past *oü*.
Gerund: *avant*.

READINGS

(The orthography of Anglo-Norman is particularly erratic, hence spellings found in the texts do not always correspond to the forms printed in the grammatical outline above. In addition, we are dealing with an evolving language. Typographical marks (accents) occur in some manuscripts.)

Lines in praise of London, from Thomas' *Tristan*, mid-twelfth century:

Lundres est mult riche cité,
London is   very rich   city,
Meliur n' ad   en cristienté,
Better   not has (is not) in Christendom,
Plus vaillante ne melz preisiee,
More worthy   not better prized,
Melz guarnie de   gent   aisiee.
Better furnished with people well-off.
Mult aiment   largesce e   honur,
Much they-love largesse and honour,
Cunteinent   sei   par grant baldur.
They-conduct themselves with great boldness (confidence).
Le   recovrer est de Engleterre:
The treasury it-is of England:
Avant d'iloc ne l' estuet   querre.
Further   not it is-necessary to-seek.
Al   pé del mur il   curt Tamise
By-the foot of-the wall it (there) runs Thames
Par la vent la marchandise
Thither comes the merchandise
De   tutes les terres   qui   sunt
From all   the countries which are

U   marcheant cristien   vunt.
Where merchants Christian go.

From a Proclamation of Henry III, dated 18 October, 1258:

Henri, par le   grace Deu,   Rey   de Engleterre, sire   de
Henry, by the grace of-God, King of England,   Lord of
Irlande, duc   de Normandie, de Aquitien,   et   cunte de Anjou,
Ireland, Duke of Normandy, of Aquitaine, and Count of Anjou,
a tuz ses feaus   clers   et   lays saluz.
to all his faithful learned and lay greeting.
Sachez ke   nus volons et   otrions ke se ke   nostre
Know that we will   and grant that that which our
conseil, u la greignure partie de eus   ki   est esluz   par nus
council, or the greater   part of them which is elected by us
et par le commun de nostre reaume,   a   fet,   u fera,
and by the people of our   kingdom, has done, or will-do,
al   honur   de Deu et   nostre fei,   et pur le profit de
to-the honour of God and our   faith, and for the profit of
nostre reaume   sicum il ordenera   seit ferm et   estable en
our   kingdom as   it shall-ordain be firm and stable in
tuttes choses a tuz jurz;   et   comandons   et
all   things to all days (always); and we-command and
enjoinons a tuz noz feaus   et leaus,   en la fei
enjoin   to all our faithful and loyal (subjects) in the faith
k' il   nus deivent, k' il   fermement teignent, et   jurent
which they us owe   that they firmly   hold,   and swear
a tenir et   a maintenir les establissemenz ke   sunt fet,   u
to hold and to keep   the statutes   which are made, or
sunt a fere,   par l' avant dit cunseil, u la greignure partie
are to-be-made, by the aforesaid council, or the greater   part
de eus, en la maniere k'   il est dit desuz . . .
of them, in the manner which it is said above . . .
Tesmoin meimeismes a Londres le   disutime   jur de Octobre,
Witness myself   at London the eighteenth day of October,
l' an de nostre regne quaraunte secund.
the year of our   reign forty   second.

From *Le Mireur a Justices – Mirror for Justices,* end of the thirteenth century:

Juges   sunt   qe unt juresdiction. Juges poent estre tuz
Judges are (those) who have jurisdiction. Judges can   be   all
ceaux a queux   lei nel   defent. As   femmes defent
those to whom (the) law not-it forbids. To-the women forbids
droit qe eles ne   seient juges, e   de   ceo est
(the) law   that they (not) be   judges, and from this is (hence
qe   femmes sunt exemptes de   fere   siutes en menues
it is) that women are   exempt   from to-do suits in petty
courtz. Dautrepart serfs ne   pount estre juges, pur les II (dui)
courts. Further,   serfs not can   be   judges, for the two
estaz qe   sunt repugnantz, ne   atteinz de faus
states (which) are   incompatible not (those) attainted for false
jugement ne   poient mie   estre juges, ne infames,
judgement (not) can   (at all) be   judges, not infamous (ones),
ne nul   demeins de age de XXI (vint e uns) anz, ne meseals
not nobody under   age of twenty-one   years, not lepers
apertz, ne fous nastres,   ne atturnez, (ne)
open,   not idiots congenital, not attorneys, not (those)
continuelement arrangez, ne sourz e muz, ne parties es
permanently   deranged, not deaf-mutes, not parties in-the
plez, ne   escomengez   de evesqe, ne homme
pleas, not (those) excommunicated by bishop, not person
criminal. Car dieu meimes quant il fu en terre entra   en
criminal. For God (him)self when he was on earth entered into
consistoire   ou   une peccheresce   devoit
consistory (held a consistory) wherein a   woman-sinner was-to
estre jugee   a la   mort, ou   dieu escrist en la terre
be   adjudged to (the) death wherein God wrote on the ground
e dist a   siuters qi la deivent juger 'Ki de vous
and said to (the) suitors who her were-to judge 'Who of you
est sanz   pecchie, la   doigne
(who) is without sin,   there (in that regard) let-(him)-give
soun jugement', en example de juges
his   judgement', in example of judges (as an example to judges)
qe empernent a juger la gent   chescun jour, dunt   il
who presume to judge the people each   day, whereby he
les apprent qe nule   nempreigne si haute nobleie a seer
them teaches that nobody (not) presume so high office   to sit

en la   chaiere dieu   pur juger   les peccheours taunt cum
in the chair   of-God for to-judge the sinners   while
eux meismes sunt de pecchie condempnables.
themselves   are   of sin   condemnable (tainted with sin).

Opening stanzas of a lament on the death of Edward I (1239–1307), written in the latter year or shortly afterwards:

Seigniurs, oiez, pur   Dieu le   grant,
Lords,   hear for (the sake of) God the great,
   Chanconete de dure   pité
   Little-song of grievous sorrow
De la   mort un   rei   vaillaunt.
For the death of-a king worthy.
   Homme fu   de grant bounté,
   Man   he-was of great goodness,
   E   que par sa leauté,
   And who by his loyalty,
Mut   grant encuntre ad sustenue.
Many-a great encounter has sustained.
   Ceste chose est bien prové.
   This thing is well proved.
De sa terre n' ad rien   perdue,
Of his land not has anything lost (lost none of his territories),
   Priom   Dieu en devocioun
   Let-(us)-pray God in devotion
   Que de ses pecchez le   face pardoun.
   That of his sins   to-him make pardon.
De Engleterre il fu   sire,
Of England   he was lord,
   E   rey qe   mut   savoit de guere.
   And king who much knew of war.
En nule livre puet home lire
In no book can one read
   De rei qe   mieuz sustint   sa tere.
   Of king who better sustained his country.
   Toutes les choses qu' il vodreit fere,
   All   the things which he wished to-do,
Sagement les   tint à fine.
Wisely   them held to end (accomplished them).

232

Ore si gist soun cors en tere:
Now here lies his body in earth:
Si va le siècle en decline.
So goes the world in decline (to ruin).

From the Holkham Bible Picture Book, *c.* 1320–30:

A la feste de paskes vyint Jhesus en Jerusalem e entrat
At the festival of Easter came Jesus into Jerusalem and enters
dedenz le temple, si trova marchanz vendanz lour darrees,
into the temple and found merchants selling their goods,
ceo est a savoyr: buchers vendanz lur chaers et autres
that is to know (say): butchers selling their meats and other
gens que vendeyent tutes maners de darrees, sicum
people who were-selling all sorts of goods, as
monoyers que changeyent lure munoye et gens
money-changers who were-changing their money and people
que vendeyent motuns et berbiz et beofves et pulalie,
who were-selling wethers and ewes and oxen and poultry[1],
et touz y(l) les encharceoyt et lur disoyt que ceo
and all he them was-driving-out and to-them was-saying that that
ne fu pas lou de marché, de vendre ne de achater, més
not was (at all) place of market to sell nor to buy, but
le lou Deux et de bons oreysons, et ceo fu par la
the place of-God and of good prayers, and that was for the
reson que nule marchandie duyt estre tenue
reason (was the reason) that no merchandise may be kept
en Seynte Eglise.
in holy church.

Report of the case 'Morris against Wilford', heard at Westminster on November 7, 1677, from the pen of Chief Justice Thomas Jones and translated by him into English in his *Reports*, 1695.

Le Testator Sterling covenant ove le Plaintiff a ne intromitter, suer, ou molester le Plaintiff, ou demand de luy alcun account touchant le estate del Garford, Pere de Marie, feme del Testator Sterling, que ad devise tout son personal estate al Plaintiff in trust pur le use del feme, Et assign fuit per breach, que Sterling en son vie en le nosme de luy dit et Marie sa feme ad sue le Plaintiff en Camera Scaccarii

1 Doves are shown in the illustration accompanying the text.

per bill Anglois touchant le dit personal estate et ad fair luy dexpender la 300 l. Le Defendant plede un release fait apres le mort de Sterling a luy mesme per le Plaintiff et Seigniur Grandison et le dit Marie donc sa feme, de lour droit title ou demand de ou en touts brewing vessels et tout le personal del dit Sterling solonque le custome de Londres ou aliter. Sur cest plea le Plaintiff demur generalment. Et resolve per Curiam que cest release ne bar le action del Plaintiff car cest extend solement aux biens in specie, claimable par le Plaintiff et les autres releasors. Et cest fuit le apparent Intent des parties.

The Testator Sterling covenanted with the Plaintiff not to inter-meddle, sue or molest the Plaintiff, or demand of him any Account touching the Estate of Garford, Father of Mary, Wife of the Testator Sterling, who had devised all his personal Estate to the Plaintiff in Trust for the Use of his Wife, and it was assigned for Breach, that Sterling in his Life-time, in the name of him and the said Mary his Wife, had sued the Plaintiff in the Exchequer Chamber by English Bill, touching the said personal Estate, and had made him expend there £300. The Defendant pleaded a Release made after Sterling's Death to himself by the Plaintiff and Lord Grandison, and the said Mary, then his Wife, of their Right, Title or Demand, of or in all Brewing Vessels, and all the personal Estate of the said Sterling, according to the Custom of London or otherwise. On this Plea the Plaintiff demurred generally; and it was resolved by the Court, that this Release did not bar the Plaintiff's Action, for it extends only to Goods in Specie, claimable by the Plaintiff and the other Releasors. And this was the apparent Intent of the Parties.

LITERATURE

J. Vising, *Anglo-Norman Language and Literature* (1923).
M. K. Pope, *From Latin to Modern French, with especial Consideration of Anglo-Norman* (1934).
M. D. Legge, *Anglo-Norman Literature and its Background* (1963).

CHAPTER THIRTEEN

Flemish

ⓖⓖⓖⓖⓖⓖ

THE Norman adventurers at Senlac in 1066 were assisted by two sizable foreign contingents, those of the Bretons and the Flemings. The former were particularly numerous, but have left no trace in the linguistic history of these islands. In the smaller group, however, were the forerunners of a population which, in a remote corner of Britain, preserved its linguistic identity for a few generations, and may thus claim our attention here.

After the final subjugation of England, the Normans beset Wales, hitherto ruled by independent native princes; the intention was to reduce the whole country. In this the Normans were entirely successful in the south, which was firmly in their hands by the end of the century. English soldiers were extensively used in this assault on Wales and English camp-followers flocked in the wake of the advancing armies. In the Gower Peninsula, secured by nine Norman keeps, the English contingent was strong enough to lead to the early anglicization of much of the region, a development doubtless encouraged, if not indeed directly projected, by the Norman authorities.

But whatever the position in Gower, a calculated eviction of the native population of South Pembroke is a historical fact. Here, in or about 1106, 1108 and 1111, and again in 1156, the country was planted with Flemings and the castles of Haverfordwest and Tenby erected for their protection. The newcomers – farmers, woollen manufacturers and traders – completely displaced the previous inhabitants. How long they retained the use of Flemish is uncertain. Ranulph Higden in his *Polychronicon*, a history down to the year 1327, states that the Flemings of West Wales had by then abandoned their language in favour of English, or 'Saxon' as he calls it: þe Flemmynges, þat woneþ (dwell) in þe west syde of Wales, habbeþ y-left here strange ('their foreign') speche and spekeþ Saxonlych ynow (John of Trevisa's translation of the Latin original, 1387).

How this change took place is as uncertain as when it took place, for how did it come about that this exotic community isolated in the south-west tip of Wales acquired English, seeing that their immediate neighbours were monoglot Welsh? We imagine that there was also a considerable English element in the important centres of Haverfordwest and Tenby. The acquisition of English by the Flemings would not have been difficult in view of the close similarity of the two languages. Possibly intercourse with the adjacent, already partly anglicized Gower played a significant part in developments. The hostility of the Welsh, which often found expression in large-scale violence, must have drawn the two non-Celtic enclaves closer together, and eventually the more influential English came to prevail in Pembroke, too. This, we suggest, happened in the thirteenth century, by which time the Norman gentry were also becoming anglicized. So what had been a Little Flanders was henceforth 'Little England beyond Wales'. The older English dialect of south Pembroke must have contained many relics of the lost Flemish, giving it an outlandish character. This will perhaps be the explanation of a sixteenth-century report that the inhabitants of that district spoke bad English.

The boundary between English and Welsh in present-day Pembrokeshire follows roughly a line drawn through Haverfordwest and Narberth. Judging by place names, the linguistic frontier has been practically stationary since the Middle Ages.

SKETCH OF MEDIEVAL FLEMISH

The Flemings of West Wales left no written records of their language. Contemporary Flemish is, however, known from literature preserved in the homeland. It goes back to the mid-twelfth century, becoming copious in the thirteenth. The dialects of Flanders and Holland at this period already constituted a single language, technically known as Middle Dutch, to which English in the twelfth and thirteenth centuries was still fairly close. Both languages shared a common Germanic, or more specifically West Germanic, vocabulary, and both were morphologically impoverished, though Dutch forms were in general not so far reduced as English.

Flemish

Phonetics

The vowels (*a, e, i, o, u*) are short in closed, but long in stressed open syllables, eg, *ses* [ses] 'six', but *seven* [se:ven] 'seven'. When long in closed syllables they are written *ae, ee, ij, oe, ue*, respectively.

The consonants are substantially the same as in English, but *ch* is the voiceless velar fricative [χ]. Before *e* and *i*, the consonant *g* is written *gh*; *c* = *k*, the latter used before *e* and *i*.

Nouns

a-stems: sg. nom. acc. *visc* m. 'fish', gen. *viskes*, dat. *viske*, pl. nom. acc. gen. *viske*, dat. *visken*. Similarly *woerd* n. 'word', except that pl. nom. acc. may be uninflected.

In other stems, old patterns have often been lost. Thus the *ō*-stems and the feminine *n*-stems have fallen together, so that the endings of, eg, *siele* f. 'soul' (*ō*-stem) are the same as those of *tonghe* f. 'tongue' (*n*-stem): sg. nom. acc. *siele, tonghe*, gen. dat. *siele(n), tonghe(n)*, pl. all cases *sielen, tonghen*. Masculine *i*-stems follow the endings of the *a*-stems, but feminines preserve their traditional inflexion, as sg. all cases *macht* 'power', pl. nom. acc. gen. *machte*, dat. *machten*. Likewise masculine *n*-stems, as sg. nom. acc. dat. *boghe* 'bow', gen. *boghen*, pl. all cases *boghen*.

Adjectives

The ancient distinction between strong and weak inflexion has been largely abandoned, the latter having yielded to the former. An exception is the optional singular termination -*e*, commoner in cases where the weak ending would be traditionally justified. Typical paradigm, *siek* 'sick':

Sg. nom.	masc. *siek(e)*	fem. *siek(e)*	neut. *siek(e)*	pl. *sieke*
acc.	*sieken*	*siek(e)*	*siek(e)*	*sieke*
gen.	*siekes*	*siekere*	*siekes*	*siekere*
dat.	*sieken*	*siekere*	*sieken*	*sieken*

The comparative and superlative are usually formed by adding -*ere* and -*est* to the positive: *siekere* 'sicker', *siekest* 'sickest'. Examples of irregular comparison: *goet* 'good', *beter* 'better', *best* 'best', *slecht* 'bad', *wers* 'worse', *werst* 'worst'.

237

Later Arrivals

Numbers

1 *een*, 2 *twee*, 3 *drie*, 4 *vier*, 5 *vijf*, 6 *ses*, 7 *seven*, 8 *achte*, 9 *neghen*, 10 *tien*, 11 *elf*, 12 *twaelf*, 13 *dertien*, 14 *veertien*, 15 *vijftien*, 16 *sestien*, 17 *seventien*, 18 *achttien*, 19 *neghentien*, 20 *twintich*, 21 *een ende twintich*, 30 *dertich*, 40 *veertich*, 50 *vijftich*, 60 *tsestich*, 70 *tseventich*, 80 *tachtich*, 90 *tneghentich*, 100 *hondert*, 1000 *dusent*.

een (inflecting like an adjective) is also used as the indefinite article.

Definite Article

Sg. nom.	masc. *die*	fem. *die*	neut. *dat*	pl. *die*
acc.	*dien*	*die*	*dat*	*die*
gen.	*des*	*der*	*des*	*der*
dat.	*dien*	*der*	*dien*	*dien*

Pronouns

Sg. nom.	*ik* 'I'	*du* 'thou'	*hi* 'he'	*si* 'she'	*het* 'it'
acc.	*mi*	*di*	*hem*	*haer*	*het*
gen.	*mijns*	*dijns*	*sijns*	*haer*	—
dat.	*mi*	*di*	*hem*	*haer*	*hem*

Pl. nom.	*wi* 'we'	*ghi* 'you'	*si* 'they'
acc.	*ons*	*u*	*hem*
gen.	*onser*	*uwer*	*haer*
dat.	*ons*	*u*	*hem*

The possessive pronouns are purely adjectives and inflect as such: *mijn* 'my', *dijn* 'thy', *sijn* 'his, its', *haer* 'her', *onse* 'our', *uwe* 'your', *haer* 'their'.

Verbs

Paradigm of a strong verb:

Infinitive: *driven* 'drive', *te drivenne* 'to drive'.

Indicative: pres. sg. 1 *drive*, 2 *drijfs*, 3 *drijft*, pl. 1 *driven*, 2 *drijft*, 3 *driven*; past sg. 1 *dreef*, 2 *dreefs*, 3 *dreef*, pl. 1 *dreven*, 2 *dreeft*, 3 *dreven*.

238

Imperative: sg. *drijf*, pl. *drijft*.

Subjunctive: pres. as indic. except sg. 3 *drive*; past as indic. except sg. 1, 3 *dreve*.

Participles: pres. *drivende*, past *ghedreven*.

Other patterns of vowel change (infin., past sg. 1, past pl. 1, past part.): *skieten* 'shoot', *scoet*, *scoten*, *ghescoten*; *bersten* 'burst', *barst*, *borsten*, *gheborsten*; *stelen* 'steal', *stal*, *stalen*, *ghestolen*; *gheven* 'give', *gaf*, *gaven*, *ghegheven*; *varen* 'go, fare', *voer*, *voren*, *ghevaren*; *laten* 'allow, let', *liet*, *lieten*, *ghelaten*.

An example of the weak conjugation:

Infinitive: *horen* 'hear', *te horenne* 'to hear'.

Indicative: pres. sg. 1 *hore*, 2 *hoers*, 3 *hoert*, pl. 1 *horen*, 2 *hoert*, 3 *horen*; past sg. 1 *hoerde*, 2 *hoerdes*, 3 *hoerde*, pl. 1 *hoerden*, 2 *hoerdet*, 3 *hoerden*.

Imperative: sg. *hoer*, pl. *hoert*.

Subjunctive: pres. as indic. except sg. 3 *hore*; past as indic.

Participles: pres. *horende*, past *ghehoert*.

The auxiliaries 'to be' and 'to have'. Typical forms are:

Infinitive: *wesen* or *sijn* 'be', etc.

Indicative: pres. sg. 1 *bem*, 2 *best*, 3 *is*, pl. 1 *sijn*, 2 *sijt*, 3 *sijn*; past sg. 1 *was*, 2 *wærs*, 3 *was*, pl. 1 *waren*, 2 *wært*, 3 *waren*.

Imperative: sg. *wes*, pl. *west*.

Subjunctive: pres. sg. 1 *si*, 2 *sijs*, 3 *si*, pl. as indic.; past as indic. except sg. 1, 3 *ware*.

Participles: pres. *wesende*, past *ghewesen* or *gheweset*.

Infinitive: *hebben* 'have', etc.

Indicative: pres. sg. 1 *hebbe*, 2 *heefs*, 3 *heeft*, pl. 1 *hebben*, 2 *hebt*, 3 *hebben*; past sg. 1 *hadde*, 2 *haddes*, 3 *hadde*, pl. 1 *hadden*, 2 *haddet*, 3 *hadden*.

Imperative: sg. *heb*, pl. *hebt*.

Later Arrivals

Subjunctive: pres. as indic. except sg. 3 *hebbe*; past indic.

Participles: pres. *hebbende*, past *ghehad*.

After the *Visioen van Tandalus – Vision of Tandalus*, about 1300:

Ijrlant is een lant ligghende in enen ende van der werelt. Dese
Ireland is a land lying in an end of the world. This
werelt is langs van suden in 't noerden gaende
world is along from south into the north going (stretches from
ende daer sijn vele rivieren ende boske. Ende
south to north) and there are many rivers and woods. And
het is een lant vul van vruchten ende van honighe ende van melc
it is a land full of fruits and of honey and of milk
ende van alderhande viskerien ende oec van wilden dieren. Ende
and of all-sorts-of fisheries and also of wild beasts. And
daer ne weet man van ghenen serpenten noch van ghenen
there not knows one of no serpents nor of no
venine. In desen lant sijn vele religieuse beide van
poison. In this land are many persons-in-holy-orders both of
mannen ende van vrouwen. Ende in der suetside van dien lant
men and of women. And in the south side of that land
staet Inghelant.
stands England.

From Jan van Maerlant's *Spieghel Historiael – Mirror of History*, 1283–88:

Nu hadde die Ghengolf ene vrouwe,
Now had that Ghengolf a woman,
Sijn wijf, die hem was onghetrouwe,
His wife, who to-him was untrue,
Die luttel vrientscepen hem dede,
Who little friendship him did (showed)
Om sine grote helichede.
For his great holiness.
Hi hadde hare¹ liever gheweset ries
He had to-her rather been sportive (she would have
    preferred him sportive)

1 older form of *haer*

240

Flemish

Ende soe[2] els   *hadde haren kies*
And she else (in another way) had   her   choice
Metten   *te speelne[3] in heimichede,*
With-whom to play   in secrecy,
Dan   hi soe langhe lach in ghebede.
When he so long   lay in prayer.

2 local form for usual *si*, 3 normalized *spelenne*.

LITERATURE

A. C. Bouman, *Middelnederlandse Bloemlezing met Grammatica* (1948).
J. Phillips, *History of Pembrokeshire* (1909).

CHAPTER FOURTEEN

Romany

⊠⊠⊠⊠⊠⊠

ROMANY is the language of the Gypsies. The name Gypsy is a corruption of Egyptian, but is a misnomer, for these wanderers came from India and their language is akin to the modern Aryan languages of that country. The date of their emigration is uncertain, but the philological analysis of their language shows that it lost contact with cognate Indian languages during the Middle Ages. Some authorities place their departure from India in the eleventh century. They first moved westward through Afghanistan and Persia, then split into a northern and a southern group. The latter continued into Syria, the former into Armenia. Parties of the northern group moved on through Asia Minor, some then entering the Balkans. Suddenly, in the early fifteenth century, a great expansion into Europe took place, about which time the first arrivals presumably crossed over into Britain.

Remarkably enough, the first record of Romany speech was made in England, as far back as 1542, when Andrew Boorde appended a few sentences to the chapter on the sights of Egypt in his *Fyrst Boke of the Introduction of Knowledge*. More informed interest in the speech of the Gypsies in Britain developed much later, chiefly in the last century, and collectors recorded what they could. By then, however, the language proper had already disintegrated. All that could be found were isolated words and some short phrases with which the Gypsies of the day freely interlarded their conversation, especially if they didn't wish to be overheard by the gentiles. But Romany as a genuine language, deep Romany as they called it, was a thing of the past.

Or so it seemed. For the Gypsies are an elusive tribe, and it later transpired that deep Romany had never ceased to be spoken by a clan of Welsh Gypsies. It was in 1894 that John Sampson chanced upon a Gypsy harper, Edward Wood, at Bala in North Wales, and from him and other members of his clan, acquired a thorough

242

knowledge of British Romany. Thanks to Sampson's devoted labours, this unique speech has been very fully recorded. The task could not have been long delayed, for the language was already moribund and with the passing of the generation of Edward Wood very few Romany speakers remained. We believe there are none surviving today.

It may be mentioned that all the Romany speakers were trilingual, having Welsh and English in addition to their native language. It is therefore all the more remarkable that they should have preserved the language so long and in such purity. Quite sixty per cent of the vocabulary is Aryan, while the grammar and general structure of the language, conservative in character, are thoroughly representative of the best European Romany and faithful to its origin in distant India.

It goes without saying that the dialects of the Gypsies have always been essentially oral media. We remember that this was the language of an impoverished community of nomads, socially ostracized and often subject to persecution. Such people could not create a written literature or maintain any considerable corpus of historical tradition. Accordingly, the most important indigenous source for older Gypsy history is the Romany language itself. We have already referred to this in connection with the date of the departure from India. Similarly, the wanderings of the Gypsies are documented in the loan words in their dialects, in the case of the Welsh Gypsies as follows. Out of a loan-word total of some forty per cent, Iranian (Afghanistan and Persia), Greek (Asia Minor) and Slavonic (Balkans) account for some five per cent each, to which add a handful of Armenian words commemorating a brief sojourn in Armenia. The absence of Turkish loans is clear evidence that the Gypsies in question preceded the Turks across Asia Minor. Over ten per cent of the total vocabulary comes from English, much less than five per cent from Welsh, indicating that the ancestors of these Gypsies must have lived for generations in England. In fact, they themselves remembered that their forebears had come from Somerset in the eighteenth century, whence the obvious inference that Romany was still current among some Gypsies in England at that time.

Phonetics

As the speech of an unlettered people, Romany has no traditional orthography. We employ the following alphabet: *a, ā, q, ā̇, b, ch, d, dd, e, ē, f, g, h, i, ī, j, k, kh, l, ll, m, n, ng, o, ō, p, ph, r, rr, rh, s, sh, t, th, tt, u, ū, v, w, wh, x, y, z, zh.* Stress is marked by the acute accent except when falling on the first syllable.

Vowels: *a, e, i, u* are as in English; *o* is closed, *q* is open [ə]; *ā*, etc., denote the corresponding long sounds.

Consonants: *b, ch, d, f, h, j, m, n, s, sh, w, y, z* are as in English. The letters *p, t, k* are pronounced without aspiration, as in French, and are thus quite distinct from *kh, ph, th* which are strongly aspirated, *kh* equaling *k+h*, etc. This contrast between aspirated and unaspirated occlusives is a traditional Indian feature and is, of course, phonemic, as *kēr* 'do!', *khēr* 'house'. The letter *g* is like *g* in *go*, *v* is bilabial like *w* in German *schwören*, *x* is like *ch* in Scottish *loch*, *l* is like *l* in *leave*, *ll* denotes voiceless *l* as in Welsh *llan*, *r* is trilled as in Scottish, *rr* is a lengthened form of *r*, *rh* denotes voiceless *r* as in Welsh *rhan*, *ng* is like *ng* in *singer*, *wh* denotes voiceless *w* as in the Scottish pronunciation of *what*, *dd* is like *th* in *that* (or Welsh *dd*), *tt* is like *th* in *thin*, *zh* is like *s* in *pleasure*.

The constants *dd, ll, rh, tt, wh, zh* are infrequent and none actually occur in the texts in this chapter. Sample words are *laddera* 'ladder' (Irish Tinker influence), *llokō* 'light (in weight)', *rhodā̇* '(I) search', *fett* 'indeed' (=faith), *whēa* 'whey', *zhozh* 'power'.

Stress may be governed by grammatical considerations: *ō phurō mūrsh* 'the old man', but *ō phurō̇* 'the old one', *phurō̇ sas ō mūrsh* 'the man was old'.

Nouns

There are two genders: masculine and feminine, and eight cases: nominative, vocative, accusative, genitive, dative, ablative, instrumental, prepositional. The nominative form may also be used for the accusative; this we term the nominative-accusative form.

In general, the cases have the usual functions, but the accusative may include those of the dative, the ablative those of the genitive. The prepositional occurs more commonly with pronouns, but with nouns prepositions are more frequently followed by the nominative-accusative form. The genitive is more accurately described as an adjective, since it inflects as such (see further under 'Adjectives'). The terminations of the singular genitive *-kō*, etc., dative *-kī*, ablative *-tē*, instrumental *-sa* (> *a* before *-s* of oblique stem), prepositional *-tī*, plural genitive *-gō*, etc., dative *-gī*, ablative *-dē*, instrumental *-sa*, prepositional *-dī*, are in origin postpositions which have become agglutinated to the oblique stem and in part slightly modified in the process.

Two basic declensional types are distinguished, according to gender.

Masculine

Sg. nom.	*phal* 'brother'	Pl.	*phalắ*
voc.	*phaláia*		*phalálē*
acc.	*phal* or *phalés*		*phalắ* or *phalén*
gen.	*phaléskō*, etc.		*phaléngō*, etc.
dat.	*phaléskī*		*phaléngī*
abl.	*phaléstē*		*phaléndē*
inst.	*phalésa*		*phalénsa*
prep.	*phaléstī*		*phaléndī*

The different accusative forms are not distinguished syntactically and may be regarded as optional alternatives. In the case of inanimates, however, the accusative form is always that of the nominative: sg. nom. acc. *vast* 'hand', pl. *vastắ*.

Nouns ending in *-ō* in the nominative change this to *-ē* in the plural, as sg. nom. *pīrō* 'foot', *gājō* 'non-Gypsy, gentile', acc. *pīrō*, *gājō* or *gājés*, pl. nom. *pīrē*, *gājē*, acc. *pīrē*, *gājē* or *gājén*.

Most nouns with the nominative endings *-is*, *-os*, *-us* change these to *-ī* in the plural and always use these endings in the accusative, whether animate of not, thus sg. nom. acc. *papíris* 'paper', *urchos* 'hedgehog', *kunsus* 'corner', pl. *papírī*, *urchī*, *kunsī*.

Nouns ending in *-ben* mostly form the oblique stem with sg. *-benás-*, pl. *-benán-*, commonly contracted to *-mas-*, *-man-* in the gen., hence sg. nom. acc. *lodibén* 'lodging', gen. *lodimáskō*, dat. *lodibenáskī*, etc., pl. nom. acc. *lodibenắ*, gen. *lodimángō*.

The common words *chōr* 'thief' and *mūrsh* 'man' remain unchanged in the nominative plural. The accusative plural is thus *chōr* or *chōrén*, etc.

Feminine

Sg. nom.	*phen* 'sister'	Pl.	*pheníā*
voc.	*phení*		*pheníálē*
acc.	*phen* or *pheníā*		*pheníā* or *pheníén*
gen.	*pheníákō*, etc.		*pheníéngō*, etc.
dat.	*pheníákī*		*pheníéngī*
abl.	*pheníátē*		*pheníéndē*
inst.	*pheníása*		*pheníénsa*
prep.	*pheníátī*		*pheníéndī*

Nouns with nominative ending in -*ī* also decline as above, except for making singular vocative in -*íā*, thus sg. nom. *rą̄nī* 'lady', voc. *rą̄níā*, acc. *rą̄nī* or *rą̄níā*, etc.

Inanimates always use the nominative form for the accusative: sg. nom. acc. *shuvél* 'broom', *kūnī* 'elbow', pl. *shuvelíā, kuníā*.

A large number of nouns decline without medial -*í*-, as *yakh* 'eye': sg. nom. acc. *yakh*, pl. *yakhǎ*, sg. gen. *yakhákō*, pl. *yakhéngō*, etc.

Nouns with nominative ending in -*a* change this to -*ī* in the plural and, whether animate or not, always use these endings in the accusative, thus sg. nom. acc. *vlija* 'village', *pishténa* 'pigeon', pl. *vlijī, pishténī*.

Adjectives

Endings are almost universally as follows:
Singular uninflected masculine -*ō*, feminine -*ī*, oblique masculine feminine -*ē*, plural -*ē*, as *bą̄rō pīrō* 'big foot', *bą̄rē pīrésa* 'big foot-with', *bą̄rē pīrē* 'big feet', *raikanī rą̄nī* 'fair lady', *raikanē rą̄níátē* 'fair lady-from', *raikanē rą̄níéngī* 'fair ladies-for'.

A handful of adjectives inflect irregularly, as *bita* 'small' unchanged throughout the singular and forming plural *bitī*, thus *bita vlija* 'little village', plural *bitī vlijī*. The English loan word *dīr* does not inflect at all: *dīr phal, phen* 'dear brother, sister'.

A traditional feature of Romany is the genitive adjective, eg, singular *phaléskō khēr* masculine 'brother's house', *phaléskī yakh* feminine 'brother's eye', *phaléskē pishténī* 'brother's pigeons', plural *phaléngō khēr* 'brothers' house', etc.

When the genitive adjective is used predicatively, the lengthened termination *-kerō*, etc., is found, hence *mē phaléskerō sī ō khēr* 'the house is my brother's'.

Adjectives can be used as nouns, sometimes with specialized meanings: *kạlō* 'black', as a noun 'Gypsy man', similarly *kạlī* 'Gypsy woman', *kạlē* 'Gypsies'. They follow the appropriate declension of nouns, eg, *kạléskī* 'Gypsy man-for', *kạlīénsa* 'Gypsy women-with'.

When a genitive adjective is used as a noun, again only the lengthened termination is applicable: *hudạr* 'door', *hudāréskerō* '(he) of door' ie, 'doorman' synonymous with *hudáréskō mūrsh* lit. 'man of door', likewise *khēr* 'house', *khēréskerī* '(she) of house', ie, 'housekeeper', *bakarō* 'sheep', *bakaréngerō* '(he) of sheep' ie, 'shepherd', *bakaréngerī* 'shepherdess'. Also inanimates: *vast* 'hand', *vastéskerō* '(thing) of hand', ie, 'handle', *īzā* 'clothes', *īzéngerī* 'clothes-line'. These formations are legion and productive, often making for succinctness of expression inimitable in English, as *kunséskerō*, *kunséskerī* 'man, woman (boy, girl) sitting in a corner (*kunsus*), occupying a corner seat', further compounds like *pạrnē-pōrīákerī* 'squirrel' lit. '(she) of white tail' (*pạrnō* 'white', *pōrī* 'tail') or highly idiomatic expressions like *tala-dandéskerō*, *-ī* 'dishonest man, woman', cf. *tala-dandéskō* 'dishonest' (*tala* 'under', *dand* 'tooth').

There are two degrees of comparison: positive, as *bạrō* 'big', *bita* 'small', and comparative which ends in invariable *-edér*, hence *bạredér* 'bigger', *bitedér* 'smaller'. The superlative degree can be expressed periphrastically, eg, with *sạr* 'all': *ō bạredér lendē sạr* lit. 'the bigger from them all', but often the comparative alone suffices. Examples of irregular comparison: *kushkō* 'good', *fededér* 'better', *basavō* 'bad', *ūsedér* 'worse'.

Definite Article

Masculine singular nominative accusative form *ō*, oblique *ī*, feminine and plural *ī* throughout. Examples: sg. nom. acc. *ō phal* 'the brother', oblique acc. *ī phalés*, dative *ī phaléskī*, etc.

There is no indefinite article.

Numbers

1 *yekh*, 2 *dūī*, 3 *trin*, 4 *shtạr*, 5 *pansh*, 6 *pạsh dūrika* or rarely *shov*, 7 *trin thā shtạr*, 8 *dūvarī shtạr*, 9 *shtạr thā pansh* or *desh bī yekh*, 10

desh, 11 *desh thā yekh,* 12 *desh thā dūī,* 13 *desh thā trin,* 14 *desh thā shtā̤r,* 15 *desh thā pansh,* 16 *desh thā pᶏsh dūrika,* 17 *desh thā trin thā shtā̤r,* 18 *deshūtō,* 19 *desh thā shtā̤r thā pansh* or *dūī desh bī yekh,* 20 *dūī desh* or less usually *bish,* 21 *dūī desh thā yekh* or *bish thā yekh,* 30 *trin desh,* 40 *shtā̤r desh,* 50 *pansh desh,* 60 *pᶏsh dūrika desh,* 70 *trin thā shtā̤r desh,* 80 *dūvarī shtā̤r desh,* 90 *shtā̤r thā pansh desh,* 100 *shel,* 1000 *bā̤rō shel.*

The first four numbers decline as follows:
Masc. fem. nom. acc. *yekh,* masc. dat. *yekhéskī,* fem. *yekhákī,* etc., there being no genitive; *dūī, trin, shtā̤r* follow the masculine declension, oblique acc. *dūīén,* etc.

Notice *panshéngerō* '(he) of five', ie, 'fiver'.

Pronouns

Sg. nom.	*mē* 'I'	*tū* 'thou'	Pl. *amé* 'we'	*tumé* 'you'
acc.	*man*	*tut*	*amén*	*tumén*
gen.	*mīrō,* etc.	*tīrō,* etc.	*amā̤rō,* etc.	*tumā̤rō,* etc.
dat.	*mangī*	*tukī*	*améngī*	*tuméngī*
abl.	*mandē*	*tutē*	*améndē*	*tuméndē*
inst.	*mansa*	*tusa*	*aménsa*	*tuménsa*
prep.	*mandī*	*tutī*	*améndī*	*tuméndī*

Sg. nom.	*yov, -lō* 'he, it'	*yoi, -lī* 'she, it'	Pl. *yon, -lē* 'they'
acc.	*les*	*lā*	*len*
gen.	*leskō,* etc.	*lakō,* etc.	*lengō,* etc.
dat.	*leskī*	*lakī*	*lengī*
abl.	*lestē*	*latē*	*lendē*
inst.	*lesa*	*lasa*	*lensa*
prep.	*lestī*	*latī*	*lendī*

The enclitic nominative forms *-lō,* etc., may be used as subjects of the verb 'to be' and of the invariable *nai* 'is, are not', as *chōr sī yov, nai-lō kek lūr* 'he's (only) a thief, he's no (bold) robber', *kā sas-lī?* 'where was she?', *sā̤r mulé sī-lē* 'they are all dead'.

There is third person reflexive, indifferent to gender: sg. acc. *pes* 'himself, herself', gen. *peskō,* etc., pl. acc. *pen* 'themselves', gen. *pengō,* etc.

The genitive functions as a possessive: *mīrō* 'my', etc., also with forms appropriate to the declension of nouns, as *yekh amā̤rendē* 'one of ours'. The first and second persons are often contracted to *mō, tō*, etc.

Verbs

The verb has four tenses of the indicative: present, imperfect, preterite and (in rather rare use) pluperfect, further, one subjunctive tense: present. There is an imperative mood and a past participle. The present tenses are based on the verbal stem, commonly identical with the imperative singular; the preterite is based on the stem of the participle, the third person plural being in fact the plural of the participle itself. The imperfect and pluperfect are regularly derived from the present and preterite respectively. The present includes the functions of a future, the preterite those of a perfect.

There are seven conjugations, differing only in details. Typical forms:

Present		Imperfect	Preterite	Pluperfect
Sg. 1	*kamắ* '(I) love'	*kamắs*	*kamdóm*	*kamdómas*
2	*kamésa*	*kamésas*	*kamdán*	*kamdánas*
3	*kaméla*	*kamélas*	*kamdás*	*kamdásas*
Pl. 1	*kamása*	*kamásas*	*kamdám*	*kamdámas*
2	*kaména*	*kaménas*	*kamdán*	*kamdánas*
3	*kaména*	*kaménas*	*kamdé*	*kamdénas*

Subjunctive sg. 1 *te kamā* 'that (I) love', 2 *kamés*, 3 *kamél*, pl. 1 *kamás*, 2, 3 *kamén*. Imperative sg. *kam*, pl. *kamén*. Participle *kamdó* 'loved'.

The verb 'to be' has three tenses of the indicative: present, future and imperfect, the last functioning as a general past tense, further two tenses of the subjunctive: present and imperfect, and an imperative.

		Indicative		Subjunctive	
Present		Future	Imperfect	Present	Imperfect
sg. 1	*shom* 'am'	*vava*	*shomas*	(*te*) *vā*	(*te*) *vās*
2	*shan*	*vesa*	*shanas*	*ves*	*vesas*
3	*sī*	*vela*	*sas*	*vel*	*velas*
pl. 1	*sham*	*vasa*	*shamas*	*vas*	*vasas*
2	*shen*	*vena*	*shenas*	*ven*	*venas*
3	*sī*	*vena*	*sas*	*ven*	*venas*

Imperative: sg. *av*, pl. *ven*.

In conjunction with the participle, the verb 'to be' forms the passive of active verbs, thus *shom kamdŏ*, also *kamdŏ shom* '(I) am loved', etc.

There is no verb 'to have', possession being commonly expressed by the verb 'to be' with the accusative (in its dative function), as *sī man khēr* 'I have a house' lit. 'is to-me house'.

READINGS

Zumavibenă – Riddles:

> *Sŏ   prechéla thā ŏ   shērŏ talé   thā ī   pīrē opré? Purum.*
> What grows   and the head down and the feet up?   Onion.
> *Sŏ   jala   bāredér kana chinésa lā? Xev.*
> What goes (gets) bigger when you-cut it? Hole.
> *Kon jala aré ī   kralishákī komŏra thā phuchéla kekéndē?*
> Who goes into the queen's   chamber and enquires none-of?
> *Ŏ   kham.*
> The sun.
> *Jidŏ alán,   mulŏ maskál, trūpos thā ŏzĭ   palál.*
> Alive before dead between body and heart (soul) after.
> *Phagē-phūvīéngerŏ.*
> Plough (lit. breaker of fields).
> *Shtār pārnē rānīă prasténas   palál vaverkéndī thā kekār*
> Four white ladies were-running after each-other and never
> *thildé vaverkén.   Ŏ   bavalīákerŏ.*
> caught each-other. The windmill.

Ŏ Dinilŏ ī Bakarénsa – The Idiot with the Sheep:

> *Odói sas bita givéskŏ khēr,   thā kushī guruvă, thā*
> There was little corn   house (farm) and a-few cows   and
> *trin phală.   Dinilŏ sas yekh phal,   thā akála dūī phală*
> three brothers. Idiot was one brother, and other two brothers
> *wąntasénas   tē   mārn les. Junénas   kek sŏ*
> were-wanting that they-kill him. They-were-knowing not what
> *te ken   Xąch' ŏ*
> that they-do (didn't know how to set about it) Said   the

phuredér phal, 'Jak, *av akái. Akē 'mē jasa kī mō*
elder (eldest) brother, 'Jack, come here. Look we go to my
dīr devél.' '*Sār java mē odói?*' '*Av aménsa.*' '*Aua*
dear god (heaven). 'How go I there?' 'Come us-with.' 'Yes
mē!' *xạch' ō dinilō.*
I (will)' said the idiot.

    Gilé te len gonố. 'Jạ aré akái' xạchē yon.
They-went that they-get (a) sack. 'Go in here' said they.
Aré ō gonố gīás. Ak' ī dūī phalắ phandéna ō
Into the sack he-went. Look the two brothers tie the
gonố. Akē jana pengī ī dūī phalắ, thā
sack. Look go (themselves-for) the two brothers and
rigerénas ō gonố. Vilé kī kirchíma. Chidế
were-carrying the sack. They-came to (an) inn. They-put
ō gonố talé thā gilé aré ī kirchíma te len dropa
the sack down and went into the inn that they-get drop (of)
lovína.
beer.

    Ak' ō gạjō vela thā bakaré. Akavắ
Look the gentile comes and sheep (ie, with sheep). This (lad,
    sas aré ō gonố. Hūpasás tạp lestī. 'Sō sī?'
ie, the idiot) was in the sack. He-called to him. 'What is
    xạch' ō gạjō. 'Akē mūrsh jala kī
(what's the matter?)' said the gentile. 'Look (a) man goes to
mō dīr devél' '*Sār man java mē odói?*'
my dear god.' 'How for-me go I (how can I go) there?'
phuchtás ō gạjō. 'Pirắ tū akáva gonố.' Piradás ō mūrsh
enquired the gentile. 'Open (you) this sack.' Opened the man
ō gonố. Ak' ō vavér vela avrí ō gonố. Chidás ī
the sack. Look the other comes out-of the sack. He-put the
vavér mūrshés aré ō gonố thā phandiás les. Ak' ō vavér
other man into the sack and tied it. Look the other (ie,
    jala ī bakarénsa kheré.
the idiot) goes the sheep-with home.

    Vavér dūī vena avrí te len ō gonố, thā jana
Other two come out that they-get the sack and go
pengī k' ō dōrīav. Ucherdế les aré ō dōrīav.
(themselves-for) to the sea. They-threw it into the sea.
Ak' ī dūī phalắ vena pạlē Vilé pạsh ō khēr
Look the two brothers come back. They-came to the house

251

odói-kā   jivénas   thā xạch' ō   phuredér phal   ī
there-where they-were-living and said   the elder   brother the
vaveréskī 'Kerása   'kaṇǎ.'
other-to 'We-do (we shall manage) now'.

  Dikhế   ō vavér phal   thā trashadế   te   dikhén
  They-saw the other brother and (they) amazed that they-see
les   ī bakarénsa. 'Kā   lián   odóla bakarén, Jak ?' 'Arế
him the sheep-with. 'Where you-got those sheep,   Jack?' 'In
ō   dōrīav.' 'Av   aménsa, Jak, te   sikavés   ō   than kā
the sea.'   'Come us-with, Jack, that you-show the place where
lián   len.'
you-got them.'

  Chidás ō   Jak ī bakarén arế   phūvīátī. Ak' ī   trin
  Put   (the) Jack the sheep into (a) field. Look the three
jana pengī   thā vilế   k' ō   dōrīav. 'Ach tạp akái'
go (themselves-for) and came to the sea.   'Stand up here,'
xạch' ō   Jak ī phuredér phaléskī. Chas   kā   phendás
said (the) Jack the elder   brother-to. He-stood where he-told
leskī, thā ō   Jak ucherdás les arế ō   dōrīav. Mērlas
him and (the) Jak threw   him into the sea.   He-was-dying
            arế ō   pānī thā ō   pānī keradás. 'Sō   kela
(drowning) in the water and the water seethed. 'What does-he
'kaṇǎ?' xạch' ō   tārnedér phal.
now?' said the younger brother. (The idiot replied that)
Kedélas   ī thuledér   bakarén. 'Ucher man talế
he-was-picking the fatter (fattest) sheep.   'Throw me down
mangkē lela   thulế bakarén sǎr.'
before he-gets fat sheep all.'

  Palál-sō uchderdás ī   dūī phalǎ` te   mērn   arế ō
  After   he-threw the two brothers that they-drown in the
pānī, kherế gīás ō   Jak akaṇǎ. Okē   sǎr!
water home went (the) Jack now. That's all!

Ō Vend – (The) Winter:
  Bita chorvanō khēr munjerdē thanéstī, thā   phurǒ thā
  Little poor house lonely   place-in and (an) old-man and
        phurí.   Chorvanế. Ō phurǒ kelas   būtí.
(an) old-woman (They) poor. The old-man was-doing work (went
        I gǎjế   na denas   les būt lovǒ.
out to work). The gentiles not were-giving him much money.

252

Rigerénas   pąsh lestē aré   phurē xolováti. Kedás
They-were keeping half of-it in (an) old   stocking. They-did
oją̃ bērshéngi. *Phukadás ī phurīákī   'Te rigerés   odovą̃*
thus years-for. (He) said the old-woman-to 'That you-keep that
ī vendéskī.'
the winter-for'.

Ō phuró   sas avrí yekh divés. Vīás phurō droméngerō k'
The old-man was out one day. Came old   tramp   to
ō hudár te mangél. Khārdás les ī   phurī   atrÉ, thā
the door that he-beg. Called   him the old-woman inside and
dīás les kushī xąbén. Phuchtás   leskō nav. 'Mīrō nav   sī
gave him a-little food. (She) asked his   name. 'My   name is
Vend', xąch' ō phuró.   'Vend sī tīrō nav?   Akái sī būt
Winter,' said   the old-man. 'Winter is your name? Here is much
lovó tukí.'   Gīás ī phurí   thā dīás les ī xolov
money you-for.' Went the old-woman and gave him the stocking
sunakái. Trashadó sas ō   phurō Vend. Līás
(full of) gold.   Amazed was (the) old   Winter. (He) took
ī xolov   thā gīás peskī.
the stocking and went (himself-for).

Kheré vīás ō phurīákō   rom,   beshtás talÉ. 'Akái
Home came the old-woman's husband, sat   down. 'Here
sas ō   Vend', xąch' ī phurí,   te lel   ō lovó.'
was (the) Winter,' said   the old-woman that he-get the money.'
'Sō   phenésa?' xąch' ō phuró, 'dián   ō lovó
'What you-say?' said   the old-man, 'you-gave the money
komonéskī?' 'Aua', xąch' ī   phurí,   'phurō mūrsh
someone-to?' 'Yes', said   the old-woman, '(an) old   man
vīás akái, thā Vend khárlas   pes.
came here and Winter was-calling himself (called himself
                    Dīóm les ī   xolov.'
Winter). I-gave him the stocking.'

'Kedán   améngī akaną̃',   xąch' ō phuró,
'You-did us-for now (now we're done for)', said   the old-man,
'jasa 'mengī.'   Avrí gilÉ,   mukdÉ ō
'we-go us-for (let us go away)'. Away they-went, left   the
khēr thā līás ō phuró ō hudár opré ō   dumó te
house and took the old-man the door onto the (his) back that
sovén   tąp lestī.   GilÉ   opré ō drom, thā sas
they-sleep on it (to sleep on). They-went up   the road, and was

Later Arrivals

len   pąshě́ra   kek.   *Rātí   vĭás*
to-them halfpenny not (they hadn't a halfpenny). Night came
opré len.   Junénas   kek kā   te   jan.
upon them. They-were-knowing not where that they-go (to go).
Vilé   kī   phuré rukéstī. 'Akái sovása   'karát
They-came to (an) old   tree.   'Here we-sleep to-night.'
(= *akarát*).' *Opré gĭás ō   phuró   ī hudārésa thā lĭás ī*
              Up   went the old-man the door-with and got the
phurí   opré, thā odói sutilé.
old-woman up   and there they-slept.
   Akána-sig shundé   godlī pīréndē. 'Akē komónī   vela',
Presently they-heard sound feet-of. 'Look somebody comes',
xąch' ō phuró   ī phurĭákī.   'Ach konyō thā phen
said the old-man the old-woman-to. 'Stand still   and say
chī   tē   meribenáskī!' Ō phuró   chidás   peskō shērō
nothing your life-for!'   The old-man put (out) his   head
te   vartín.
that he-watch.
   Dikhás   mūrshén te   vilé   talál   rukhéstī. 'Akē
(He) saw men   who came beneath (a) tree.   'Look (a)
than te   ken   yąg. Shukó sī akái. Xąbén
place that they-make (to make) (a) fire. Dry   is here. Food
wąntasénas   ī   mūrsh. Xą́lé.   Kedé   te   xąn.
were-wanting the men.   They-ate. They-made that they-eat (they
finished eating).
   Ō   shērnō mūrsh phendás ī   vaveréngī te   tārdén
The head   man   told   the others   that they-bring-out
ō   lovó.   Chidé   les sąr talé.   Ak' ō mūrsh ginéla les.
the money. They-put it all down. Look the man   counts it.
Odói sas būt sunakái te   lurdé   Dĭás
There was much gold   which they-stole (had-stolen) (He) gave
kushī sąkon yekhéskī. Rigerdás yov dosta kokoréskī.
a-little every one-to.   Kept   he plenty self-for.
   Chingerénas   vaverkénsa   trushal ō lovó.
They-were arguing each-other-with about the money.
Chinimángerī.   Wąntasénas   te   pąravén
(There was a) sovereign. They-were-wanting that they-change (to
   lā. 'Lava te   pąravá lā,   te java
change) it. 'I-get that I-change it (I'll have it changed), if go

254

mē k' ō beng te pāravā   lā.'
I   to the devil that I-change (to change) it.'
    Sār kekār sas ō   lav   phendiló, ō   phuró   mukdás ō
    As-soon-as was the word spoken, the old-man let   the
hudǎr te   perrl talé.   'Tū   khārdán ī   bengés.   Akēkó vīás!'
door that it-fall down. 'You called   the devil.   Lo-he came!'
Trashadé   thā prastilé. Mukdé sǎr   odói.
(They) amazed and ran.   They-left everything there.
    Ō   phuró   thā ī   phurí   niserdé talé.   'Akē   dosta
    The old-man and the old-woman climbed down. 'Look plenty
'mengī', xǎch' ō   phuró,   'te   rigerél amén vendéngī.'
us-for,' said the old-man, 'that it-keep us   winters-for (to
                         Pǎlē gilé   k' ō   phurō khēr
keep us for (many) winters)'. Back they-went to the old   house
ī   lovésa,   thā odói jivéna   akaná, te nī   mērdé   kek.
the money-with, and there they-live now,   if not they-died not
(if they are not dead).

LITERATURE

There is no general textbook of British Romany. Our information is
derived from J. Sampson, *The Dialect of the Gypsies of Wales* (1926),
reprinted 1968, a work addressed primarily to the specialist in Romany
and Aryan linguistics. It contains no reading passages, the texts upon
which the analysis of the language is based being printed at various
times since 1907 in the *Gypsy Lore Society Journal*.

ROMANY IN ENGLAND

As explained above, the Romany language proper was early lost in
England, much to the chagrin of such enthusiasts as George Borrow.
His novels on Gypsy life, *Lavengro* 'Philologist' and *Romany Rye*
'Gypsy Gentleman', are widely read classics, but another work of
his inspired by the same wandering people *Romano Lavo-Lil* 'Gypsy
Word-Book' is not surprisingly less well known. It contains an
English–Romany vocabulary running to some 1400 items, a number
of single sentences and some pieces of prose and poetry accompanied
by English renderings. It must be emphasized, however, that the
connected passages are essentially synthetic, giving an idealized pic-

ture of the jargon of the nineteenth-century Gypsy in England. But they are admirably done, nonetheless, as our specimen – jargon with translation – may illustrate:

The Dooee Chals

Dooee Romany Chals were bitchenee,
Bitchenee pawdle the boree pawnee:
Plato for koring,
Lasho for choring
The putsee of a boree rawnee.

And when they well'd to the wafoo tem,
The tem that's pawdle the boree pawnee,
Plato was nasho
Sig, but Lasho
Was lell'd for a rom by a boree rawnee.

You cam to jin who that rawnee was,
'Twas the rawnee from whom he chor'd the putsee:
The Chal had a black,
Chohawniskee yack,
And she slomm'd him pawdle the pawnee.

The Two Gypsies

Two Gypsy lads were transported,
Transported across the great water:
Plato for rioting,
Louis for stealing
The purse of a great lady.

And when they came to the other country,
The country that's across the great water,
Plato was hanged
Forthwith, but Louis
Was taken for a husband by a great lady.

You wish to know who that lady was,
'Twas the lady from whom he stole the purse:
The Gypsy had a black,
Bewitching eye,
And she followed him across the great water.

A handful of Gypsy words have entered the English language. As one would expect, they occur chiefly in substandard usage. Examples, with Welsh Romany parallels in brackets, include cock 'mate' (*kǫk* 'uncle'), cosh (*kǫsht* 'stick'), cove (*kova* 'chap'), lolly (*lolī* 'red', ie, 'copper (coin)'), mush, moosh (*mūrsh* 'man'), pal (*phal* 'brother'), rum (*rom* 'husband') – originally '(Gypsy) man' then 'queer man' then as adjective 'queer' – to which also the term Romany itself (*Romanī chib* 'Gypsy tongue'). The above are all purely Aryan words. Lastly we mention the well-known Gypsy name Petulengro 'Smith' (*Petaléngerō* 'blacksmith' lit. 'he of horse-shoes' which goes back to Greek *pétalo* (> Rom. *petalō*) 'horse-shoe').

The Paternoster (Matthew vi, 9–13) in the languages of the British Isles

🐚🐚🐚🐚🐚🐚

BRITISH CELTIC

Welsh

9 Ein tad, yn hwn wyt yn y nefoedd: sancteiddier dy enw.
10 Deled dy deyrnas. Gwneler dy ewyllys, megis yn y nef, felly ar y ddaear hefyd.
11 Dyro i ni heddiw ein bara beunyddiol.
12 A maddau i ni ein dyledion, fel y maddeuwn ninnau i'n dyledwyr.
13 Ac nac arwain ni i brofedigaeth, eithr gwared ni rhag drwg. Canys eiddot ti yw'r deyrnas a'r gallu a'r gogoniant yn oes oesoedd.

Middle Cornish (normalized)

9 Agan tas ny, us yn nef: benygys re bo dha hanow.
10 Re dheffo dha wlascor. Dha voth re bo gwres, y'n nor kepar hag y'n nef.
11 Ro dhyn ny hedhyu agan bara pup deth oll.
12 Ha gaf dhyn agan camwyth, kepar del aven nyny dhe'n re na us ow camwul er agan pyn ny.
13 Ha na wra agan gorra yn temptasyon, mes delyrf ny dyworth drok. Rag dhyso jy yu an wlascor ha'n gallos ha'n gordhyans bys vyken ha bynary.

IRISH CELTIC

Middle Irish, c. twelfth century

9 A athair fil hi nimib: noemthar th' ainm.
10 Toet do flaithius. Bíd do thoil i talmain, amal atá i nnim.

11 *Tabair dún indíu ar sásad cechlaithi.*
12 *Ocus log dún ar fiachu, amal logmaitne diar féchemnaib.*
13 *Ocus nír lecea sind i n-amus ndofulachtai, acht ron soer ó cech ulc.*

Modern Irish (*in the two scripts*)

9 Ⱥʀ n-ⱥⱦⱥıʀ, ⱥⱦⱥ ⱥʀ neⱥ́ṁ: ᵹo nⱥoⱃⱥɼ ᴅ'ⱥınm.
10 ᵹo ᴅⱦⱥᵹⱥ ᴅo ʀíoⱦⱦ. ᵹo nᴅéⱥnⱦⱥʀ ᴅo ⱦoıl ⱥʀ ⱥn ⱦⱥlⱥ́ṁ, mⱥʀ ᴅéⱥnⱦⱥʀ ⱥʀ neⱥ́ṁ.
11 Ⱥʀ n-ⱥʀⱥ́n lⱥeⱦıúl ⱦⱥⱱⱥıʀ ᴅúınn ınnıu.
12 Ⱥᵹus mⱥıⱦ ᴅúınn ⱥʀ ⱱⱃıⱥⱨⱥ, mⱥʀ ṁⱥıⱦımıᴅ ᴅⱥ́ʀ ⱱⱃéıⱨıúnⱥıⱦe ⱃéın.
13 Ⱥᵹus nⱥ́ lıᵹ sınn ı ᵹⱨⱥⱦú, ⱥⱨ sⱥoʀ sınn ó olⱨ. Óıʀ ıs leⱥⱦ ⱃéın ⱥn ʀíoⱦⱦ ⱥᵹus ⱥn ⱨuṁⱥⱨⱦ ⱥᵹus ⱥn ᵹ́lóıʀ ᵹo síoʀⱥı́.

9 *Ár n-athair, atá ar neamh: go naofar d'ainm.*
10 *Go dtaga do ríocht. Go ndéantar do thoil ar an talamh, mar dhéantar ar neamh.*
11 *Ár n-arán laethiúl tabhair dúinn inniu.*
12 *Agus maith dúinn ár bhfiacha, mar mhaithimid dár bhféichiúnaithe féin.*
13 *Agus ná lig sinn i gcathú, ach saor sinn ó olc. Óir is leat féin an ríocht agus an chumhacht agus an ghlóir go síoraí.*

Scottish Gaelic

9 *Ar n-athair a tha air nèamh: gu naomhaichear d'ainm.*
10 *Thigeadh do rìoghachd. Dèantar do thoil air an talamh, mar a nithear air nèamh.*
11 *Tabhair dhuinn an diugh ar n-aran lathail.*
12 *Agus maith dhuinn ar fiachan, amhuil mar a mhaitheas sinne d'ar luchd-fiach.*
13 *Agus na leig am buaireadh sinn, ach saor sinn o olc. Oir is leatsa an rìoghachd agus an cumhachd agus a' ghlòir gu sìorruidh.*

Manx

9 *Ayr ain, t'ayns niau: casherick dy row dt'ennym.*
10 *Dy jig dty reeriaght. Dt'aigney dy row jeant er y thalloo, myr te ayns niau.*
11 *Cur dooin nyn arran jiu as gagh laa.*
12 *As leih dooin nyn loghtyn, myr ta shin leih dauesyn ta jannoo loghtyn nyn oi.*
13 *As ny leeid shin ayns miolaght, agh livrey shin veih olk. Son lhiat's y reeriaght as y phooar as y ghloyr son dy bragh as dy bragh.*

Appendix

Old English, late tenth century

9 Fæder ūre, þū þe eart on heofonum: sī þīn nama ġehālgod.
10 Tōbecume þīn rīċe. Ġeweorþe þīn willa on eorþan swā swā on heofonum.
11 Ūrne dæghwāmlīċan hlāf sielle ūs tō dæġe.
12 And forġief ūs ūre gyltas, swā swā wē forġiefaþ ūrum gyltendum.
13 And ne ġelæd þū ūs on costnunge, ac ālīes ūs of yfele, forþæm þīn is þæt rīċe and sēo miht and þæt wuldor āwa tō ealdre.

Middle English, thirteenth century

9 Fader oure þat art in hevene: ihalgeed bee þi nome.
10 Icume þi kingriche. Yworthe þi wille, also is in hevene so be on erthe.
11 Oure iche dayes bred gif us to-day.
12 And forgif us our gultes, also we forgifet oure gultare.
13 And ne led ows nowth into fondingge, auch ales ows of harme . . .

Medieval Flemish, mid-thirteenth century

9 Onse vader, die best in den hemele: gheheiligt si dijn name.
10 Toe comende si dijn rike. Ghescien moet dijn wille beide in hemelrike ende in ertrike.
11 Onse daghelicske broet gheef ons heden.
12 Ende vergheef ons onse sculden alsoe ghelike alsoe wi si vergheven den ghenen, die ons sculdich sijn.
13 Ende en begheef ons niet in coringen, maer verlose ons van arghe . . .

Old Norse, early twelfth century

9 Faðir vár, þú sem ert í himnunum: helgist nafn þitt.
10 Komi ríki þitt. Verði vilji þinn, svá á jǫrðu sem á himni.
11 Gef oss í dag várt daglegt brauð.
12 Ok gef oss upp skuldir várar, svá sem vér ok hǫfum gefit upp skuldunautum várum.
13 Ok leið oss ekki í freistni, heldr frelsa oss frá illu . . .

Appendix

Shetland Norn, late eighteenth century

9 *Fy vor o er i chimeri: halaght vara nam dit.*
10 *La konungdum din cumma. La vill din vera guerde i vrildin sindaeri chimeri.*
11 *Gav vus dagh u dagloght brau.*
12 *Forgive sindorwara sin vi forgiva gem so sinda gainst wus.*
13 *Lia wus ike o vera tempa, but delivra wus fro adlu idlu. For doi ir konungdum u puri u glori . . .*

Orkney Norn, early eighteenth century

9 *Favor i ir i chimeri: helleut ir i nam thite.*
10 *Gilla cosdum thite cumma. Veya thine mota vara gort o yurn sinna gort i chimeri.*
11 *Ga vus da on da dalight brow vora.*
12 *Firgive vus sinna vora sin vee firgive sindara mutha vus.*
13 *Lyv vus ye i tumtation, min delivra vus fro olt ilt . . .*

ITALIC

Latin

9 *Pater noster, qui es in caelis: sanctificetur nomen tuum.*
10 *Adveniat regnum tuum. Fiat voluntas tua, sicut in caelo, et in terra.*
11 *Panem nostrum quotidianum da nobis hodie.*
12 *Et dimitte nobis debita nostra, sicut et nos dimittimus debitoribus nostris.*
13 *Et ne nos inducas in tentationem, sed libera nos a malo. Quoniam tibi est regnum et potestas et gloria in saecula saeculorum.*

Norman French, early thirteenth century

9 *Li nostre pere, qui ies es ciels: saintefiez seit li tuns nums.*
10 *Avienget li tuns regnes. Seit faite la tue voluntét, sicum en ciel e en la terre.*
11 *Nostre pain cotidian dun a nus oi.*
12 *E pardune a nus les noz detes, eissi cume nus pardunums a noz deturs.*
13 *E ne nus mener en temtatiun, mais delivre nus de mal . . .*

Appendix

ARYAN

Welsh Romany

(In the absence of a traditional text, we submit a synthetic version of our own; asterisked items are unattested in the surviving material.)

9 Amā̧rō dad kā shan arȩ̄ ō ravnos: tīrō nav te avél parikedó.
10 Tīrō *kralishéskerō te avél. Tīrō lav te avél kedó arȩ̄ ō them ojā̧-sār arȩ̄ ō ravnos.
11 Dē amén kedivés amā̧rō diveséskō mā̧rō.
12 Thā ātav amén amā̧rō mizhibén ojā̧-sār ātavása amáia odolén kā kena mizhibén améngī.
13 Thā mā̧ and amén arȩ̄ *temptibén, thā riger amén avrī basavibén. Odoléskī tīrō sī ō *kralishéskerō thā ō zhozh thā ō *ravalibén sā̧r ō chēros.

*kralishéskerō < kralíshos 'king', *temptibén < *temptin- 'tempt', *ravalibén < ravalō 'noble, splendid'.

262